Psychoanalysis: The First Ten Years

PSYCHOANALYSIS:

The First Ten Years

1888–1898

WALTER A. STEWART, M.D.

LONDON: GEORGE ALLEN & UNWIN LTD

FIRST PUBLISHED IN 1969

SBN 04 131021 7

ACKNOWLEDGMENTS

For permission to quote from *The Standard Edition of the Complete Psychological Works of Sigmund Freud*, Vols. 1, 2, 3, 5, 7, 12, 14, 15, 20, 22, and 23, © James Strachey, 1959, 1962, and 1964, published by The Hogarth Press, Ltd., London, author and publisher wish to thank Sigmund Freud Copyrights, Ltd., Mr. James Strachey, and The Hogarth Press, Ltd., and, in addition, Allen & Unwin, Ltd., for quotations from *Interpretation of Dreams*.

Acknowledgment with thanks is also made to Basic Books, Inc., for permission to quote material from *Interpretation of Dreams*, by Sigmund Freud; from *Studies on Hysteria*, by Josef Breuer and Sigmund Freud; from *Collected Papers of Sigmund Freud*, edited by Ernest Jones, Basic Books, Inc., Publishers, New York, 1955, 1957, 1959; and from *Origins of Psycho-Analysis, Letters to Wilhelm Fliess, Drafts and Notes; 1887–1902*, by Sigmund Freud, edited by Marie Bonaparte, Anna Freud, Ernst Kris; translated by Eric Mosbacher and James Strachey, Copyright, 1954, by Basic Books, Inc., Publishers, New York.

An Outline of Psycho-Analysis was published by W. W. Norton and Company, Inc., New York, Copyright 1949 by W. W. Norton and Company. *Beyond the Pleasure Principle* was published by Liveright Publishing Corp., New York.

PRINTED IN GREAT BRITAIN
BY PHOTOLITHOGRAPHY
BY JOHN DICKENS AND CO LTD
NORTHAMPTON

Contents

Chart 1: Chronological List of Freud's Analytic Papers

	Published Books and Papers		Letters and Drafts first published in *The Origins of Psycho-Analysis* (1954)	Comments
1888	Preface to the translation of H. Bernheim's *De la Suggestion et de ses applications à la thérapeutique* (Paris 1886; 2d ed. 1887). German translation 1888–89. *Die Suggestion und ihre Heilwirkung (Suggestion and its Therapeutic Effects)* S.E. *1* 75 (1888–89)	*1888*	Letters 4 and 5	
1889	Review of August Forel's *Hypnotism* S.E. *1* 91	*1889*		Freud treated Frau Emmy von N. Visited Dr. H. Bernheim at Nancy
1890	Psychical (or Mental) Treatment S.E. 7 281.	*1890*	Letters 6 and 7	
1891	Hypnosis S.E. *1* 105	*1891*	Letter 8	Freud treated Katarina (Jones, *Life and Work of Freud*, vol. 1, p. 332)
1892	Letter to J. Breuer (written June 29, 1892) S.E. *1* 147 (1941*a*) On the Theory of Hysterical Attacks November 1892 S.E. *1* 151 (1940*d*) Note III (1941*b*) Undated but believed to have been written late in 1892. The title refers to its being the third section of the Preliminary Communication S.E. *1* 149	*1892*	Letters 9–11 *Draft A*–Problems	Used later in a Reply to Criticism (1895*f*) Freud treated Fraulein Elizabeth von R. and Miss Lucy R.
1893	Preface and Notes to J.M. Charcot's *Poliklinische Vortrage* S.E. *1* 133 (1892–93*a*) A Case of Successful Treatment by Hypnotism S.E. *1* 115 (1892–93*b*) (1) With Breuer, J., On the Psychical Mechanism of Hysterical Phenomena: Preliminary	*1893*	Letters 12–15 *Draft B*–The Ætiology of the Neuroses *Draft C*–Report on Work in	Used later in On the Grounds for Detaching (1895*b*)

Year	PUBLISHED BOOKS AND PAPERS		LETTERS AND DRAFTS FIRST PUBLISHED IN *The Origins of Psycho-Analysis* (1954)	COMMENTS
	Communication (1893*a*) S.E. *2* 3 (published in two installments January 1 and 15, 1893) (2) Lecture delivered at Wiener Medizinscher Club, January 11, 1893. On the Psychical Mechanism of Hysterical Phenomena S.E. *3* 25 (1893*f*). Some Points for a Comparative Study of Organic and Hysterical Motor Paralyses S.E. *1* 160 (1893*c*) Charcot S.E. *3* 11 (1893*f*)		Progress	
1894	The Neuro-Psychoses of Defence S.E. *3* 45	*1894a*	Letters 16–21 *Draft D*–On the Ætiology and Theory of the Major Neuroses *Draft E*–How Anxiety Originates *Draft F*–Collection III	Both Drafts D and E used in On the Grounds for Detaching 1895b
1895	On the Grounds for Detaching a Particular Syndrome from Neurasthenia under the Description "Anxiety Neurosis" S.E. *3* 87 (1895*b*) Obsessions and Phobias S.E. *3* 74 (1895*c*)	*1895*	Letters 22–38 *Draft G*–Melancholia *Draft H*–Paranoia	

Chronological List of Freud's Analytic Papers

	Published Books and Papers		Letters and Drafts first published in *The Origins of Psycho-Analysis* (1954)	Comments
	Studies on Hysteria (? May) S.E. *2* (1895*d*) A Reply to Criticisms of My Paper on Anxiety Neurosis S.E. *3* 121 (1895*f*)		*Draft I*—Migraine *Draft J*—Frau P.J. Project for a Scientific Psychology	Used in Further Remarks (1896*b*)
1896	Heredity and the Ætiology of the Neuroses S.E. *3* 143 (February 5th; published March) (1896*a*) Further Remarks on the Neuro-Psychoses of Defence (published? —May) S.E. *3* 159 (1896*b*) The Ætiology of Hysteria S.E. *3* 189 (1896*c*)	*1896*	Letters 39–53 *Draft K*—The Neuroses of Defence	Beginning of seduction theory Writing paper on paralysis in children for Nothnagel Used in Further Remarks (1896*b*)
1897		*1897*	Letters 54–80 *Draft L*—Notes I *Draft M*—Notes II *Draft N*—Notes III	Letter 52—early picket fence model Letter 58—believed father seduced sibling (See Jones, *ibid*., 1, 324) Letter 69—abandoned seduction theory, (Jones, *ibid*., 1, 265) Letter 71—discovery of oedipus complex Letter 75—discovery of infantile sexuality First beginning insight into fantasies and drives Finished paper on paralysis in children Occupied with self-analysis (see S.E. *3* 262)
1898	Sexuality in the Ætiology of the Neuroses (finished February 9) S.E. *3* 261 The Psychical Mechanism of Forgetfulness (S.E. *3* 287)	*1898*	Letters 81–100	Letter 85—beginning to write *The Interpretation of Dreams*

Psychoanalysis: The First Ten Years

1. The Setting: Freud's Early Analytic Concepts

THIS BOOK PRESENTS a systematic formulation and a disscussion of the major ideas Freud developed during the period between 1888 and 1898.

During this ten-year period, representing one-fifth of his professional life devoted to psychoanalysis, Freud published fifteen papers and one book on the subject. In addition, many of his ideas were formulated in a series of letters and drafts of paper that he wrote to his "friend in Berlin," Dr. Wilhelm Fliess. This material has only recently been published in English.[1] The relationship between these two men stressed the sharing of their ideas, a most fortunate fact for the student of Freud's work: at one point in his life Freud gleefully burned most of his working papers with the pleasure of knowing he was making it hard for his future biographers. He had exposed himself more than most men would have been willing to do in the recording and analyzing of his own dreams (*The Interpretation of Dreams*, 1900, *S.E.* 4–5); more than this he did not feel was warranted.

Volume I of Ernest Jones's life of Freud[2] gives a brief his-

[1] Freud, *The Origins of Psycho-Analysis* (hereafter referred to as *Origins*) and, later, in *The Standard Edition of the Complete Psychological Works of Sigmund Freud* (hereafter referred to as *S.E.* with volume number and page numbers where needed). Draft C and other letters not published in the *S.E.* are published in *Origins* only and such references are to that volume.

[2] Jones, *Life and Work of Freud*, vol. 1.

tory of how the letters to Fliess narrowly escaped the same fate. They were saved by the recipient, and after his death in 1928 his widow sold them to a Berlin book dealer named Mr. Stahl, with the provision that they would not be resold to Freud, who certainly would have destroyed them. The bookseller had in turn sold them for $480 to Princess Marie Bonaparte, an analysand, colleague, and close friend of Freud and his family. When Freud learned of their existence from her,[3] he advised that they be burned and wrote on January 3, 1937, "I don't want any of them to become known to so-called posterity." Because of the war and the danger that the letters might be destroyed by the Nazis, they were taken from a bank in Vienna and brought secretly to Paris, where they were left with the Danish legation. Immediately after the war the documents were sent to England. Because there still were mines in the English Channel, the papers were wrapped in waterproof material and made buoyant so that they would not be lost if the ship were sunk.

During the period from 1888 through 1898, ninety-seven letters and fourteen drafts of articles were written. Some of the letters and many of the drafts amount to the working papers that preceded published articles and thus show us not only the product but also the process of work in progress. Other drafts contain tentative formulations that were found to be inadequate and were discarded. Some of them contain ideas formulated at this time that were developed and published only many years later. Finally concepts are described which, in spite of their evident value, were not developed further because of a lack of time or a shift in interest. These remain as important clues to further research and thought.

One of these drafts is an untitled hundred-page manuscript that the editors of *Origins* have given the title "A Project for a Scientific Psychology" (Project).[4] This in itself is an

[3] Schur, *Drives, Affects, Behavior*, vol. 2, p. 13.

[4] Published in *Origins* and *S.E. 1* 175. Rerefences to the Project in this study refer to *S.E.*

extraordinary document, written by Freud in 1895 with feverish intensity and great hope, but abandoned within a few months as an unsuccessful effort. Most of Freud's papers have to be read paragraph by paragraph. Of this highly condensed manuscript it can accurately be said that it has to be read and reread sentence by sentence and even word by word. It contains Freud's most closely reasoned and intricate thoughts and is the basis for many of Freud's fundamental concepts, which he developed in a different vocabulary during the remaining forty-two years of his life.

Finally there are three posthumously published "fragments" written in 1892. The first is a letter to Dr. Joseph Breuer, Freud's Vienna colleague and collaborator in his earliest papers; the next two fragments are notes written jointly with Breuer, but in Freud's handwriting. All three fragments are condensed notes made in preparation for writing their first analytic paper, "Preliminary Communication."

The value of these posthumously published letters and drafts is beyond calculation. The papers Freud published at the time give only an incomplete picture of the intellectual work and creative ferment in his mind; the new papers allow a further insight into his intellectual life during these early years, which were not only the formative years, but also the most creative. Jones writes that the year 1897 "was the acme of Freud's life." The papers illustrate what Heinz Hartmann[5] has described as Freud's capacity for fruitful theorizing, which he states was on a level with his clinical genius.

Freud seldom attempted any systematic presentation of his concepts or even a careful definition of his terms. In this first decade, complex and intricately interrelated ideas were tentatively formulated, abandoned, revived, and modified from week to week. Freud was opposed to a preoccupation with consistency and preferred a fragmentary treatment of a subject that encouraged further exploration rather than

[5] Hartmann, *Essays on Ego Psychology*, p. 276.

premature closure. This was particularly and necessarily true of the early period in his work, when he was searching for the most fruitful concepts that he could apply to his observations of human behavior and feelings. Concepts developed in the first period are often now referred to by different terms. Also, the same terms may be used now, but frequently have a new or subtle difference in meaning. Even more confusing is the fact that Freud would develop an idea, lay it aside only to take it up again in connection with another problem even as much as forty years later. Freud seldom stopped to annotate these differences or integrate the past with the present. As a result of these changes in terms and discontinuity of discussion, many of Freud's later views can be fully understood only when the early formulations are known. The genetic point of view is as important to the understanding of the growth of psychoanalytic theory as it is to the theory itself. One of the aims of this book is to show the continuity and modification that occurred as Freud developed his ideas.

Another reason for providing a detailed review of these early papers, drafts, and letters is to offset the tendency for the ideas to be robbed of their detail. This is often the fate of complex ideas as is perhaps even more likely to occur in dealing with ideas that challenge man to face the detailed knowledge of the ways in which he is not master in his own house. It may be an unavoidable historical fate that Freud's ideas will suffer partial or complete distortion. The history of psychoanalysis, with its splinter groups of neo-Freudians who, with their "new discoveries," ignorantly restate parts of Freud's ideas and throw out other essential parts, would lend support to this possibility. Paradoxically, recent additional knowledge of the problems Freud faced in his early years of work may decrease the study of this period, since it invites a stereotyped and codified view. The tendency has been to dismiss the early papers as a false start, based on Freud's "need to neurologize"; the detail and complexity of the thoughts can be ignored by viewing them as of historical interest only and by referring to them only with catch phrases such as the seduction theory, toxicological theory, strangulated affects, and so on.

The value of the historical approach is that it is an antidote to both uncritical acceptance and ignorant rejection of the ideas. The study of these papers counteracts the danger of a doctrinaire attitude that leads to a sterile approach to the unsolved problems. The reader who retraces the path that Freud first followed and shares the problems, understands the errors he made, the partial truths and the fundamental discoveries, is less likely to distort the material, discard the good with the bad, or confuse rediscovery with new advances.

A final reason for reviewing this material—somewhat less practical than those already mentioned—is that it offers an exciting intellectual experience. The letters and drafts in particular give a close-up of Freud in this searching period of creative excitement. In these ten years Freud originated the basic concepts with which he began to organize his observations. These led to elaborate formulations of great intellectual beauty, which were then succeeded by newer, equally elaborate theoretical formulations. It quickly becomes apparent that not all his efforts were successful and that the successes were not easily won. It may not be a typical form of creative genius to make only fundamental errors and fundamental discoveries, but it was certainly Freud's way. For example, at one time Freud erroneously believed that the prerequisite etiological factor in the psychoneuroses was a seduction of the individual as a child, and that without this premature sexual experience a psychoneurosis could not occur. The seducer was most often thought to be the patient's father, and when Freud's own sister showed clear evidence of a psychoneurosis, he felt that this implicated *his* father! This has come to be known as the seduction theory. Perhaps only a person who could pursue the seduction theory to its bitter end, in spite of its implausibility, could discover the "undiscoverable" existence of the unconscious. Other formulations, such as the concept of the actual neurosis (nonpsychogenic adult sexual pathology due to deleterious sexual practices), represent an early and unsuccessful effort to delineate the biological level of sexual illness. That problem is still unsolved and remains an important challenge to present and future students.

At the beginning of the period under discussion Freud was thirty-two years old. He had been married for two years and was the father of one child, Mathilde, named after Breuer's wife and born in 1887. His next five children, all born during the period under study, were: Jean Martin, named after Charcot and born in 1889; Oliver, named after Cromwell and born in 1891; Ernst, named after Ernst Brücke and born in 1892, the year of Brücke's death; Sophie, named after Freud's niece, Sophie Schwab, and born in 1893, the year of the publication of the first of Freud's truly analytic papers, the "Preliminary Communication"; and Anna, named after a daughter of Hammerschlag's and born in 1895, the year in which Freud's and Breuer's *Studies on Hysteria* was published and the Project was written. Had his last child been a boy, he would have named him Wilhelm after Fliess (*Origins*, Letter 37).

Drs. Brücke, Breuer, Jean Martin Charcot, and Fliess were of great importance in determining Freud's scientific attitude in his study of the neuroses. Freud's contact with the first of these men, Dr. Ernst Brücke, began in the late 1870's. At that time Freud, in his early twenties, was in medical school in Vienna and doing special research work under Brücke at the Institute of Physiology on the histology of the nerve cells of a fish, Amoecetes (Petromyzon). The work led to his first scientific publication, which appeared in the January, 1877, *Bulletin of the Academy of Sciences*. Dr. Brücke was described by Freud as "the greatest authority who affected me more than any other in my whole life."[6] Brücke, a small man with a large head, was a German Protestant. He was thought of as a strict, undemonstrative, and uncompromising man, yet his pupils were devoted to him and it is said that none was ever disloyal.

When he was a demonstrator at the Institute of Physiology, Freud sometimes reached the laboratory late. One day Brücke was there at the hour of opening and reprimanded Freud for being late. Freud recalled this episode in an association to a later dream, in *The Interpretation of Dreams.* He wrote, "His words were brief and to the point. But it was not they that mattered. What overwhelmed me were the terrible blue eyes with which he looked at me and by which I was reduced to nothing" (S.E. *5* 422).

Brücke, along with Carl Ludwig (1816–95), Emil Du Bois-Reymond (1818–96), and Hermann Helmholtz (1821–94), formed a group of scientists devoted to a physical-chemical approach to science as opposed to the vitalistic school of their teacher, Johannes Müller. When Brücke moved to Vienna, the members of his group who stayed in Berlin considered him their "Ambassador in the Far East." It was from Brücke rather than Breuer or Charcot that Freud obtained the scientific philosophy that governed his studies.[7]

It was during the six years that Freud worked at Brücke's Institute in Vienna that he first met Dr. Joseph Breuer (1842–1925). Breuer, fourteen years older than Freud, was a well-known practicing physician in Vienna who had earlier been successful in research and teaching. Siegfried Bernfeld in a valuable small paper[8] points out that in most references to

[6] Jones, *Life and Work of Freud,* vol. 1, pp. 28, 39.

[7] *Ibid.,* p. 45. Freud was conditioned by the principles of causality and determinism of the Helmholtz school, as is evidenced by his unwavering belief in the strict determinism he applied to the understanding of "free association." At the same time he was able to emancipate himself from the narrower implications of the attitude and deal with such human imponderables as wish, purpose, intention, and aim.

[8] Bernfeld, "Freud's Earliest Theories and the School of Helmholtz," *Psychoanalytic Quarterly, 13,* (1944), 341.

Breuer, psychoanalysts speak of him as simply a practicing physician in Vienna. In fact he was a distinguished teacher and made numerous important discoveries, of which the self-regulation of respiration by the vagus and the function of the semicircular canals of the ear are probably the best known. He was the family physician for Brücke, as well as for other famous Viennese of the time. Freud and Breuer quickly became friends. They had in common a devotion to the deterministic school of science and soon began sharing their intellectual interests. Because Freud was at times almost penniless, Breuer began to "lend" him regular monthly sums of money. This apparently began in 1881, and by 1886 it amounted to over $1,000 (2,300 gulden).

Freud described Breuer during this time as his friend and helper, "the ever-loyal Breuer." Freud often depended on Breuer's advice about his future, and even accompanied Breuer when he visited his patients.

After considerable delay because of his special research interests, Freud obtained his medical degree on March 31, 1881. This made little difference to his plans and he continued to work under Brücke for another fifteen months. Then, partly on Brücke's advice, he left the Physiological Institute and entered the General Hospital in order to get the further practical training that would make it possible for him to earn his living as a physician. Brücke had pointed out to Freud that his extremely restricted financial circumstances made a theoretical and research career impractical. As Jones points out, the immediate event which precipitated the decision was that Freud had met Martha Bernays in April, 1882, and was in love with her.[9] On June 17, 1882, they became secretly engaged. This, more than any other determinant, forced Freud to face the necessity of planning to earn an income.

At the General Hospital, Freud first served under the professor of medicine, Carl Wilhelm Nothnagel, for six and one-half months. His letter of introduction was written by

[9] Jones, *Life and Work of Freud*, vol. 1, p. 61.

Theodor Meynert (1833–92), the professor of psychiatry. He began there on October 12, 1882.

An important event occurred on November 18, 1882, for that was the day that Breuer first told Freud of a case he had treated. This is the famous case of Fraülein Anna O., reported later by Breuer in the joint work of Breuer and Freud, *Studies on Hysteria.* This patient, now known to be Bertha Pappenheim and an old friend of Freud's wife, later became the first social worker in Germany. Breuer treated her from December, 1880, to June, 1882. Breuer decided to end the treatment when he became aware of his wife's jealousy. To his horror, the patient developed a pseudopregnancy. Breuer, profoundly shaken by the event, calmed the patient but left the next day on a second honeymoon with his wife.

The details of this case captured Freud's imagination, particularly the observation that Anna O.'s bizarre symptoms could be made to disappear permanently when, under hypnosis, the circumstances surrounding their origins were recalled and the emotions involved were relived and thus discharged (see chapter 4).

Breuer's account of his experience with Fraülein Anna O. was unquestionably a major determinant in turning Freud's attention and interest to the problem of the psychoneuroses, although the incident apparently lay relatively dormant in his mind for a number of years.

In May, 1883, Freud transferred from the department of medicine to Meynert's psychiatric clinic. At this time, and even later, after the relationship had deteriorated considerably, Freud always held Meynert in the highest esteem. He described him as "the great Meynert in whose footsteps I followed with such veneration," and felt he was "the most brilliant genius he had ever encountered."[10]

Dr. Gregory Zilboorg[11] points out that as an undergraduate

[10] *Ibid.*, p. 65.

[11] Zilboorg, "Freud's Fundamental Psychiatric Orientation," *International Journal*, 35, (April 1954), 91.

Freud's psychiatric training consisted of only one five-hour course a week under Meynert. Meynert was a brilliant brain anatomist, but a poor psychiatrist.[12] All the psychoses were thought by Meynert to be diseases of the forebrain, the anatomical pathology of which was unknown. Catatonia was caused by meningitis at the base of the brain. Psychiatry at this time was "anatomico-physiological cerebral mythology".[13] Fortunately for Freud, neuroanatomy and neuropathology were his interests then, rather than psychiatry.

Freud served in Meynert's clinic studying neurology for five months and then moved to Von Zeissl's department of dermatology for three months. On January 1, 1884, he transferred to the department of nervous diseases under Superintendent Franz Scholz, and remained there for the next fourteen months. On July 18, 1885, at the recommendation of Brücke, Meynert, and Nothnagel, he was appointed to the position of *Privatdozent* in neurology, a highly prized position that allowed him to lecture. He reluctantly left Scholz's department at the superintendent's request, over a difference of opinion on how to run the department. On March 1, 1885, he began to work in the department of ophthalmology. On March 3, 1885, he decided to apply for a traveling grant which would pay him $240 (600 gulden) and allow him six months' leave. His plan was to travel to Paris and study under Charcot, the famous French professor of neurology. His chances of receiving this grant seemed extremely small, but after some delay and because of Brücke's "passionate intercession" on his behalf, the committee's vote, taken on June 19, 1885, was in his favor.

On August 31, 1885, Freud left the General Hospital for good, after having served there for three years and one month. During this time he had published original research and achieved recognition as a neurologist. He had published in June, 1885, a paper on the connections of the acoustic

12 Jones, *Life and Work of Freud*, vol. 1, p. 65.
13 Zilboorg, "Freud's Fundamental Psychiatric Orientation," p. 91.

(auditory) nerve, which he had explored in the medulla of foetuses of five to six months in age. Two other papers on anatomical aspects of the brain stem were published a few months later.

When Freud set off for Paris these interests in brain anatomy were still uppermost in his mind, and in fact his purpose in visiting Charcot was to learn more about neurology. Fortunately for the historian, Freud wrote a "Report on My Studies in Paris and Berlin" (*S.E. 1* 5), which describes some of his experiences while studying under Charcot. He arrived in Paris on October 13, 1885, and stayed there, except for a Christmas week with his fiancée, until February 1886.

Charcot, whose specialty was the organic illnesses of the nervous system, was at the height of his career, and his interest had recently turned to those patients suffering from hysteria. Before he began to investigate these symptoms, physicians had felt that hysteria did not deserve their attention and patients with this diagnosis were considered malingerers or worse. As a result of Charcot's prestige, his interest in the disease made it a respectable area for the interest of other doctors. In addition, Charcot began to use hypnosis as an experimental procedure in his investigations. An interest in hypnosis had not been acceptable to the medical profession either, until he made it at least partly so. It is somewhat confusing in our present state of knowledge to realize that Charcot's interest in hysteria was still in line with his training in neurology. Charcot believed the nature of the illness was organic rather than psychologically determined. He felt that the capacity to develop the illness was inherited and involved some form of congenital deterioration of the brain, although the symptoms were of a psychic nature. His main interest lay in the traumatic hysterias—those which followed a railway accident, for example. The patients showed "neurological" symptoms, such as paralyses and fainting fits, for which no clear specific organic basis could later be discovered. Since there appeared to be a specific precipitating cause, however, these illnesses were more understandable and acceptable to most physicians. Possibly this leniency was also attributable to the fact that these patients were the center of litigation for compensation.

Charcot's research and study led to two useful results. One was the detailed description of the classical picture of hysteria, which clarified the criteria for making the diagnosis. His second contribution was to show that the disease could be imitated when suggestions were given while the patient was in a hypnotic trance and that symptoms could occasionally be removed or altered by hypnotic suggestion; that is, that they were psychic phenomena.

Freud was fascinated by Charcot's eloquence and his mastery of the subject. The technique of teaching used by this histrionic Frenchman must have been quite a change from the austere and aloof manner of the usual teacher in Vienna.

That Freud, in his plan to study under Charcot, expected to continue his *neurological* interests is borne out because shortly after his arrival in Paris he began some studies on brain anatomy in the laboratories of the Salpêtrière. His subject was the descending fibers of the spinal cord. However, he found the work in this dismal and poorly equipped setting difficult and unrewarding and he soon gave it up.

Charcot's lectures and clinical illustrations on hysterics must have aroused in Freud's mind the memory of Breuer's case, Fraülein Anna O. He mentioned the case to Charcot, who seemed unresponsive, and Jones feels this "damped his own enthusiasm about the discovery."[14] Yet it is clear that Charcot's interest in the subject of hysteria also contributed to Freud's freedom to investigate the problem.

Freud returned to Vienna by way of Berlin, where he studied the general diseases of children at Adolf Baginsky's clinic. When he reached home, in April, 1886, he was invited to use the facilities of Meynert's clinic, and he worked there each morning, continuing his anatomical studies. He was also

[14] Jones, *Life and Work of Freud,* vol. 1, p. 226.

employed by Max Kassowitz as the director of a new neurological department in the Institute for Children's Diseases. Finally he set up a private practice. As Jones Points out, Freud sent out notices of his practice on Easter Sunday, April 25, 1886! Breuer was the main source of referrals.[15]

In spite of his precarious financial situation, Freud was finally able to marry. The civil marriage was on September 13, 1886, and the religious marriage the next day.

On October 15, 1886, Freud presented a paper, "On Male Hysteria," before the Vienna Gesellschaft der Aertze. He regarded it as a scientific report on his visit to Paris, but in fact no report was required and the action was somewhat tactless. The paper, which was never published (*S.E. 1* 24), was poorly received, arousing a mixture of ridicule and resentment. One surgeon criticized Freud for not knowing that since the term hysteria came from the Greek word for uterus, the disease of necessity was limited to women.[16] His seniors resented Freud's attitude, which so clearly reflected his feeling that he had a great deal to teach them. Meynert was antagonized on at least two accounts. He ridiculed the idea of male hysteria, although he later privately admitted to Freud that he suffered from the illness himself. He was also offended by Freud's interest in hypnosis and felt that Charcot's influence had corrupted him in his devotion to the exact sciences.

Meynert challenged Freud to present a case illustrating his thesis, which Freud did on November 26, 1886. This paper was published under the title, "Observation of a Severe Case of Hemi-anaesthesia in a Hysterical Male" (*S.E. 1* 23). Meynert's opposition to hypnosis was fierce and irrational. He had as a mortal enemy a Dr. Leidesdorf, the superintendent of Obersteiner's sanatorium, who was known as a hypnotizing doctor.[17]

[15] *Ibid.*, p. 143.
[16] *Ibid.*, p. 231.
[17] *Ibid.*, p. 237.

Freud not only became increasingly interested in hypnosis, but also worked with and was a friend of Leidesdorf. Meynert began referring to Freud as if he were only a hypnotist (*S.E. 1* 95 fn. 2) and made it clear that he was no longer welcome in the clinic. Freud quite understandably took offense at the numerous personal attacks and defended himself in his papers against this biased and ignorant attitude (*S.E. 1* 12, 94, 105).[18]

Meynert was a great neuropathologist, and he respected Freud's competence in this field. His own interests had shifted to the study of the neuroses, which he naturally felt would be understandable in neuroanatomical terms.[19] In order to pursue his new interest, he would gladly have turned over many of his teaching obligations to Freud and given him an important position in his department. Freud, however, was also interested in the neuroses, but in terms which were mostly foreign to Meynert.[20] They were not only competitors, but Meynert and all he stood for was being defeated by a person whom he had befriended, using hypnosis, which he abhorred. The quarrels with Freud seem to have been only a symptom in Meynert's illness. Toward the end he was a heavy drinker, jealous, and according to Jones "had difficulty in retaining any self-control."[21]

During the next few years Freud translated two of Charcot's books, one of which appeared in 1886 and the other

[18] This view of Freud's relationship to Meynert (and later to Breuer) is very much influenced by the reports of Jones and Strachey and is in danger of becoming uncritically accepted. It is important to keep in mind how devoted Freud was to Meynert and to Breuer and their high regard for Freud. Both Meynert and Breuer were distinguished, competent, and admirable men. There may be a tendency to ignore the complexity of the relationships. There is some reason to doubt the accuracy of the current view; for example, the concept of male hysteria was well known in the medical circles of Vienna, therefore the need for Freud to prove its existence seems to be a distortion of historical fact.

[19] Jones, *Life and Work of Freud*, vol. 1, p. 232.

[20] Meynert wrote a paper in 1884 not dissimilar to Freud's Project, in which he described the ego and the important role of activity in perception (Hartmann, *Essays* 274).

[21] Jones, *Life and Work of Freud*, vol. 1, p. 238.

in 1892–93. He also translated two of Dr. H. Bernheim's books and for one, which was published in 1888 (*Suggestion and Its Therapeutic Effects*), he wrote a valuable preface (*S.E. 1* 73).[22]

In 1891 Freud published a book on aphasia, which he dedicated to Breuer, and which in its dynamic approach already showed the nature of the intellectual style that proved so valuable in his study of mental functioning. Freud later referred to it as his most valuable neurological contribution.

In the fall of 1887 an event of considerable significance occurred. This was the beginning of Freud's friendship with Dr. Wilhelm Fliess (1858–1928), a man two years his junior. They met as a result of Breuer's advice to Fliess that he should attend some lectures that Freud was giving on the anatomy and function of the central nervous system.

The two men soon became friends, their friendship being expressed mostly in their exchange of letters. They had in common a devotion to the Helmholtz school and a wish to develop "The Foundations for an Exact Biology" (actually the subtitle of one of Fliess's books).

The simplest description of the debt of gratitude we owe to Fliess is that he was the recipient of the letters and drafts written during Freud's formative period and that he (and his widow) preserved them. In addition he appeared at an opportune moment in Freud's life. Freud's relationship with Breuer had deteriorated. He had only with difficulty, unpleasantness, and suffering[23] persuaded Breuer to agree to a publication of the 1893 "Preliminary Communication," and by the time their joint work, *Studies on Hysteria*, appeared in 1895 all semblance of real cooperation had disappeared. The editors of the letters to Fliess have preferred to keep from public view most of Freud's hostile and bitter com-

[22] Preface to the translation of H. Bernheim's *De la Suggestion et de ses applications a la thérapeutique* (Paris 1886; 2d ed. 1887. German translation 1888–89). *Die Suggestion und ihre Heilwirkung (Suggestion and Its Therapeutic Effects) S.E. 1* 75 (1888–89).

[23] Jones, *Life and Work of Freud*, vol. 1, p. 307.

ments about his erstwhile loyal friend and benefactor. Freud's financial indebtedness may have played some part in this hostility, but even more important was Breuer's caution and indecisiveness. Freud, in "An Autobiographical Study," states that at this time Breuer's attitude toward him "oscillated for some time between appreciation and sharp criticism; then accidental difficulties arose, as they never fail to do in a strained situation, and we parted" (*S.E. 20* 26). Since, in retrospect, many of Freud's ideas, to which he was passionately devoted at the time, have turned out to be quite incorrect, one can sympathize with Breuer.

One of the puzzles in analytic history is why Breuer was assigned the theoretical chapter in the *Studies on Hysteria*. As is clear from the letters and drafts sent to Fliess, Freud had already developed a complicated, clinically oriented, and carefully reasoned dynamic and economic theory. The most obvious reason for assigning this chapter to Breuer was that Freud felt obliged to continue the guise of collaboration begun in 1892. Had Freud written this chapter as well as the chapter on therapy, Breuer's contribution to their "joint work" would have consisted of only one case, treated in 1881–82 (Fraülein Anna O., 1859–1936). Even the therapeutic result in this case was ambiguous. Although the treatment lasted one and a half years, it was abruptly terminated and the outcome was for a long time quite unsatisfactory.[24]

The difficulty in the collaboration was evident from the very beginning. According to Freud, even the writing of the "Preliminary Communication" was "a long battle" (Letter 11). These difficulties between Breuer and Freud have been described by the editors of the *Standard Edition* in their introduction to the *Studies on Hysteria* and more fully by Jones,[25] as well as by Freud.

It is generally agreed that differences over theoretical formulations could not account for the amount of tension

[24] *Ibid.*, p. 223–226.
[25] *Ibid.*, p. 253.

in the relationship, which apparently reached tempestuous levels in Freud, although most of the letters to Fliess that deal with this have not been published. In the clash of personalities, Breuer's wavering indecisiveness is usually stressed. It is, however, easy to sympathize with him. He was being led along by a mind that could soar like a hawk,[26] pursue a false idea indefatigably, and produce the most creative and basic ideas at a prodigious rate. Freud describes himself at this period as having tried "to take the citadel by storm" (Letter 125).

It is interesting to speculate about what could have been the intellectual area of disagreement at this time. Freud himself discusses the question at some length in his "Autobiographical Study." He first comments on Breuer's preference for a physiological approach (hypnoid state) to his own predilection for viewing the material in terms of conflict and defense. This description by Freud is of course not intended to explain the later, deeper alienation that occurred; but even as a statement of a most superficial difference between the two, it does not ring fully true. Breuer was not limited to a physiological orientation, nor would this seem to be an issue about which Freud would be likely to object, since only a few months later he was busy writing the very neurologically oriented Project.

The deeper source of alienation Freud attributes to Breuer's shrinking away from recognizing the sexual etiology of the neuroses, and Jones appears to agree with this.[27] Since Breuer on a number of occasions expressed his belief in the importance of the role of sexuality in the psychoneuroses, however, Jones suggests that Breuer specifically balked at accepting the idea that the sexual factor was *essential*, or at Freud's views concerning the incestuous seduction.[28] Since the seduction theory did not occur to Freud until October,

[26] *Ibid.*, p. 242.
[27] *Ibid.*, p. 253.
[28] *Ibid.*, p. 254.

1895 (Letter 29), it could not have been the cause for the earlier difficulties.

We know from Letter 19, June 22, 1894 (*Origins* 94), how deeply dissatisfied Freud was with Breuer's contribution to the studies. In this letter he writes, "The book with Breuer will include five case histories, a chapter by him—*from which I dissociate myself*—on the theories of hysteria, summarizing and critical, and one by me on therapy which I have not started yet . . ." (italics added).

This fact of disagreement was marked enough so that it is mentioned even in the preface to the first edition of the *Studies on Hysteria*, and of course each chapter is separately signed: a most unusual "joint effort."

In order to understand what the disagreement may have been, we can turn to the letters and drafts to see what was foremost in Freud's mind. Previous to the bitter letter of June 22, 1894, Freud had been wholly preoccupied with the formulations concerning the actual neurosis, the role of masturbation in neurasthenia and of coitus interruptus, in the anxiety neurosis.

Breuer made perfectly clear in *Studies on Hysteria* the importance he attached to sexuality in the origin of neurosis (*S.E. 2* 200, 246). He differed with Freud on the concept of the actual neurosis and did not accept the exclusive origin of neurosis from the sexual life.

It is also necessary to remember that whatever reservations Breuer had about accepting Freud's conviction concerning the role of sexuality, Breuer's reservations are now universally accepted; neither the actual neurosis nor the later seduction hypothesis and the associated formulations concerning the timing of the scenes and the delayed response have remained in their original form as part of current psychoanalytic theory. There is a temptation to equate Breuer's reservations about analysis with an unwillingness to accept the existence of *infantile* sexuality, when in fact that had not yet been discovered by Freud.

If we consider the nature of Freud's complaints about

Breuer, they seem to be derived from Freud's impatience with his less talented colleague. We know that shortly after the publication of *Studies on Hysteria*, Freud was writing the "Project for a Scientific Psychology" at a white-hot tempo. It seems quite likely that the Project is an elaboration of the theoretical chapter that Freud would have wanted to write for the *Studies*, and that his dissatisfaction with the limited nature of Breuer's product may have provided some of the intensive drive under which it was written. It is understandable that Freud would be impatient with "good advice" from his senior partner and benefactor. Had he listened, he would have saved himself the errors of the seduction hypothesis and possibly the toxicological theory of anxiety, but might well have missed the discovery of infantile sexuality.

Whereas Breuer was undoubtedly frightened by Freud's creative genius (and errors), he was still able to enjoy his success. The description of Breuer's pleasure when he heard of Freud's clinical success (Letter 135) is very touching.

It is noteworthy that Breuer did not subscribe to Freud's nonpsychodynamic concept of the actual neuroses, feeling that the symptoms represented hysterical conversion. Freud, on the other hand, repudiated Breuer's nonpsychodynamic concept of the hypnoid state, believing that the dissociated state was the consequence of conflict that had not been abreacted and (later) proof of the unconscious that exists in everyone. The differences no longer seem relevant today, mostly because we ignore the problem of the physiological substrate to the psychoneuroses. Neither the concept of the actual neurosis nor the concept of the hypnoid state was successful in dealing with the nonpsychogenic aspects of mental illness. The problem remains as important today as it was then, and just as far from solution. However, it appears to have been swept under the rug and conveniently ignored, while psychodynamic explanations are offered as the etiology of everything from schizophrenia to war.

Breuer, in any event, was not able to give Freud the type

of encouragement he now needed. In a sense, Fliess replaced Breuer and served as an idealized image of him,[29] successful but not conservative, and in particular not afraid of speculative concepts which involved sexuality. In 1887, Freud had had to leave Brücke, accept Meynert's disapproval and criticism, and become aware of Breuer's pussyfooting limitations. It was also at this time, in spite of Breuer's generous attitude, that Freud became unwilling to be in Breuer's debt and began to repay him for the earlier "loans." He needed a friend who was unabashedly wholehearted in his support, not niggardly and critical.

In these terms the imaginative, successful, and permissive Fliess was exactly the right man for Freud. Just as Charcot had made the study of hysterias respectable for many doctors, including Freud, Fliess made it personally possible for Freud to try out his early, shocking, and implausible theories concerning the importance of sexuality in their etiology. Breuer would have clipped Freud's wings, in spite of the fact that he had described his intellect as "soaring at its highest";[30] Fliess, who was a spellbinder and incapable of self-criticism, served as an indulgent audience who put no limitations on Freud. One senses that the rather self-preoccupied adolescent style of some of Freud's letters to Fliess was in imitation of Fliess, since this style is so different from that of Freud's letters to others.

For his part, Freud also hoped that Fliess would be valuable to him, since as a biologist Fliess might be able to provide him with a physiological basis on which his psychological observations could rest. During the time of the correspondence with Freud, Fliess, a nose and throat specialist, was interested in what he termed a nasal reflex neurosis. He had noticed that he could cure a host of symptoms, especially gastric neuralgia and painful menstrual bleeding, by anesthetizing with cocaine an area of the nasal mucosa. The

[29] Jones, *Life and Work of Freud*, vol. 1, p. 296.
[30] *Ibid.*, p. 242.

cause of the symptoms could be the aftereffects of nasal infection, or it could be entirely functional, dependent on nasal congestion associated with menstrual periods. These observations led to a greater generalization concerning the periodicity of phenomena in human life: for women a twenty-eight-day periodicity and for men a twenty-three-day cycle. Soon Fliess elaborated his laws governing periodic phenomena until, with an understanding of these laws, one could predict the dates of birth, conception, illness, and death. The delusional component of the later formulations seems clear. At the beginning of Fliess's work, however, this was not yet evident. Fliess was a prominent medical man, with wide and impressive knowledge of biology. Freud had every reason to respect him and hope the relationship would be mutually profitable. Their interests seemed to overlap and be somewhat different approaches to the biology, psychology, and psychopathology of sexuality.

Freud's personal attachment to Fliess was considerable. An artificial and self-conscious tone often appears in Freud's praise of Fliess in the letters; sometimes they sound as if Freud were part of a mutual admiration society to which he was flattered to belong. Yet it is clear that Fliess was a great intellectual stimulant for Freud, probably because Fliess was so unafraid of grandiose formulations.

We see in retrospect that Brücke had given Freud an appreciation of precision and a deterministic approach to the sciences; Meynert had helped him in his interest in neurology; Breuer, besides emotional and financial support, had interested him in the subject matter of the psychoneuroses and suggested the method of pursuing memories until the origins of the symptoms could be arrived at. Charcot's interest in hysteria and hypnosis made these areas respectable and freed Freud to pursue his interests (Freud had written to his future wife when he was in Paris that he was changing a good deal and that Charcot was "simply uprooting my aims and opinions"). And from Fliess, Freud obtained intellectual stimulation and uncritical approval for ideas which had frightened Breuer and were later to shock the world.

In spite of the important influence that each of these men had on Freud, by the turn of the century none of them remained in his life. Both Brücke and Meynert died in 1892, and Charcot died the following year. Although Breuer lived until 1925, the collaborative relationship ended in 1895, and after this Freud grew bitterly critical of him. Fliess lived until 1928, but for all practical purposes the relationship ended in 1900.

The termination of the relationship with Fliess has been intimately related to Freud's self-analysis (Ernst Kris *Origins* 43).[31] The self-analysis, Freud's hardest analysis, began in the summer of 1897, less than a year after his father's death (October 23, 1896), and while Freud was writing *The Interpretation of Dreams.*

Jones considers Fliess to be the figure onto whom Freud transferred his unconscious anger directed in childhood toward his father, and writes that only with self-analysis was Freud able to become truly independent and self-reliant. In my opinion, this formulation overemphasizes the neurotic aspect of the relationship and ignores the fact of Fliess's increasing emotional difficulties and his growing rivalry with Freud. The main accomplishment of Freud's self-analysis was not to free him from Fliess, but rather to free him from the narrower aspect of the seduction theory. The increasingly evident implausibility of this theory was of great concern to Freud, and his self-analysis showed him that the seductions reported were most often fantasies behind which lay the world of infantile sexuality.

Freud published two more papers before the turn of the century, in addition to the momentous work, *The Interpretation of Dreams.* In 1898 he wrote a brief paper, "The Psychical Mechanism of Forgetfulness," in which he reported

[31] See also *ibid.*, p. 324.

the dynamics around his inability to recall the name of the artist Signorelli. This material was first mentioned in his correspondence to Fliess (Letters 96, 97) and later became the basis of the first chapter to *The Psychopathology of Everyday Life* (*S.E.* 6), which appeared as a book in 1904. In 1899 he published a paper, "Screen Memories" (*S.E.* 3 303), in which he relates an incident from his own childhood, although in a disguised form.

Both papers are more closely related to *The Interpretation of Dreams* than they are to the material described here. The same basic dynamics that operate in dreams and in symptom formation are described in the two papers. This involves the repression of one idea or memory and the displacement of its energy onto a substitute. This basic idea had been present from the very beginning of Freud's writings and has been discussed in terms of his case histories. It was the mechanism that had first allowed him to understand symptom formation. Although not new to his understanding, it became the key to his combining the economic and dynamic views and showed the relationship between dreams, symptoms, slips of the tongue, wit, forgetfulness, the unusual clarity of certain childhood memories, and in fact all mental processes in which one could discern the difference between manifest content and a latent content in any thought process.

The ten years under discussion were years of relative intellectual loneliness for Freud, although he later described them as a time of splendid isolation. He began to emerge from this period of isolation by 1901, at which time he was forty-five years old. In 1901 he overcame an inhibition that had kept him from visiting Rome. Although he had traveled extensively in northern Italy, he had never got farther south than Trasimeno, the same town in which centuries earlier Freud's childhood hero Hannibal had also been stopped in his efforts to reach Rome.

This increased freedom and self-assertion may also have played a part in his being appointed to a professorship in

1902. Drs. Nothnagel and Krafft-Ebing supported him again, as they had done five years earlier. But in addition he also had to accept the help of two women, both patients of his. One was Elsie Gomperez; the other, unnamed, was an influential woman and a patron of the arts.

Also in 1902 Freud began to have a small group of young students who came to him to learn the practice of psychoanalysis. The first group, according to Jones, consisted of Max Kahane, Rudolf Reitler, Wilhelm Stekel, and Alfred Adler. Paul Federn joined the group in 1903 and was followed, among others, by Otto Rank (1906), Carl Jung (1907), A. A. Brill, Ernest Jones, Fritz Wittels (1908), and Sandor Ferenczi (1909).

In 1905 Freud published an observation that was of great importance to the theory of the developmental nature of sexuality. The seduction theory was an earlier and erroneous effort toward understanding the central role of infantile sexuality in the etiology of the psychoneuroses. Only when Freud realized the biological developmental aspects of infantile sexuality that culminated in genital primacy, could he integrate with normal development the actions in perversion and the symptoms in the psychoneuroses. The details of this development took many years to discover. The role of autoerotic impulses and the biological concept of genital primacy was described in 1905, the narcissistic stage in 1911, the anal-sadistic stage only in 1913, the oral stage in 1915, and the phallic stage as late as 1923. It is impressive that these stages in infantile sexuality that are now taken for granted took twenty years to be understood. Perhaps it is even more impressive that these discoveries could be made by employing the research method of psychoanalysis as applied to adults.

2. *First Observations*

THE FIRST PROBLEM Freud faced in his study of the neuroses was how to deal with the baffling question of the relationship of the biological-physiological level of observation to the psychological level. The issue was being fought over in connection with the problem of hypnosis, and Freud took up the problem in his translation of Bernheim's book, *Suggestion and Its Therapeutic Effects* (*S.E. 1* 75). The phenomenon of hypnotism was still so suspect that he first had to point out that it was "a subject which can no longer be neglected by physicians," even though his former professor, Meynert, was still maintaining that it was surrounded by a "halo of absurdity." Meynert and most other doctors still attributed the realities of hypnotic phenomena to simulation by the patients and gullibility in the observers. Only a few had come to realize the intimate relationship of the hypnotic state to the illness hysteria, and hoped to use the former to study the latter.

At the time of the translation there was a difference of opinion between Bernheim and Charcot on the role that suggestion by the doctors played in the production of symptoms during hypnotic trance. Charcot believed that the basic problem was physiological. Freud wrote, in a review of August Forel's *Hynotism* (1889), "it is the great authority of Charcot which supports this exclusively somatic view of hypnosis" (*S.E. 1* 97). Charcot felt that most of the manifestations were physiological, that is, based on changes in the excitability of the nervous system, and were not associated with consciousness. In contrast, Bernheim maintained that all the phenomena in hypnosis were the result of suggestion, either direct or indirect. This meant that they originated from ideas, that is, were psychological and associated with consciousness.

Bernheim most profitably related hypnotism to sleep and so had placed it in the context of normal psychic functioning. In addition he had shown it to be a "powerful therapeutic method."

The difficulty was that if Bernheim's views were correct, the "laws" governing hypnosis, and by implication hysteria, were not accurate and useful observations of a clinical syndrome. Each physician produced any symptom or "clinical entity" of which he had a predetermined idea; in fact there was no clinical entity to describe.

Freud agreed with Charcot that there must be a core of symptoms (stigmata, in the nonreligious sense) common to many patients and not the consequence of suggestion. In proof of this assertion, he cited the similarities in the clinical picture from patient to patient and even in hysterics from "past times and distant lands." After other arguments he concluded that there are objective physiological phenomena in hysteria. Freud then used his two colleagues' difference of opinion to discuss the basic problem. Since there were both mental and physiological phenomena in hypnosis and hysteria, what was the connecting link or relationship between the two? He pointed out that suggestions, whether direct or indirect, are external influences, whereas the term autosuggestion is useful because it emphasizes the inner readiness of the subject to accept external influences.

Current studies of perception have rediscovered this fact when they describe perception as an active rather than a passive process. The concept has always been of central importance in psychoanalytic theory. It was most clearly stated in chapter 7 of *The Interpretation of Dreams*, in which the reflex model, stimulus-response, is modified by the insertion of the unconscious into the circuit. The implication is that the meaning of the stimulus is understandable only when allowance is made for the nature of the appetitive state of the organism, which is primarily determined by somatic factors (needs or drives).

After emphasizing the role of internal processes (functional peculiarities of the subject's nervous system), Freud asks whether these need to be mental. He points out that the difference between the mental level and the physiological level is based on the criteria of consciousness and concludes that the question is no longer meaningful, since there can be executive activity of the brain (both cortical and subcortical) not associated with consciousness. These processes would then be described as physiological rather than psychological. If, however, the same processes occurred *and* were associated with attention, they would involve consciousness and would be described as being psychological.

As early as 1891, in his book *On Aphasia*, Freud described the physiological and psychological as dependent concomitants or parallel processes. He wrote, on page 55, "The relationship between the chain of physiological events in the nervous system and the mental processes is probably not one of cause and effect. The former do not cease when the latter set in; they tend to continue but, from a certain moment, a mental phenomenon corresponds to each part of the chain, or to several parts. The psychic is, therefore, a process parallel to the physiological, a 'dependent concomitant'." Much later, in 1915 in his paper "The Unconscious," Freud pointed out that to equate mental with consciousness was impractical and, he wrote, "plunges us into the insoluble difficulties of psycho-physical parallelism" (*S.E. 14* 168).

More recently Hartmann has emphasized the fact that the psychological is not the antithesis of the physiological.[1]

The problem was one of the issues that the topographical theory attempted to resolve. It was most fully discussed in *The Interpretation of Dreams* and in "The Unconscious."[2]

In the early years most German psychiatrists in general, and Meynert in particular, aimed at understanding mental illness only in terms of a physiological orientation. In contrast the French view as expressed by Charcot and Bernheim, Freud said, "relegates physiological considerations to a second place" (Freud, 1892–93*a*, *S.E. 1* 135).

[1] Hartmann, *Ego Psychology and the Problems of Adaptation*, pp. 34–35.

[2] In the topographical theory the psychical apparatus was divided into three systems—the system unconscious (Ucs), the system preconscious (Pcs), and later the system conscious (Cs). The goal of the topographic approach was to describe for "any given mental act within what system or between what systems it takes place" (*S.E. 14* 173). Memory traces were considered to have an unconscious registration and that "a very great part of this preconscious originates in the unconscious, has the character of its derivatives and is subjected to a censorship before it can become concious" (*S.E. 14* 191).

The essence of the topographic theory was a sequential (spatial or temporal) and hierarchic ordering of a perceptual registration that might first be organized in terms of simultaneity and next in terms of similarity and finally in causal terms.

One implication of the theory, which involved transpositions of an idea from one system (or locality) to a new system, was that each transposition involved a fresh registration in a new locality "alongside of which the original unconscious registration continues to exist" (*S.E. 14* 174). Freud considered this hypothesis and, both in 1900 (*S.E. 5* 610) and in 1915 (*S.E. 14* 180), felt an economic view was superior to the concept of double registration. The economic view maintained that there was only a single registration but the energic organization was what distinguished the unconscious form from the preconscious one.

Even the economic view that described mobile energies as characteristic of the system Ucs in contrast to bound energies in the system Pcs turned out to be unsatisfactory. Freud then concluded that the difference between an unconscious presentation and a conscious one was not that they are "different registrations of the same content in different psychical localities, nor yet different functional states of cathexis in the same locality" (*S.E. 14* 201), but that preconscious registration differs from unconscious registration by the fact that the former are linked to words. Finally the problems that the topographic theory attempted to solve were somewhat sidestepped when Freud advanced the structural hypothesis in 1923 in his paper, "The Ego and the Id" (*S.E. 19* 12–66).

Freud's position, modeled after that of the famous British neurologist Hulings Jackson, was to recognize the two views as "separate but equal." This imposed a double burden on Freud, who had an early hope that both the physiological and the psychological aspects of mental functioning could be described. He felt that to study the psychological aspect alone was to deal with only the superstructure.

Freud's interest in the physiological level has been falsely described as his need to "neurologize" his psychological understanding. According to this view, Freud was inhibited in his exploration of the psychological factors and clung to the safer physiological formulations, and only his self-analysis freed him from this inhibition. His early papers are viewed as reflecting his need to neurologize, when, so the theory goes, his observations could better have been formulated in purely psychological terms. The "Project for a Scientific Psychology" is cited as representing the culmination of the need to remain neurologically oriented. The Editor's Introduction to the *Standard Edition* translation of *Studies on Hysteria* describes Freud at the "halfway stage in the process of moving from physiological to psychological explanations of psychopathological states" (*S.E. 2* xxv). It goes on to contrast the two papers on anxiety neurosis (1895*b*, 1895*f*), with their "toxicological" explanation (poisonous damming up of the libido), and the two papers on the neuropsychoses of defense (1894*a*, 1896*b*), with their emphasis on dynamic psychological formulations.

The order of the publication of these papers would tend to contradict the belief that Freud went from a physiological orientation to a psychological one. The first paper on the neuropsychoses of defense was published in early 1894, the first anxiety paper in early 1895 (although the basic ideas were described earlier in Drafts B, E, and G). The second anxiety paper appeared in March, 1895, and the second paper on defense in 1896. Thus the order of publication does not corroborate the thesis that Freud "abandoned" the physical level of explanation and "discovered" the psychological. The two approaches were *clearly intended to supplement each other.*

Freud's goal at this time was a "complete psychological explanation." As he used the term, this involved both a clinical (psychological) understanding and an understanding of the underlying physical "mechanics" of the phenomenon. Part of Freud's enthusiastic belief in Fliess was based on his hope that Fliess, being interested in biology, would help him in this endeavor. For example, in Letter 38 (*Origins* 136), he writes that obsessional ideas are "invariably *self-reproaches*, while at the root of hysteria there is always *conflict* (sexual pleasure versus an accompanying unpleasure). . . . That is a new formula for expressing the *clinical explanation*" (italics added). In Letter 36 (*Origins* 134), when Freud expresses disillusionment about the Project, he writes, "the clinical explanation . . . will probably stand, after some modifications." Later, in Letter 48 (*Origins* 169), Freud writes in a depressed state saying that he hopes for further help from Fliess, and then adds, "Anxiety, chemical factors, etc.–perhaps you may supply me with solid ground on which I shall be able to give up explaining things psychologically and start finding a firm basis in physiology!" In Letter 51 (*Origins* 172), he still talks of the hope of putting "my column on your base." By Letter 96 (*Origins* 264), he is writing that he has "no desire at all to leave the psychology hanging in the air with no organic basis. . . . I have no idea yet why I cannot yet fit it together."

Freud increasingly became convinced that questions concerning the biological basis of mental function were currently insoluble. In "The Unconscious," he writes (*S.E. 14* 174), "every endeavour to think of ideas as stored up in nerve-cells and of excitations as travelling along nerve-fibres, has miscarried completely. . . . There is a hiatus here which at present cannot be filled, nor is it one of the tasks of psychology to fill it." Yet he remained convinced of the central importance of the physiological substrate in the genesis of emotional illness. This can be seen by his belief in the injurious effects (somatic) of masturbation, and in the existence of the actual neuroses.[3]

Freud's dissatisfaction with his understanding of the physiological level of the neuroses can be seen in his comment that our theory of instincts is, so to speak, our "mythology" (*S.E. 22* 95), by which he meant that, although incomplete, it had to suffice until the organic substrate could be discovered. What was for Freud an unavoidable restriction has been accepted by many analysts and is unquestioned. As a result analysis has dealt exclusively with psychogenic explanations and even "overstretched psychogenicity" ("Contributions to a Discussion on Masturbation," *S.E. 12* 248). Unlike Freud, we limit even the nature of the questions we ask: for example, the study of anxiety focuses almost entirely on its use by the ego as a signal of danger and ignores the problem of its origins.

Freud never found a "solution" to the question of "at what distance these parallel processes were to be studied" (Kris *Origins* 44). He had to accept his ignorance of the physiological substrate and his lack of any means for its investigation. Accordingly he put aside his original ambitious program and limited himself to the study of the psychological level alone. This decision was a difficult one for him, equivalent to what every medical analyst goes through, since it involved some giving up of the security of the "hard sciences" in which he had been trained.

The biological basis of psychoanalytic theory, although incomplete, is still of central importance. The biological and somatic factor is most obviously represented in the instinct or drive orientation of psychoanalysis. Another common

[3] The term "aktuelle neuroses" and later "Aktualneuroses" is best translated as "present-day neuroses," and emphasizes that the etiology is a current sexual practice that fails to bring about adequate discharge of sexual tension. These neuroses are in contrast to the psychoneuroses, whose sexual etiological factor derives from childhood experiences.

basis that psychoanalysis has with biology is the emphasis on "an original bisexuality in human beings (as in animals)" (*S.E. 18* 171). More recently, as Hartmann has pointed out,[4] the concept of the primary autonomy of the ego and its "centralized functional control" provides a biological orientation to ego psychology.

Freud's hope in these early years was that a clear understanding of both the physiological and psychological factors in the neuroses would also provide an answer to their etiology. The expectation was one of finding a single cause that produced a specific effect, probably of a neurological nature. Charcot's work with hysterical paralyses of traumatic origin became prototypical. He had shown that the precipitating event that produced the hysterical symptoms was a frightening experience, a psychic trauma. The clinical picture of the hysterias could also be exactly reproduced by suggestion in patients in a hypnotic state. This proved that the hysterias were functional in origin (psychic) and influenced by experience (the trauma). In contrast to the traumatic hysterias, there were the "common hysterias," those in which no precipitating traumatic factor could be discovered. Because of this, the etiology of these common hysterias was thought to be entirely the result of hereditary factors. To Charcot this proved that the basic etiology in both cases was a hereditary factor and that the traumatic experience was a nonspecific precipitating event. The capacity to develop the disease was based on a hereditary taint and the disease itself was evidence of some degeneracy.

Freud described his work in this field as a continuation of Charcot's studies, but his studies did not support Charcot's belief in the significance of the hereditary factor. Freud wrote in "The Aetiology of Hysteria" (*S.E. 3* 191), "In the view of the influential school of Charcot, heredity alone deserves to be recognized as the true cause of hysteria, while all the other noxae of the most various nature and intensity

[4] Hartmann, *Essays on Ego Psychology*, p. 268.

only play the part of incidental causes, of '*agents provocateurs.*'" (See also "Heredity and the Aetiology of the Neuroses," *S.E. 3* 143.) Freud came to disagree with this formulation because, unlike most of his colleagues, but following Breuer's example from 1882, he *listened* to his patients. The particular nature of Freud's dialogue with his patients had convinced him that many symptoms in the common hysterias could also be understood as determined by experience and that many so-called hereditary hysterias were in fact traumatic in origin, not the consequence of a single and obvious trauma, but the result of many small and cumulative traumas.

Freud's first contribution was the statement that there was a complete analogy between traumatic hysteria and the common hysterias. The common hysterias were also "acquired" rather than hereditary in origin, and psychic trauma played a role, except that instead of one major and obvious trauma, as in the traumatic hysterias, there were many small traumas acting by summation.

Freud was also convinced from what his patients told him that these traumatic experiences involved the patient's sexual life. He became convinced that the sexual life was the specific factor in the etiology of the neuroses and psychoneuroses and that the hereditary factor was of only secondary, nonspecific importance. He set himself the goal of describing these various determinants of the neurosis and their relative importance. For this purpose he devised what he called his "aetiological formula."

Even a casual reader of these early papers is impressed by the importance that Freud attached to this idea. It is the main topic of Drafts A and B, and in Draft C he writes that he is pleased that Wilhelm Preyer "does not know our aetiological formula," which he describes a few lines later as the "key that unlocks everything." (See also *S.E. 3* 104, 1895*b*.)

In Draft B Freud distinguished the necessary precondition (the sexual factor) from the precipitating factors. The two factors were additive: if the necessary precondition is present, but in an insufficient amount, then the quantitative lack can be made up by an abundance of the secondary precipitating factor. For example, in acquired neurasthenia (always and only a sexual neurosis), sexual exhaustion due to masturbation is the necessary precondition and can by itself be sufficient to produce the neurosis. If qualitatively present but quantitatively inadequate, such nonspecific factors as overwork and physical illness may bring the latent illness into the open. Later, in the closely reasoned second anxiety paper *S.E. 3* 123–139, 1895*f*), he considerably elaborated the etiological factors, dividing them into four categories: (1) preconditions, (2) specific cause, (3) concurrent causes, and (4) precipitating or releasing cause.

The terms in summary are defined by Freud in the following fashion:

(1) Preconditions are those factors in whose absence the neurosis would never come about and that when present are "incapable of producing the effect by themselves alone, no matter in what amount they may be present. For the specific cause is still lacking" (*S.E. 3* 136). Hereditary factors are under this heading.

(2) Specific cause is defined as never absent in any case where the effect takes place. It can alone, if present in sufficient quantity, produce the illness, when the precondition is fulfilled. Sexual noxae fall into this category and include both early sexual experience and current sexual practices.

(3) Concurrent causes are generally defined as chronic stressful experiences, quantitatively able to *supplement* the specific cause, but not able to produce the illness in the absence of the specific cause: typically, chronic fatigue, overwork, and the like.[5]

[5] A similar distinction is met again in Freud's later description of dream formation, in which wish fulfillment of infantile unconscious sexual factors is specific to the dream and the day residue acts as the precipitating nonspecific factor.

(4) Releasing causes are acute forms of concurrent causes and act as sudden precipitants to the symptomatology.

Both 1 and 2 are necessary causes, but can be distinguished since the precondition exhibits no special relation to the effect (i.e., does not determine the form) and is of long standing in contrast to the specific cause.

Freud applied to this formulation the term "aetiological equation" (*S.E. 3* 135) because each factor was capable of a quantitative change—that is, increase or decrease—and from a quantitative point of view could result in a final sum that passed the threshold level—"the total load on the nervous system in proportion to its capacity to carry the load" (*S.E. 3* 131). The etiological equation implied a primitive type of dynamic and economic point of view and therefore could be described as an early metapsychological formulation.

As an economic formulation its imperfections are quite apparent. Although it involves an equation with a variety of theoretical variables, none of these variables can be quantified or even distinguished except on theoretical grounds: each is independently variable and only subjectively and post hoc estimatable.

The pseudomathematical nature can be seen when the role of hereditary factors is compared with that of the acquired disability. The hereditary factor was described as working like a "multiplier introduced into an electric current" (*S.E. 3* 139 1895*f*, 147 1896*a*, 252; also, Draft A, *S.E. 1* 177). What was inherited was a defective *vita sexualis*, an inability of the nervous system to tolerate the usual quantity of somatic sexual excitation. However, this defective functioning could equally well be the result of an acquired disability. It could be the consequence of masturbation or of the practice of coitus interruptus, which led to a disability in the discharge or distribution of the somatic excitation: the results were the same.

Since the specific factor and the stock factors could combine quantitatively to produce the illness, their separation was of little real value. Freud wrote (*S.E. 3* 138), "whether a neurotic illness occurs at all depends upon the total load on the nervous system as compared with the latter's capacity for resistance." Since none of the individual components of the load, or the total load, or the resistance, could be measured, the "equation" was from this point of view worthless.

A further defect in this primitive "quantitative" view is that it was without clear dynamic implications. An economic view must be more than an assumption of the existence of some type of energy serving as a driving force. A dynamic concept of function presupposes energy and structure, just as energy must posit structure and function. All three concepts are inseparable in a dynamic system. To be meaningful, an economic viewpoint must deal with the vicissitudes of the energy and relate these vicissitudes to clinically observable phenomena.

It is a question why Freud attached so much importance to his etiological formula in these early years. The answer is not hard to find. The most immediate value of the etiological formula was the impetus it gave for further study of the patients. As long as hereditary factors were considered of prime importance, little could be hoped for in the study or treatment of the disease. The etiological formula was a way of stating and defending the thesis that the specific precondition for the genesis of the neurosis lay in the sexual life and gave hope of further knowledge. It was not a dynamic formulation, or a meaningful economic one, but it was a beginning toward both. The etiological formula also reduced the importance of various secondary complaints—preoccupation with bowels, bladder, brain, and so forth (*Origins* 74)—behind which lay the omnipresent and essential sexual factor.

The etiological formula has survived in psychoanalytic theory in the concept of the "complemental series." This states that there are multiple determinants in the etiology of the psychoneuroses and that they are reciprocally related to each other in a quantitative way (*S.E. 16* 347, 362; *22* 126). The most important and immediate effect of the etiological formula was that in all hysterical patients (both those with traumatic and those with common hysterias) a traumatic factor could be uncovered. As a result all hysterias might be helped by therapy. This in turn had important implications concerning treatment.

In his first months of practice (1886), Freud treated his hysterical patients, as others did, with baths, massage, and local electrical stimulation. This electrical treatment had been described in a textbook by Dr. W. Erb, the famous neuropathologist. Electrodes were applied to the affected areas, and the mild electric current produced a local tingling sensation or occasionally a muscle jerk.

The method achieved little success and Freud felt "absolutely helpless" (*S.E. 14* 7–66). Jones reports his saying that the only reason he could not agree that the results were due to suggestion was that he did not have any results to explain.[6]

In December, 1887, Freud began to employ hypnosis with most of his patients. Freud, like others, had used the hypnotic trance occasionally even before his 1885 trip to Paris. He had seen a public demonstration of "magnetism" by Hansen (*S.E. 20* 161) and of course he knew of Breuer's use of hypnosis in the treatment of Anna O. Only during his studies with Charcot did he see it accepted as a regular technique in the treatment of patients.

In his preface to Bernheim's book (1888; *S.E. 1* 75), Freud describes hypnosis as a "powerful therapeutic method." The method was to tell the patients while they were in the hypnotic trance that their symptoms would disappear. Using hypnosis in this manner Freud had what he termed "small but unusual successes" (*Origins*, Letter 2). The technique is well illustrated in his 1892–93 paper, "A Case of Successful

[6] Jones, *Life and Work of Sigmund Freud*, vol. 1, p. 235.

Treatment by Hypnotism" (*S.E. 1* 119). The patient was a young mother who had been unable to breast feed her first child. The difficulty reappeared at the birth of her second child three years later and was associated with vomiting, lack of appetite, irritability, and insomnia. Breuer, her family physician, recommended that she try once more to feed the child with the help of hypnotic suggestion, and Freud was brought in on the case. Freud describes his therapeutic comments to the patient during the hypnotic trance. "I made use of suggestion to contradict all her fears and the feelings on which those fears were based: 'Have no fear! You will make an excellent nurse and the baby will thrive. Your stomach is perfectly quiet, your appetite is excellent, you are looking forward to your next meal, etc.'" The results were so immediate and successful that Freud was told there were no longer any problems and he need not continue with the case. The impression is that his role in the patient's recovery was ignored or minimized and he was hardly thanked.

A year later a third child was born and the symptoms reappeared. Again Freud was successful in his hypnotic therapeutic efforts. This time both the patient and her husband were grateful and recognized his role in her recovery.

Freud uses this example to consider psychical mechanisms at work in the patient. His formulation is a dynamic one, in which two forces are at work: the conscious wish of the patient was to feed the child, but another, antithetical force led her to expect failure. The healthy person is self-confident and expects success. The neurotic with lowered self-confidence and a tendency to depression fears failure, but in the hysteric this fear remains unconscious and becomes apparent only in bodily symptoms. In the neurasthenic patient with a similar problem the fears would have been conscious and expressed as a dread of the task and doubts of success. The patient would have felt exhausted and might even have given up the job. Thus the neurasthenic shows a weakness of will, the hysteric a perversion of will.

Freud does not offer any specific explanation of the origin of the antithetic impulses (later called ambivalence). He implies that these impulses are present in everyone and become manifest only in states of general exhaustion. In fatigue states, the conscious impulse is weakened more than the suppressed ideas, which then are able to gain the upper hand.[7]

The limited nature of the technique, as well as its limited success, left Freud dissatisfied. In a footnote to his translation of Charcot's *Leçons du Mardi* (*Poliklinische Vorträge* 1892 192), he wrote, "Neither physician nor patient can for any length of time be satisfied or tolerate the contradiction existing between the denial of illness during suggestion and its recognition outside that situation." On another occasion, in "Hypnosis" (1891), he wrote, "Physician and patient grow tired . . . as a result of the contrast between the deliberately rosy coloring of the suggestions and the cheerless truth" (*S.E. 1* 113).

Because of his dissatisfaction, Freud revived the technique that he had heard of from Breuer of attempting, under hypnosis, to trace the symptoms back to their origin during a traumatic experience. Breuer had discovered the method in 1882 while treating Anna O. and had described it to Freud. The technique is known as Breuer's cathartic method and depends for its therapeutic success on the patient's recall of the circumstances and feelings associated with the first appearance of the symptom. In the hypnotic trance, memories that otherwise were not available to the patient were recalled (*S.E. 1* 112). During the emotional reliving of the traumatic experience the "strangulated" affects that kept the symptom in existence could be expressed and discharged (abreacted).

[7] This dynamic concept is elaborated in *The Interpretation of Dreams* (1900). In sleep the forces of censorship are weakened, and unconscious impulses find expression in the dream. It is also contained in the dynamic concept of repression, in which drive impulses find expression in symptoms in the form of the return of the repressed. The problem is more fully discussed in Freud's paper of 1912, "Types of Onset of Neurosis" (*S.E. 12* 231).

It seems most likely that Freud first systematically applied Breuer's technique to his treatment of Frau Emmy von N., which he began on May 1, 1889. Even as he began to employ this method, he also began to modify it, for he had found that many of his patients could not be hypnotized. When he visited Bernheim at Nancy in 1889, he was accompanied by a patient whom he had not been able to hypnotize. Bernheim also failed in his attempts to hypnotize this patient and told Freud that he was most successful with his clinic patients and less successful with patients in his private practice. These latter were apparently more sophisticated and less impressionable. Freud felt embarrassed and dissatisfied by his failures, apparently most so with Emmy von N. (*Studies on Hysteria*, *S.E. 2* 101). He abandoned the goal of producing a hypnotic trance and substituted "a state of concentration" (*S.E. 2* 108), often aided by "pressure technique," in which he would press his hand on the patient's forehead and ask the patient to report whatever thoughts or images came to mind (*S.E. 2* 270). This technique seems to have been used first with his patient Fraülein Elizabeth von R. (*S.E. 2* 145 and fn. 110). Certainly by 1900 and probably before, he had given up touching his patients or using hypnosis and had developed the procedure of free association as the method of choice.

It is puzzling that Freud delayed so long in applying Breuer's method to his own patients. Why, if he was so impressed by Breuer's revelation of the technique and consequences of his treatment under hypnosis of Anna O. as early as 1882, did Freud, when he was treating patients by hypnosis in 1887, not use this more productive and more precise form of treatment?

Jones suggests that it was Charcot's lack of interest when Freud told him of Breuer's discovery that accounts for the delay.[8] In "An Autobiographical Study," Freud attributes

[8] Jones, *Life and Work of Freud*, vol. 1, p. 235.

his use of Erb's electrotherapy to his "innocent faith in authority," from which he was not yet free (*S.E. 20* 16).

Whatever the cause, the result was a slow acceptance of the value of inquiry over a more direct assault on the symptom, and Freud's inquiry became more and more centered on the delicate subject of the details of the patient's sexual life. It seems possible that the incentive and even self-permission to inquire into the patient's sexual conflicts was not possible for Freud until he surmised that the sexual life was of central etiological importance. Only when he was convinced of the importance of this line of inquiry was he free to pursue it in face of society's prohibition and his own inhibitions. This may account for the delay; certainly it leads us directly into the question of Freud's early views concerning the role of the sexual life in the etiology of the neuroses. It is a subject in which he made his greatest discoveries and his grandest errors.

3. *Early Views on Sexuality—The Actual Neurosis*

PART OF FREUD'S genius lay in his remarkable ability to select new and fruitful concepts with which he could organize and explain his observations. He could take a few facts, see the central issue, and offer a basic formulation on even the slimmest of evidence. This creative approach can be seen in *The Interpretation of Dreams*, where, after examining a handful of dreams, he was able not only to describe the dynamic forces which lead to dream formation, but also to construct from this a basic theoretical model of the mind and show the manner of its functioning. The same almost magical creativeness was shown many years later in his study of fetishism, where, like an artist, with a few deft strokes he was able to show the basic issues involved, leaving to his followers little to do but fill in details and admire his skill.

There is a danger to this form of inquiry. Only if the basic postulates and the ordering of the facts are correct (and this has to be almost intuitional) are the formulations trustworthy. A false step can lead to nonsense, and if the formulation is maintained against further evidence, it can end in delusion. Freud made a number of bold but false formulations. He was saved from any serious consequences because when he was wrong he did not ignore his error and become addicted to his erroneous ideas. Unlike Fliess, he was able to recognize and correct his mistakes. It is interesting too that even when he was wrong, his formulations often contained an important truth, and when the error was corrected this fundamental discovery would emerge. The seduction theory—a complex set of hypotheses related to the etiology of the psychoneuroses, the reasons for repression, and the choice of the neurosis—is the outstanding example. When this error was corrected (Letter 69, *S.E. 1* 259), it led to the discovery of infantile sexuality and the role of fantasy in symptom formation. It took less than two years to correct this error. A second error in Freud's early formulations was maintained for thirty years before he finally corrected it. It involved what is referred to as the toxicological theory of anxiety, in which repression caused a damming up of somatic libido that was toxic or poisonous to the organism. The libido was then transformed and discharged through somatic channels in the form of an anxiety attack. In the first theory, repression caused anxiety, whereas later (1926) anxiety was seen as the cause for repression.

The early erroneous concept of the origin of anxiety was the basis on which the concept of the actual neuroses rested. The term designated neurotic illnesses, the symptoms of which Freud considered physical in origin and the consequence of *current* deleterious sexual practices. Since the symptoms were unrelated to psychological conflict, they did not have symbolic meaning and were not treatable by psychological techniques. The erroneous formulation was the result of Freud's lack of awareness at this time of the existence of unconscious mental processes and of infantile sexuality. Even after his discovery and investigation of these factors, he remained convinced of his ideas concerning the actual neuroses, and only in 1926 did he retract the theory of transformation of libido into anxiety. His clinging to the theory seems to have been motivated by his desire to include the physiological level of understanding with the psychological. Because the theory turned out to be incorrect, there is a tendency to ignore the observations on which it was based, and the details of the complex hypothesis. Nevertheless, it is rewarding to follow the line of reasoning that led Freud to the formulation.

Throughout his life, in the method common to scientists, Freud naturally based his theories on the insights he gathered from the observation of his patients. In dealing with them, Freud was impressed, as others had been, with the fact that neurotics were disturbed in their sexual functioning as well as in other areas.[1] Unlike previous investigators, he made a point of inquiring into all aspects of the patient's life. This and his increasing willingness to listen made it possible, or even unavoidable, for the patients to speak of those life situations that were most on their minds. This receptiveness gradually opened up a new world for observation. The first impact on Freud was a conviction that the disturbance in the adult sexual life was not a *consequence* of the illness, but rather the cause. This conviction is all the more impressive because, as Freud admitted in 1933, it was not accurate. Nevertheless, Freud felt he had more than a grain of truth and held to the basic idea.

In order to understand Freud's clinical and theoretical formulations, it is necessary first to look at his concept of normal sexual functioning. This is presented in Draft G (*S.E. 1* 200) and summarized later in his first paper on anxiety (*S.E. 3* 108 1895*b*). In this draft he presents the first of a series of models with which he attempts to illustrate and explain his theory of psychic functioning.

Freud begins his presentation by assuming the existence of a chemical sexual substance produced in the body, which gradually accumulates until it passes a threshold level, at which time it is capable of creating an awareness of sexual desire. This chemical substance is referred to as somatic

[1] Earlier casual statements concerning the central importance of sexuality in the etiology of the neuroses had been made to Freud by Breuer, by the gynecologist Rudolf Chrobak, and by Charcot (*S.E. 14* 13).

sexual substance and/or somatic libido. It provides the *energy* that "runs" the model. The *structure*, Freud postulates, consists of a terminal organ in which somatic sexual substance is stored. The implication is that it is the accumulation in this storage compartment that produces the awareness of "tension." (See "Three Essays on Sexuality," *S.E.* 7 213–216.) In the psychical sphere the structure is the "psychosexual group of ideas." This group of ideas also has its own mental energy—psychical libido, which can vary in amount and quality. The terminal organ is linked via a "spinal center" to the psychosexual group of ideas. The chemical substance produced in the body accumulates in the terminal organ and when it passes the threshold level it excites the psychosexual ideas. It is then "worked over psychically" (linkage occurs—Draft E, *S.E. 1* 194) and becomes an affect or sexual desire. This leads to a search in the external world for the sexual object. The presence of the sexual object further stimulates both the psychosexual group of ideas and the psychical libido and increases the production of the somatic sexual substance, which in turn also further stimulates the psychosexual group of ideas. When the sexual object is in "a favorable position," sensations from the genitals act on the terminal organ and provide another source of reflex stimulation of somatic sexual substance. The accumulated interrelated stimulation from the terminal organ, genital sensation, and sexual object builds to a crescendo ending in orgasm. The sexual act is the specific action that has as its function the discharge of the tension which has accumulated from somatic sources. At the time of orgasm, what Freud calls "voluptuous feelings" are transmitted from the terminal organ to the psychosexual group of ideas, where they become conscious. These feelings which occur at the time of orgasm are to be distinguished from pleasurable sensual feelings before orgasm. Voluptuous feelings are a direct indication of the efficiency of the orgasm in serving its function of discharging the chemical sexual substance (somatic sexual excitation—

S.S.E.). The fact that these feelings register in consciousness means that they will become bound as a pleasurable memory to the psychosexual group of ideas. This leads to pleasurable anticipation of the next experience, contributes to the stability and availability of the ideas, and creates a desire for repetition of the experience. Freud describes this when he states that "the psychical sexual group is strengthened by the introduction of [voluptuous feelings] and weakened by its omission" (*S.E. 1* 203).

Freud suggests that the terminal organ in this theoretical model may be related in men in some way to the testes or seminal vesicles and in women to the ovaries. Characteristically Freud was quite content to develop a model and leave the relationship to actual anatomy quite uncertain. He was not limited by the necessity to make concrete psychophysical parallels. This freedom is at times a problem to his more literal-minded critics.

This model of sexuality described in Draft G, with its energic, structural, and functional formulations, foreshadows the models developed later. These include the neuronic model in the Project (1895), the topographical model presented in *The Interpretation of Dreams* (1900), and the structural model presented in *The Ego and The Id* (1923). In fact many aspects of the structural hypothesis have their origins in this first schematic picture. The somatic sexual substance can be equated with the drives, the terminal organ with the id, and the psychosexual group of ideas with the preconscious of the topographical model or with the ego concept of the structural hypothesis. An even more remarkable parallel exists between this early model and recent neurophysiological discoveries of periodic stimulation of the subcortical and cortical areas of the brain by the reticular system. The terminal organ can be equated with these brain-stem sources of stimulation.

The fundamental hypothesis in this "schematic picture of sexuality" is that the function of orgasm is the unburdening of the model of internal excitation. The complexity of this deceptively simple model derives from the fact that the sexual cycle is presented as a chain reaction or a programmed series of steps leading to orgasm. There are a number of feedback systems or reverberating circuits that aid in the required progressive building up and final discharge of tension. Freud's early understanding of neurotic and psychoneurotic illness was based on this schematic model, and the illness was seen as the consequence of interference in the normal sexual cycle it described.

Freud's belief that current sexual practices were etiological for the neuroses came from his observation that neurasthenic symptoms, chronic fatigue, and bodily worries occurred most often in young men who were chronic masturbators. Attacks of anxiety, on the other hand, characteristically occurred in married couples, who, in order to avoid conception, practiced coitus interruptus, the withdrawal of the penis just before ejaculation. On the basis of these observations he suggested that neurasthenia and anxiety neurosis were two distinct clinical entities with different sexual etiologies (1895*b*).

Freud soon realized that although these sexual practices might precipitate the onset of the symptoms, their relation to the form and the etiology of the illness was ambiguous and indirect. Freud needed a more comprehensive theory that could include the wide variety and mixture of symptoms in both the actual neuroses and the psychoneuroses as well. He then advanced the more fundamental and unambiguous hypothesis that illness was related to inadequate unburdening, psychical insufficiency, or defense accompanied by substitution (*S.E. 3* 114 1895*b*).

These three alternatives are at different levels of theoretical explanation: inadequate unburdening is the most general statement and could include unburdening at too low a level of psychical tension (neurasthenia) or incomplete discharge (anxiety neurosis). Psychical insufficiency is one reason for incomplete discharge; another, for example, is psychical alienation. Defense accompanied by substitution refers to the psychoneuroses and leaves this diagnostic group outside the general formulation as a special case not directly connected with the concept of inadequate unburdening.

This led Freud to a complicated hypothesis that can best be understood if his most fundamental idea of the unburdening of the apparatus is related to two variables. The first is the problem of the linkage (later described by the term "cathectic investment") of the somatic libido with the psychosexual group of ideas. The second is the problem of the level of tension of the somatic libido at which this linkage occurs. Focusing on the issue of linkage and the level of tension, permits the illnesses to be divided into three major groups (see Chart 2), in which: (1) linkage between somatic and psychical libido occurs too easily (i.e., at too low a level of excitation), leading to excessive discharge; (2) incomplete linkage between somatic and psychical libido occurs because of (*a*) psychical insufficiency and (*b*) psychical alienation, and results in inadequate unburdening; and (3) linkage between somatic libido and psychical libido occurs but is not maintained as a functional unit.

Situations (1) and (2) lead to simple quantitative imbalance as a result of faulty unburdening and result in the actual neuroses, neurasthenia, anxiety neurosis, and some forms of melancholia. Group (3) represents the neuropsychoses of defense.

(1) *Linkage occurs at too low a level of excitation, leading to frequent discharge, a chronic depletion of somatic excitation, and the clinical picture of neurasthenia.*

Freud's *clinical observations* were that neurasthenia occurred often in young unmarried men who, being afraid of contracting gonorrhea or syphilis, would resort to masturbation for the relief of sexual tension. This also fitted in with the observation that young unmarried women tended to masturbate much less often and that there were many fewer

Chart 2 Relationship of Somatic to Psychic Libido in the Neuroses and Psychoneuroses

Nature of Linkage between Somatic and Psychical Libido	Quantitative Level of Somatic Libido	Quantitative Level of Psychical Libido	Etiology	Diagnosis
Linkage too easily achieved	Low because of poor tolerance of excitation	Low because of frequent discharge	Masturbation. Discharge occurs too easily at low level of excitation (low threshold).	Neurasthenia, usually in men before marriage, due to depletion of S.S.E.
Linkage not achieved	Usually high	Low	Psychical insufficiency or psychical alienation—occurs in virgins, prudes, or married couples practicing coitus interruptus. Symptoms are not psychogenic—i.e., they do not have symbolic meaning.	Anxiety neurosis; also common phobias. Draft E, p. 92, or *Origins* and S.E. *3* 74.
	Low level of tension in terminal organ	High or low, but of poor quality. The psychosexual group of ideas is imperfectly and precariously invested since it is not sustained by somatic libido nor reinforced by voluptuous feelings.	Psychical libido withdrawn from other investments to reinforce precarious investment of psychosexual group of ideas. Occurs in women in whom the object arouses only psychical libido; therefore these women have narcissistic rather than genital demands.	Melancholia
Linkage achieved but not maintained as a conscious sexual unit	High	High	Psychosexual energy discharged through somatic channel. Symptom ideogenic or symbolic.	Hysteria
			Displaced in time and onto other analogous situation.	Obsession
Linkage achieved and maintained	Low	Low	Unknown	Frigidity—no neuroses. S.E. *3* 102; Origins 107

neurasthenic females. Thus Freud accounted for his clinical observation that in the first ten years after puberty, there were more neurotic men than neurotic women.

Another clinical observation seemed to confirm the close relationship of masturbation and neurasthenia. This was that some lucky young men who had been seduced by older women at an early age did not develop neurasthenia.

The deleterious effect of masturbation was that it was less than a fully satisfactory form of orgastic discharge. Its easy availability meant that it did not require a strong arousal or investment of the psychosexual feelings. In fact, frequent masturbation occurred in people who could not tolerate the optimum level of excitation. In this sense, masturbation, being easily available without struggle, was described as an addiction (Letter 79, *S.E. 1* 272). Freud described masturbation as the first of the sexual noxae and stated that it was the "specific factor" leading to neurasthenia, which was "always *only* a sexual neurosis." The less frequent the act of masturbation the less damaging the consequences, but this quantitative reduction in the specific factor could be offset by an increase in the nonspecific sources of strain such as illness, overwork, and other depleting experiences.

The therapeutic problem consisted of persuading the patient to abandon this path of inferior satisfaction and to establish the normal and more complete form of sexual gratification ("Sexuality in the Aetiology of the Neuroses" (1898), *S.E. 3* 276).

Freud's *theoretical explanation* for neurasthenia was an extension of an idea put forward by G. M. Beard, a British neurologist who in 1884 had published a book titled *Sexual Neurasthenia (Nervous Exhaustion)*. Beard had suggested that the characteristic neurasthenic symptom of chronic fatigue was due to a *physiological* exhaustion of the nerve cells. Freud's view was that what was exhausted was somatic libido. But in order to explain why repeated masturbation produced symptoms whereas equally frequent enjoyable sexual relations did not, Freud needed a hypothesis that went beyond this ambiguous formulation. He advanced the theory that in the person potentially susceptible to neurasthenia there was too great an ease in forming a linkage between somatic libido and psychical libido; that is, the threshold of arousal was too low in terms of the accumulation of somatic sexual substance in the terminal organ. This led to "an impoverishment owing to the excitation running out, as it were, through a hole. . . . What is pumped empty is somatic sexual excitation." The basic cause for this impoverishment could be a hereditary factor (poor *vita sexualis*) or spontaneous emissions (*S.E. 3* 150 1896*a*, 275 1898), but more often it was the direct consequence of masturbation. The process was circular, however, since the act of masturbation was thought to accustom the model (neuronic system or mental apparatus) to expect and finally to *require* disburdening at a low level of excitation. If the masturbation had been frequent and occurred over a prolonged period, it led to a permanent impairment of potency and in marriage very often to the symptom of premature ejaculation. Thus premature ejaculation could occur as a hereditary or acquired inability to tolerate optimum sexual tension. Since the discharge occurs at a low level of excitation, and before optimum tension develops in the psychosexual group of ideas, the individual would have a poorly developed sexual affect: at first a need to discharge somatic and *psychical libido* at low tension and later an increased propensity for low-tension-level discharge, that is, facilitation would have occurred.

The model for Freud's concept of discharge is a combination of physical, hydraulic, and neurological images. The physical image of discharge is taken from the male's ejaculation at orgasm. The closely associated hydraulic image is clear from the remark that somatic sexual excitation is "pumped" out (*S.E. 1* 206). The neurological image is similar to Breuer's formulation in his chapter in *Studies on Hysteria.* It implies that a chemical secretion in the body produces a local area of high electrical potential in the brain. This local area of high potential produces the intense idea and affect associated with sexuality (psychical linkage). The term discharge then refers to an electrical discharge that achieves a reduction in the local high-potential area.

This formulation might appear to be simply a more "scientific" restatement of the Victorian view of the danger of masturbation. It is true, however, that the chemical, biological, and psychical consequences of frequent masturbation are still not fully known. Freud, who can hardly be considered a moralistic prude, continued to feel that some damaging somatic factor was involved and that to ignore this was to "overstretch psychogenicity" (*S.E. 12* 248–253; *9* 199). These comments illustrate Freud's reluctance to limit himself to the psychological level in his attempts to explain the malfunctioning of the mental apparatus.

(2) *Incomplete linkage between somatic libido and psychical libido occurs and results in inadequate unburdening. The resultant accumulation of somatic sexual excitation (somatic libido) is discharged through somatic channels, giving the picture of anxiety neurosis.*

Freud was first tempted to explain anxiety attacks as hysterical symptoms in which concern about pregnancy played the etiological role. Anxiety about pregnancy having been put out of consciousness then returned as a symptom. Such an explanation would mean that the anxiety attacks were symptoms of a psychoneurosis (neuropsychosis of defense). A number of other clinical examples, however, convinced Freud that this formulation was untenable. For example, he observed anxiety attacks in women who had no fear of pregnancy and in fact wanted children. If pregnancy fears were not the source of anxiety, Freud thought the anxiety might be caused by conflict over sexual impulses aroused during intercourse. This was also unlikely, since Freud observed as many anxiety attacks in women who were anesthetic during intercourse as in those who had sexual sensations. The most convincing clinical demonstration that sexual conflict was not the cause of anxiety attacks was "a remarkably pure case of anxiety-neurosis, after coitus interruptus in a placid and entirely frigid woman." Since this woman was not sexually aroused psychically, Freud reasoned *that her anxiety attacks could not be psychological in origin.*

Another case which led to the same conclusion, that anxiety attacks were not psychological in origin, was that of a "gay old bachelor who denies himself nothing." He had a "classical anxiety attack after allowing his thirty-year-old mistress to induce him to have coitus three times" (*Origins*, Letter 15, 79–80). Freud reasoned that the man had been psychosexually stimulated beyond his own somatic or endogenous needs and this must in some way be the source of his anxiety attack. Freud was led by these and other cases to write, "I have come to the opinion that anxiety is to be connected, not with mental, but with a physical consequence of sexual abuse."

Freud's theoretical explanation of anxiety neurosis had to explain a wide variety of clinical examples. He had observed anxiety attacks in virginal persons, in people who were deliberately abstinent (most often prudish people), and in those who were abstinent from necessity. The obvious factor common to the three groups was that the patients described had no outlet for their sexual tension. The greatest number of anxiety attacks, however, occurred in one or the other partner of a newly married couple. The problem was why these persons should develop anxiety, since they had the opportunity for the discharge of sexual tension. Each case Freud studied showed that some difficulty in the current sexual life led up to the same point—the inadequate discharge of sexual tension that led to the accumulation of an excess of somatic sexual substance. Since this excess was not bound to the psychosexual group of ideas, it could not emerge as a sexual wish, and became instead a burden to the psychical apparatus.

Freud's explanation, again employing the schematic sexual model, involved two explanations. The first concerned the variety of ways in which the inadequate unburdening came about. Freud showed that in all the clinical cases in which anxiety attacks occurred, there was an inadequate unburdening of somatic sexual excitation. Next he explained why the accumulated sexual substance (somatic libido), after it reached a certain threshold, resulted not in sexual desire but in an attack of anxiety. To explain inadequate unburdening and the accumulation of unbound somatic libido, Freud separated his cases into two major groups: those in whom there was "*psychical insufficiency*" and those who had "*psychical alienation.*"

The group with psychical insufficiency developed adequate amounts of somatic libido but these cases were deficient in the psychicical sphere. Freud writes (Draft E, *S.E. 1* 193): "The physical tension increases and reaches the threshold value at which it can arouse psychical affect; but for some reasons the psychical linkage offered to it remains insufficient; a *sexual affect* cannot be formed, because there is something lacking in the psychical determinants."

Freud felt that his clinical observation supported his theoretical formulation, since persons with anxiety neurosis regularly complained of a loss of sexual interest, that is, they were apparently deficient in psychical libido.

The concept of "psychical insufficiency" explained attacks of anxiety in virginal persons, especially girls, in whom some early psychical awareness of sexuality had only just begun. In these persons the "field of ideas which ought to take up the physical tension is not yet present or it is only insufficiently present" (Draft E, *S.E. 1* 193; see also *S.E. 9* 181 pp. 197–201 particularly). Other examples illustrating the problem of psychical insufficiency included people who suffer enforced abstinence and then actually achieve a lack of psychical desire; older persons who as a result of age have lost the capacity for summoning up sufficient psychical desire;

and finally prudes, in whom sexual ideas are unpleasurable.

In both the male and female climacteric, Freud postulated only a *relative* insufficiency of psychical libido. In the first paper on anxiety (1895*b*), he suggested that, at this age, there is so marked an increase in the production of somatic sexual excitation "that the psyche proves relatively insufficient to master it" (*S.E. 3* 102, 110). This is also the mechanism of "Anxiety Type x," in which somatic sexual excitation is induced by the partner's stimulation (*Origins*, Letter 15, 79, and Draft E).

A normal person stimulated to excessive sexual activity would experience only sexual exhaustion. Both somatic libido and psychical libido would be produced and discharged at an even pace, leaving no undischarged surplus. In a similar situation a person who had practiced masturbation to excess earlier in life would, because of the low threshold level for somatic discharge, develop neurasthenia.

Freud's explanation of the development of anxiety in an older man induced to perform sexually beyond his own inclination is ingenious and the reverse of what would seem the usual explanation. It might seem that he would be psychically stimulated but somatically "exhausted." Freud suggested that the opposite occurred. The older man would respond to his partner's sexual seductiveness by producing an excess of somatic libido that he could not master or bind by psychical interest; that is, Freud felt the man became aroused somatically, but was not able to be really interested. The limiting factor was the reduction in the quality or quantity of psychical libido.

This explanation might be hard for a man to understand, since he would rather explain his difficulty on the basis of a somatic depletion than on a lack of interest. But Freud's explanation seems correct because, although the older man may want to perform sexually, it is more that he strives to perform than that he is driven to it by his own sexual needs. Even though he may achieve an ejaculation, the quality of the orgasm is reduced. The lack of adequate orgasm results in incomplete discharge of somatic libido; the somatic arousal is greater than the psychical release and the differential is the sexual noxa. Forced performance (Draft F) from a sense of duty produces a similar undesirable ratio between excessive somatic stimulation and lowered psychical desire. The result is inadequate unburdening of the somatic libido.

Anxiety symptoms occurring in married couples had a more complex explanation. Freud observed that in newly married couples in which the wife developed symptoms that the man had previously been neurasthenic. After marriage he might continue neurasthenic or improve as a result of achieving adequate gratification without undue strain, despite a remaining potency disturbance (premature ejaculation) resulting from his masturbatory history. His new wife, however, was very likely to become ill, either with anxiety neurosis or with hysterical symptoms. Her illness was due to incomplete arousal and satisfaction and occurred as a result of the potency disturbance of her husband. To the extent that the sexual arousal was only somatic and did not achieve psychical representation (no sexual wishes), she developed anxiety neurosis; to the extent that she became aware of her sexual wishes which were not gratified and "put them out of her mind," she developed hysterical symptoms.

Freud felt that his explanation not only was supported by the individual cases he studied, but was also confirmed in another way. Just as he explained the greater incidence in men of neurotic illness in the first decade after puberty (ages thirteen to twenty-three), as due to the damaging overindulgence in masturbation, he was also able to explain why the situation was reversed in the second decade after puberty (ages twenty-three to thirty-three). In this decade there were more neurotic women than neurotic men and this could now be understood as a result of the husband's potency disturbance, which resulted in the wife's lack of psychosexual arousal and gratification.

In the next decade (thirty-three to forty-three), the difficulty a married couple had to face was the problem of pregnancy. By this time they might have had all the children they wanted or could afford, and it became necessary to practice some form of incomplete intercourse in order to prevent further pregnancies. Either partner might become ill depending on the sexual practice involved. The use of a condom, because it interfered with full sensual stimulation and according to Freud resulted in an orgasm of reduced intensity, was considered a sexual noxa. Actually condoms were not in general use and the usual practice was coitus interruptus.

This practice ignored the wife's need for an orgasm. During intercourse she would be stimulated sufficiently to increase the somatic level of excitation, but, expecting her pleasure to be interrupted, was not stimulated psychically. The somatic libido was in excess of the psychical libido and could not be fully absorbed in a linkage nor discharged in orgasm. The excess of somatic libido was transformed and discharged as anxiety.

On the other hand, if the husband controlled his sexual arousal and did not have an ejaculation until his wife achieved orgasm, then it would be he who would develop anxiety. This occurred because of his nonsexual preoccupation, which had as its result a diminished arousal of psychical libido and an excess of unlinked somatic sexual excitation. In describing this situation, Freud wrote: "It [the preoccupation with his wife's orgasm] introduces alongside of the task of mastering the sexual affect another psychical task, one of a deflecting sort" (*S.E. 3* 110 1895*b*).

Thus insufficiency of psychical libido occurred in either the wife or the husband; in the wife if the husband practiced coitus interruptus and in the husband if he attempted to delay his orgasm in order to ensure his wife's full pleasure (*S.E. 3* 111). The reduction in psychical libido led to a failure in linkage with, or binding of, the somatic sexual tension. As a result, the unbound somatic tension was not adequately discharged and a surplus accumulated. In this vicissitude of sexual life then, in which a reduction in psychical libido resulted in an inadequacy in the mastering or binding of somatic libido, illness could result without a sexual etiology, but as a result of a sexual mechanism.

This formulation also showed that anxiety neurosis was an *acquired* neurosis, as opposed to those due to hereditary factors, and could be treated by a change in the sexual life. Many men solved the problem by having intercourse with prostitutes and, not needing to be concerned with the possibility of pregnancy, were therefore able to have an adequately gratifying sexual experience. For women this solution was not available.

Again Freud found his theoretical explanation supported by his observation that more women than men in this later age group were neurotic. This consistency seemed to him to validate his basic hypothesis.

The second and greater source of pathology leading to anxiety neurosis occurred in those in whom linkage failed because of *psychical alienation.* Again the crux of the matter was the failure of the somatic sexual excitation to become "bound" by achieving psychical representation through linkage (Draft E, *S.E.* *1* 193). In this case the lack of linkage occurred in spite of there being adequate amounts and quality of both somatic and psychical libido. Simple alienation is very similar to psychical insufficiency, except for the quantitative difference in the amount of psychical libido. It may occur in persons who during the sexual act are preoccupied with worries or concerns that interfere with their sexual pleasure, for example, the fear of conception, concern about the sexual pleasure of the partner, and similar preoccupations. The enjoyment of sexual excitation and the circular effect of voluptuous feelings are disrupted and incomplete sexual involvement ensues, with, as a consequence, a less than complete sexual discharge. This is one reason why the practice of coitus interruptus or *retardato* (delay in ejaculation) is defined as a sexual noxa (*S.E. 3* 110). The man's reduced potency (premature ejaculation, often the result of earlier masturbation) acted for the woman in a manner very similar to coitus interruptus, particularly when the latter was performed without concern for the woman's experiencing full sexual pleasure ending in orgasm.

A more complex form of psychical alienation occurred in women whose husbands, suffering from some degree of impotence, were unable to produce in them the *anticipation* of pleasure. The endogenous excitation was induced from the outside, but was not sufficient to arouse psychical affect. Women who experienced some somatic arousal during intercourse, but in an insufficient amount to arouse psychical affect, were thought to develop an incapacity for psychical working over of somatic excitation (artificial or habitual alienation). Then at a later date, when the endogenous excitation increased on its own account, the defect for psychical working over continued to interfere and no linkage occurred. This was an example of facilitation in which the defect became habitual. The consequence of the lack of linkage was once again a chronic excess of unbound somatic libido.

Freud next explained how this situation led to an anxiety attack. Anxiety symptoms could occur only if the somatic libido found some way of discharge through somatic pathways. Freud postulated that there must be a *transformation* of excess somatic libido into anxiety. Somatic libido was conceived of as a chemical secretion (Letter 75, *S.E. 1* 269); the transformation was also thought of as a chemical action in which one chemical compound (somatic libido) was altered into another compound (anxiety or unpleasure). In "Three Essays on the Theory of Sexuality," Freud compared this transformation with the change of wine into vinegar (*S.E.* 7 224; footnote added 1920). The transformation concept is first mentioned in Letter 16 (*Origins* 80) and again in more detail in Letter 18. He then sent to Fliess an outline of a possible paper on "The Aetiology and the Theory of the Major Neuroses" (Draft D). The paper was to discuss etiology in terms of the etiological formula, "the key that unlocks everything," and theory (of anxiety neuroses) in terms of inadequate unburdening, the accumulation of libido, its transformation into anxiety, and its discharge through somatic pathways. The theory of constancy, by which Freud also set great store, was to account for the need for discharge.

Fliess apparently responded to the draft with some uncertainty and raised questions about Freud's explanation of the origin of anxiety, that is, the transformation of somatic libido into anxiety. In answer (Draft E) Freud agreed that this was the weak point in the theory and then attempted to answer the basic question. First he showed that the hypothesis of transformation of libido into anxiety fits the clinical material; that is, the mechanism accounts for such diverse examples as virginal anxiety, anxiety in prudes, and so forth. Then he simply restated the hypothesis that accumulated somatic libido (quantity of excitation) can be discharged through somatic channels, producing dyspnea, palpitations, and simple feelings of anxiety. His only argument in favor of the hypothesis was that these are the same pathways that would have been used for the discharge of sexual tension even after it had been worked over psychically (i.e., bound, that is, the energy is no longer mobile). By this Freud meant that in the act of intercourse there would have been rapid breathing, increased heart rate, and the like.

Fliess remained dissatisfied with the hypothesis and Freud agreed that it would not do and was not ready for publication (*Origins*, Letter 19, 94). He stated that he would like to write a preliminary study of the grounds for differentiating anxiety neurosis from neurasthenia, but since this would require a discussion of somatic libido, its depletion in neurasthenia, and its transformation in anxiety neurosis, he did not plan to publish such a study. In spite of this, within six months he wrote and published a paper with this title (1895*b*).

It is easy to sympathize with Freud in his impatience. The theory seemed to account for the clinical facts, it was consistent, beautifully flexible (too much so, in fact), and provided the physiological basis for his psychological knowledge.

Freud did not include in the 1895 paper the explanations he had worked out for what at this time he believed to be a third type of actual neurosis. This was associated with the symptom of melancholia.

Freud considered the possibility that the melancholias, like the anxiety neuroses, were a consequence of a failure of adequate linkage between somatic libido and psychical libido (psychical alienation). The two differed, however, in that the production of somatic sexual libido which is in excess and unbound in anxiety neurosis is in melancholia abnormally low. The problem was not one of unburdening via transformation and somatic discharge, but almost the reverse. The danger was thought to arise from a weak and precarious (poor quality) investment of the psychosexual group of ideas.

Freud's theoretical explanation for the varieties of melancholia was again made in terms of his schematic picture of sexuality. His formulation becomes clearer if two facts are kept in mind. First, in referring to his schematic picture of sexuality, it becomes apparent that the stimulation (recycling) of the model toward orgastic discharge can occur from three independent sources: (1) the tension in the terminal organ; (2) the memory of voluptuous feelings; and (3) the stimulation provided by the presence in the external world of the sexual object. Each source can contribute to the arousal of sexual interest. A quantitative reduction in one factor can be offset by an increase in one or other of the other sources. If the sum from all three sources is insufficient, however, the result is melancholia. The second fact to keep in mind is that even though the "charge" or tension in the psychosexual group of ideas by psychical libido may be present in adequate quantity, it may be precarious or of poor quality (impoverished), suggesting a *qualitative* factor rather than simply a quantitative one.

Freud begins his formulation by stating that "melancholia is a mourning" over loss of (somatic) libido, is *related* to the absence of somatic sexual excitation, and finally that the main prerequisite to melancholia is a low level of tension (S.S.E.) in the terminal organ. These are three ways of stating essentially the same thing. Freud does *not* mean a low level of tension in the terminal organ *causes* melancholia. Rather it is the beginning of a series of events that lead to melancholia. As a result of the low level of tension in the terminal organ (low somatic libido), the psychical-sexual group of ideas (plus psychical libido) is inadequately or precariously charged. Since this sexual group of ideas is energically undercharged, it could easily be subjected to inhibition (because of the lack of adequate support from somatic sexual excitation). Aware that the desire will tend to fade away ungratified, the organism tries to sustain its investment by drawing off psychical libido from adjacent neurones. This drawing off of energy from adjacent neurones is described as an "indrawing in the psyche which resembles internal bleeding." Pain occurs when these surrounding neurones give up their excitation, since it also means a loss of their function, that is, an uncoupling of the associative patterns in which they were functioning. Freud states that "The uncoupling of associations is always painful" (Draft G, *S.E. 1* 205). This concept shows a basic similarity to Freud's later (1917) concept of depression, "Mourning and Melancholia" (*S.E. 14* 243–258), in which the mourning process is compared to depression. Both require the painful detachment of libido from the lost object, or more precisely, the object representation.

The idea of "internal bleeding" as a reaction of the mental

apparatus is again mentioned by Freud thirty-five years later in *Beyond the Pleasure Principle* (*S.E. 18* 30), where he speaks of the reaction to overstimulation. "Cathectic energy is summoned from all sides to provide sufficiently high cathexis of energy in the environs of the breach. An 'anti-cathexis' on a grand scale is set up, for whose benefit all the other psychical systems are impoverished, so that the remaining psychical functions are extensively paralyzed or reduced." He then describes the ego's function of binding this influx of energy through its capacity to master, bind, immobilize, or store energy. It is also referred to in "Inhibitions, Symptoms and Anxiety" (*S.E. 20* 171), where pain is said to "empty the ego."

Having presented this formulation of the basic *mechanism* of melancholia, Freud enumerates the various situations that can lead to it. They involve interruptions of any one of the three sources of stimulation to the psychical-sexual group of ideas.

(1) *Melancholias Subsequent to a Low Level of Somatic Libido*

(*a*) Narcissistic melancholia

The first example involves immature, demanding women who are sexually anesthetic. Women in general are more likely to be sexually anesthetic than men, since their upbringing aims at not arousing somatic sexual excitation or an awareness of voluptuous feelings independent of the presence of the object. In addition there is a constitutional difference between men and women in the nature of their sexual arousal. Women generally play a passive role, awaiting the arousal of feelings by the man's actions. In the normal sexual situation the excitation aroused by the man's actions acts to increase both the psychical libido and the somatic libido (Draft G, *S.E. 1* 200). In some demanding and easily frustrated women (those we would now call narcissistic), the stimulation from the presence of the sexual object increases the investment of the psychosexual group of ideas (by psychical libido) only and does not act to increase the production of somatic sexual excitation in the terminal organ (somatic libido). The consequence is an accumulation of high psychical tension (psychic desire), but low physical sexual tension. The psychical libido is poorly and precariously invested in terms of true (genital) sexual desire. Desire takes the form primarily of narcissistic demands, rather than genital sexual wishes. Since the psychical libido is poorly and precariously invested, energy is "borrowed" from adjacent neurones, the function of these adjacent neurones is lost, and melancholia follows. Since the patients are also sexually anesthetic, the experience of voluptuous feelings that binds the memory of a pleasant and full sexual experience is also absent and adds to the poor quality of the psychical libido.

The failure in linkage here is based on both quantitative (low somatic libido) and qualitative (poor quality of psychical libido) factors. The quantitative situation is the reverse of virginal anxiety, where Freud postulated an excess of somatic libido and a lack of psychic libido because of the individual's inexperience and the consequent undeveloped nature of the psychosexual group of ideas. The formulation of the *mechanics* of this type of melancholia foreshadows some aspects of Freud's *dynamic* explanation of melancholia, in "Mourning and Melancholia," in which libidinal regression to the oral stage and narcissistic sensitivity was a central part. As early as 1895, in Draft G, Freud relates *anorexia nervosa* (neurotic self-starvation) to melancholia and explains it as the consequence of a loss of libido that is experienced in oral terms *(S.E. 1* 200).

(*b*) Idiopathic melancholias

The idiopathic melancholias are a group in which the etiology is unknown. In this condition there is a cessation of the production of sexual excitation resulting in inadequate energic charge of the psychical-sexual group of ideas. This is the determinant of "common severe melancholia" (periodic or cyclical hereditary forms). The reason for the decreased production of somatic sexual excitation is unknown (i.e., idiopathic).

(*c*) Neurasthenic melancholia

Excessive masturbation can finally effect a lasting diminution in the production of somatic libido. This permanent lowered production gives a partial but inadequate stimulation to the psychosexual group of ideas. The "indrawing" from adjacent neurones leads to *neurasthenic melancholia.*

(*d*) Anxious melancholia

Diversion and discharge of somatic sexual libido into somatic channels (anxiety neurosis) also can result in a diminished and imperfect stimulation of the psychosexual group of ideas. This leads to *anxious* melancholia.

In each of these cases the chain of events began with a reduction, for a variety of reasons, in the quantity of the somatic libido (quantity of somatic excitation). As a consequence the psychosexual group of ideas is poorly invested with psychical libido. In an effort to maintain the investment of the sexual ideas, libido is withdrawn from adjacent neurones (psychical bleeding). This requires the uncoupling of other associations and resulting loss of function that is always mentally painful. The melancholia is the equivalent of the person's mourning over this painful loss.

(2) *Melancholia Subsequent to a Reduction in Stimulation from Voluptuous Feelings*

Whereas in the previous group of melancholias the chain of events leading to "psychical bleeding" began with a low level of somatic libido, in this group the chain of events begins with an interference with the production of, or transmission of, voluptuous feelings.

Anesthesia is the lack of voluptuous feelings. The quality of the voluptuous feelings can vary (relative or partial anesthesia) and is a direct indication of the quantity of discharge (adequacy of orgasm).

Anesthesia (the lack of voluptuous feelings) can lead to an imperfect or inadequate investment of the psychical-sexual group of ideas with psychical libido. This in turn leads to the "indrawing in the psyche" that drains the adjacent neurones, resulting in melancholia.

Freud lists three possible mechanisms that interfere with voluptuous feelings:

(*a*) Voluptuous feelings are reduced when the terminal organ is insufficiently charged; as a result only a limited orgasm can occur. This relative reduction in voluptuous feelings (anesthesia) describes the condition known as frigidity.

(*b*) Voluptuous feelings are reduced when the pathway from sensations in the genitals that are carried via the reflex arc to the terminal organ is damaged. This damage can be the result of frequent masturbation or coitus interruptus: stimulation of the terminal organ is reduced, which in turn means a reduction in stimulation of the psychosexual group of ideas.

(*c*) Although the terminal organ is adequately charged and the sensation in the genitals is sufficient, the *transmission* of voluptuous feelings from the terminal organ to the psychosexual group of ideas is interfered with by being linked to disgust, or the like. This leads to hysterical anesthesia.

Freud points out that it is possible to be anesthetic without being melancholic. The lowered stimulation of the psychosexual group of ideas accruing from the lack of voluptuous feelings can be quantitatively offset by an increase in the production of somatic sexual substance (tension in the terminal organ) or the stimulation from the sexual object in the external world.

The elaborate formulations concerning the actual neurosis are made even more complex in order to account for the coexistence of both neurasthenia and anxiety. Freud postulated a change in the rate of production of the somatic substance as well as a change in the threshold level for discharge. A lowered threshold of discharge came about as a result of facilitation. Repeated anxiety attacks increased the ease of transformation of libido into anxiety and made the somatic pathways available at a lower level of tension. By this means the symptoms became chronic. The steady somatic release at this lower level also produced the neurasthenic symptoms.

The four patterns of discharge which have been summarized are schematically represented in Chart 3.

When Freud distinguished the actual neuroses from the psychoneuroses, he described the distinction as the "first great contrast in the etiology of the neuroses." However, he also saw that the relationship between the two was quite complex. There was considerable similarity between the concept of the transformation of libido leading to anxiety neurosis and the concept of the conversion of libido with conversion hysteria as its consequence. He wrote (Draft E, *S.E. 1* 195): "There is a kind of *conversion* in anxiety neurosis just as there is in hysteria . . . but in hysteria it is *psychical* excitation that takes a wrong path exclusively into the somatic field, whereas here it is a *physical* tension, which cannot enter the psychical field and therefore remains on the physical path." Both conversion hysteria and anxiety neurosis used the same somatic channel for discharge. What was being discharged, however, differed.

Since somatic libido in the actual neuroses was never linked with psychical libido, it could have no psychical representation, but only a physical one, and was easily discharged through somatic channels. In hysteria, linkage had occurred that required conversion of the psychical libido for its discharge through somatic channels. The discharge retained the mark of having achieved psychical representation and there-

Chart 3

Actual Neurosis

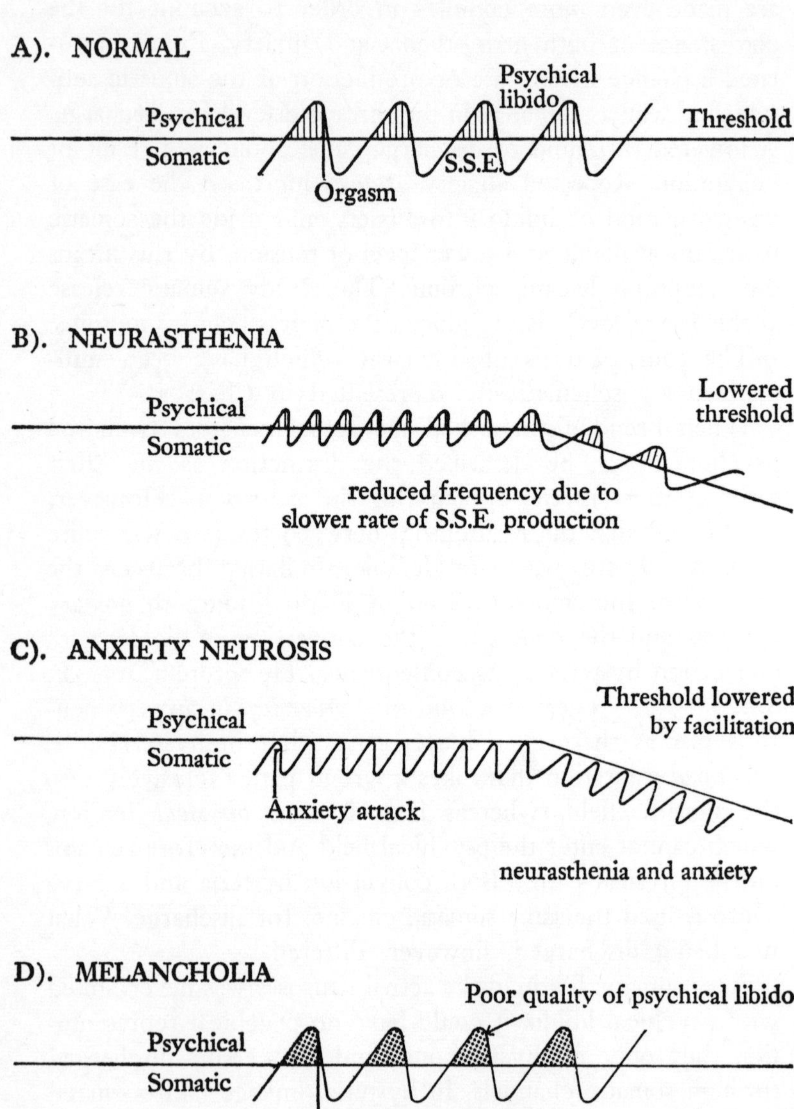

fore could have symbolic meaning. Hence conversion hysteria was described as "psychical excitation which takes a wrong path in an exclusively somatic direction" or "the somatic representation of an idea" (Draft E, *S.E. 1* 195). The cause of the conversion was conflict and therefore it was one of the psychoneuroses of defense.

In spite of having made this careful distinction between anxiety neurosis and conversion hysteria, Freud left open the possibility of greater complications. He pointed out the close connection between the anxiety neuroses and conversion hysteria, referring to the former as "the somatic counterpart to hysteria" (*S.E. 3* 115 1895*b*), and then suggested that the actual neurosis and the psychoneuroses of defense could be intermingled in a most complex fashion. The actual neuroses could even be *maintained* "not by current sexual noxae, but, instead solely by the persisting effect of a memory of childhood traumas"(!) (*S.E. 3* 168 1896*b*; see also *S.E. 11* 224).

It was not until 1909, while discussing the diagnostic problem in the case of Little Hans (*S.E. 10* 115), that Freud made a further division of the group of psychoneuroses, distinguishing for the first time anxiety hysteria from conversion hysteria. This delay can be attributed in part to his unshakable belief in the actual neuroses.

This "first great contrast" was further complicated by Freud's belief that many of what he called the "common phobias" (*S.E. 3* 92, 99), like the symptoms in neurasthenia (*S.E. 3* 90) and in pure anxiety neurosis, were also "*not further reducible* by psychological analysis, nor amenable to psychotherapy" (*S.E. 3* 97). In these common phobias the affect did not originate from a repressed idea, as occurred in the phobic symptoms in the neuropsychoses of defense. In both there was a transposition of affect (i.e., displacement), but in the common phobias this came about at a physiological level, whereas in the psychologically determined phobias, past experience and defense were the reason and purpose for this transposition.

The "common phobias" in Freud's scheme seemed to lie somewhere between the actual neuroses and the psychoneuroses. Since the symptom involved the transposition of affect it must be at a psychic level; yet the purpose of the transposition was not defensive. Perhaps Freud was searching for some concept similar to the "innate releasing mechanism," now described as a determinant of animal behavior. A child's fear of snakes, loud noises, heights, and the like, would seem to have this innate quality, which is then secondarily reinforced in the later psychological phobic symptoms.

Freud felt that this view of the "common phobias" took into account the biological level, of which he was constantly aware, as well as of the psychological elaborations brought about by experiential factors.

Freud also hoped that the distinction between the actual neuroses and the psychoneuroses of defense which was based on their difference in etiology might also carry implications about their treatment (*S.E. 3* 275 1898). The neurasthenic patient had to be told of the effect of his masturbation on his sexual capacity; married couples, the consequences of practicing coitus interruptus, and so on. Since the neuroses (neurasthenia and anxiety neuroses) were physical in origin, and often the consequence of sexual practices aimed at preventing pregnancy, they might be prevented by correcting the sexual practices, but they could not be cured by psychological therapy (*S.E. 1* 183).

From this review it is clear that there are certain specific requirements which would have to be met to fulfill Freud's early definition of the actual neuroses. There would have to be a *chemical basis* (*S.E. 18* 243) for the sexual urge. In those who develop neurasthenic symptoms, the chemical substance must excite sexual feelings at an abnormally low threshold level and be depleted by frequent ejaculation. In those who develop anxiety neurosis, the major portion of the chemical substance must not achieve psychic representation as conscious or unconscious sexual affect, and its accumulation must lead to discharge through the vegetative nervous system with the production of symptoms of anxiety. Only if these requirements are met can one speak of an actual neurosis in Freud's original meaning of the term. There is no evidence that such a condition exists, and since 1926, at which time Freud reformulated the problems of anxiety, analysts have generally agreed that anxiety is a signal of dangers related to castration fears, separation anxiety, or more primitive fears about the sense of self, and are not the consequence of somatic discharge.

Freud set considerable value on the concept of the actual neuroses (*S.E. 12* 248, *20* 26). A critical assessment of its value is not easy, since the meaning of the term changed somewhat over the years. Also the concept became part of Freud's new formulation of the problem of anxiety.

Freud abandoned the narrower concept of the transformation of libido into anxiety in 1926 (see also *S.E. 22* 94). He continued to hope, however, that some chemical basis for drive energy might be discovered. He had originally hoped to study psychological factors in detail, always with the expectation that the observations could be correlated with what was known about brain organization and chemical factors. Psychical manifestations, both normal and pathological, were to be related to their biological roots. The original energy concept was formulated at a physiological level, first employing electrical discharge concepts and later chemical concepts. Even as late as 1920 in a paragraph added to the "Three Essays on the Theory of Sexuality" (*S.E. 7* 215), Freud expressed his hope was that a sexual chemistry would be discovered that would account for the source of sexual energy and give a solid base to his theories. He complained, in "On Narcissism," of the "total absence of any theory of instincts which would help us to find our bearings," but still hoped that "all our provisional ideas in psychology will presumably some day be based on an organic substructure" (*S.E. 14* 78). When the sexual hormones were discovered it looked as if Freud's hopes might be justified. But, as we now know, the problem was not to be so easily settled.

Because of the lack of knowledge of any chemical substrate, Freud was forced to restrict himself to the psychological level, and in his writings replaced the idea of special chemical substances with the concept of special psychical forces. That is, the original and more literal energy concept formulated in physiological terms was replaced by the more theoretical concept of psychical energy.

The earlier formulation involved a "two-stage" description in that it invoked somatic excitation (somatic libido) which had to achieve psychical representation by linkage. Only then did it become evident as a need or a wish. In the later drive concept this two-stage formulation was condensed into a single one. Drive energy was still assumed to have a somatic origin, but was only known by its aims (*S.E. 14* 123). How or when the drive became psychical was no longer clearly stated. There was no point in referring to psychical libido in order to contrast it with somatic libido, and the term libido was used rather ambiguously. Later in the structural hypothesis this ambiguity was even greater. The contents of the id could be thought of as somatic and/or as psychical. The lines between somatic and psychical, id and ego, were never clarified.

This ambiguity about the relationship of the somatic origins of drives and their psychical representation was extremely useful, in light of our ignorance, then and even now, about somatic processes. It bypassed the unknown, reserving it for later understanding, and encouraged the study of the psychological level. One disadvantage, however, has been that until recently most studies seem to ignore this lacuna in our knowledge and assume that the psychological level of explanation by itself is adequate.

A number of observations show that the psychological approach alone is incomplete. One example is early childhood fears. Another is what is termed the stigmata of hysteria. This term refers to "the permanent symptoms of hysteria"[2] *(S.E. 2* 244, 265 1895*d*; 3 137 1895*f*; 192 1896*c*). As early as 1892 in a letter to Breuer, Freud had described the nonpsychogenic symptoms as "highly obscure." In "The Neuro-Psychoses of Defence" (*S.E. 3* 50), the disposition for hysteria is defined as the *capacity* for conversion and is described as being "still unknown."

This puzzling and obscure aspect of hysteria, the nonpsychogenic permanent symptoms, has been almost entirely overlooked and the disease is now treated as if it were fully understandable in terms of experiential factors alone.

More recently the physiological aspect of mental functioning has again begun to receive attention. This is illustrated in the neurophysiological studies of the reticular activating system, of the brain stem, and of the limbic brain. Another promising approach involves local chemical stimulation of the brain.[3] Research concerning the sleep-waking cycle and the associated sleep-dream cycle[4] has opened an entirely new field in which physiological and psychological investigation can be coordinated. Also relevant is Greenacre's work on "The Predisposition to Anxiety,"[5] as well as more recent reports on the significance of the stimulus barrier[6] and studies of the consequences of early maternal neglect.[7]

[2] Charcot, *Leçons sur les maladies du système nerveux*, vol. III, p. 255 (quoted in *S.E.* 192, footnote 2).

[3] A. Fisher, "Chemical Stimulation of the Brain," *Scientific American*, **210** 6 (June 1964), 60–69.

[4] C. Fisher, "Psychoanalytic Implications of Recent Research on Sleep and Dreaming," *Journal of the American Psychoanalytic Association*, **13** 2 (April 1965), 197–303, and Snyder, "Progress in the New Biology of Dreaming," *American Journal of Psychiatry*, **122** 4 (October 1965), 377–391.

[5] Greenacre, *Trauma, Growth, and Personality.*

[6] Bergman and Escalona, "Unusual Sensitivities in Very Young Children," *Psychoanalytic Study of the Child*, 3–4 333–352.

[7] Provence and Lipton, *Infants in Institutions*, and Spitz, "Hospitalism: An Inquiry into the Genesis of Psychiatric Conditions in Early Childhood," *Psychoanalytic Study of the Child*, 1 53–74.

4. *Early Views on Sexuality—The Neuropsychoses of Defense*

THE TERM NEUROPSYCHOSES of defense referred to what today are called the psychoneuroses. This diagnostic group included the conversion hysterias, the obsessions, paranoia, and hallucinatory confusion. Freud described the neuropsychoses as the second great group of mental illnesses, which he contrasted to the actual neuroses. They were distinguished from the actual neuroses by the fact that the sexual factor belonged not to the present day, as in the actual neuroses, but "to an epoch of life which is long past" ("Sexuality in the Aetiology of the Neuroses," *S.E. 3* 267).

In this early period there was an obvious split between the *dynamic* understanding of the illnesses, which emphasized conflict and defense, and the *economic* "explanation," by which symptom formation was explained. The dynamic approach made the case histories read like detective novels; the economic view was modeled on the formulations Freud had used for the actual neuroses. Dynamic and economic views were both contained in the theory that a traumatic experience was the etiological factor in the formation of a hysterical symptom. This idea was taken over from Charcot.[1]

[1] The term trauma has had a number of different meanings in psychoanalytic history. At first it meant quite literally an injury. At the time of these case histories (1895), it meant a frightening experience that was not adequately mastered. Trauma next referred to an unmastered conflictual

A clinical example in which the symptom is precipitated by a trauma occurs in the case of Anna O., whom Breuer treated between 1880 and 1882. The patient had found herself unable to drink water. Each time she put a glass of water to her lips she would push it away with an expression of disgust. The symptom disappeared when, under hypnosis, she recalled a "scene" in which she had seen her hired English companion allow her "horrid little dog" to drink water from a drinking glass.

The exploration of the patient's life history centered more and more on the search for a traumatic scene, or a series of such scenes, which could be the cause of the symptom. Freud's clinical experience led him to the conviction that behind the current scene or traumatic experience that the patient felt was the cause of the illness lay an earlier, similar but forgotten scene which was really the cause.

Three examples illustrate this early genetic and dynamic approach.

The first example (Draft J, *S.E. 1* 215) concerns a Frau P.J., a twenty-seven-year-old woman, who had been married three months. Her husband, a commercial traveler, had left her a few weeks after the marriage on one of his business trips. She came to Freud because of an anxiety attack that had developed while she was accompanying herself on the piano. Freud suspected that she had felt a sexual longing for her husband and that the attack "was no more than a state of erotic effusion." This he called Scene I, and from previous experience with other cases he was convinced that behind this scene and the thoughts she remembered there must be another deepgoing train of thought that was not conscious and that would lead to the traumatic Scene II. A

(sexual) impulse. Finally it designated an experience that aroused such a quantity of excitation that it could not be bound, and as a result overwhelmed the psychic apparatus. In this latter meaning it was often compared with physical pain, which breaks down all barriers and against which there is no defense.

history of an earlier attack four years before was elicited. At that time the patient had been singing at a rehearsal. That afternoon she had had an anxiety attack following a vision. By pressure and concentration, it emerged that the tenor in the company had, at a previous rehearsal a few days earlier, put his hand on her breast. The investigation of the case went no further, since it was interrupted by the patient's flight from treatment.

Another clinical vignette is reported in the Project *(S.E. 1* 353). The patient, Emma, was unable to enter a shop alone. She felt that the symptom related to an experience which had occurred when she was twelve years old. She had gone into a shop in which there were two shop assistants. She noticed that they were laughing. She became frightened and ran out of the shop, feeling that the men were laughing at her clothes. She confessed that one of them had been sexually attractive to her. This was, for this case, Scene I. Freud uncovered another scene, Scene II, which had occurred when Emma was eight years old. On *two* occasions she had gone into a candy shop and the owner, with a leering grin, had "grabbed at her genitals through her clothes."

The relationship of the two scenes is of importance. Scene I was composed of shop assistants, laughter, clothes, sexual excitement, fear, and flight. Scene II, which was repressed, consisted of the grinning candy store man, assault, clothing, and only after puberty, an awareness of the meaning of the scene with a release of sexual affect. The scenes are linked together by their occurring in a similar setting (shop and store) and by the laughter (the grinning of the candy store man and the laughter of the shop assistants).

The assault that was the center of the traumatic scene was not allowed into consciousness, but was represented in the second scene by the patient's concern about her clothing. Two false connections allowed Scene I to have some semblance of rationality, even though its real meaning was only comprehensible in terms of the repressed scene it represented. First, the laughter was falsely connected with her concern about her clothing; second, the sexual arousal was falsely related to her interest in one of the shopkeepers. The elements of the earlier scene are thus preserved in the later scene, but related to each other in an altered manner.

Freud theorized that the two scenes existed in two different states of consciousness (split in consciousness) and the earlier traumatic scene, for reasons of defense, was not allowed to exist in the normal conscious state. The second scene both threatened to bring the earlier scene to consciousness (return of the repressed) and provided an outlet for the energies associated with it, thereby aiding repression, and functioned to hide the original and more traumatic memory. Since the second experience acted as a screen for the first experience, it was termed a screen memory.

Another noteworthy fact is that the original scene became traumatic only after puberty. This deferred effect became the basis for Freud's early explanation that defense was always and only directed against early sexual experiences.

A third clinical example, in *Studies on Hysteria*, is that of Miss Lucy R. (*S.E. 2* 106). This young English girl, who worked as a governess for a Viennese family, complained of an hallucinated smell of burnt pudding. This symptom led to a recent experience in which a pudding had actually been burnt. Because of some difficulties with the other servants, the patient had been planning to leave her employment and return home to her mother. One day she and the children she cared for were cooking a pudding. While it was in the oven, a birthday letter arrived from her mother. The delivery of the letter distracted everyone from their care of the pudding until the smell of its burning drew their attention back to it. The conflict that the hallucinated smell of the pudding seemed to represent was between her wish to stay with the children and her wish to leave because of the attitude of the other servants. The conflict was all the more intense because she had promised their mother on her deathbed that she would devote herself to the children and take their mother's place with them.

Freud was not fully satisfied with this explanation, because the conflict seemed inadequate to justify the need for repression and the emergence of a hysterical symptom. He felt that some idea must have been present which the patient wished to forget. He then made the bold interpretation that the conflict which was repressed, but represented in this scene, involved the patient's love for her employer, a widower. The patient confirmed this interpretation and this first symptom gradually cleared up. However, another symptom hidden behind it then emerged: this consisted of the hallucination of the smell of cigar smoke. This also led to a specific scene in which a visitor, an accountant, had, while smoking a cigar, kissed the children on the mouth. The father-employer was strongly opposed to this, lost his temper, and scolded the visitor. Behind this scene lay still another, a third and earlier scene, in which the patient herself had been scolded for letting a woman visitor kiss the children. She was told if it happened again she would be fired. The fact that her employer could behave in this way to her made it quite clear that he was not in love with her as she had hoped. When as a result of this knowledge she was able to deal with her repressed wishes and accept the fact that her hopes for marriage were unrealistic, her symptoms vanished and her good spirits returned.

The reconstructed order of events was then as follows. For the first two years the patient had worked happily in the house. Then she had a conversation with her employer about her good care of the children. Usually reserved, he was on this occasion less formal and indeed quite cordial. She became aware of loving him and mistakenly felt he might reciprocate her feelings. Next was the scene in which she was scolded (Scene III). This was the "operative trauma," since it showed quite clearly that her hopes were unjustified. The scene did not have any immediate manifest effect, although it may be that her low spirits began then. This scene and her hopes were banished from her mind. The incompatability between the wish and reality was only too clear. But the idea was not truly given up; instead it was placed out of consciousness, where it remained as a center for the "formation of a psychical group divorced from the ego." Two months later Scene II occurred, in which the accountant kissed the children and was scolded. The scene was reminiscent of her own scolding and threatened to bring about a temporary convergence of the two divided psychical groups (now described as a threatened return of the repressed). The affect was converted into a somatic channel, with the formation of the symptom, the hallucinatory smell of cigar smoke. This allowed the incompatible impulse to remain unconscious. Next occurred Scene I, the burnt pudding experience. It was the most recent memory and was also connected with the main conflict, since it again brought to mind the conflict over leaving her employment and revived her repressed hopes for marriage. A second symptom was formed that covered the first.

In most cases the problem was even more complicated. The symptoms were found to be linked to a whole series of "scenes," strung together by a common theme. It was necessary in these cases to start with the most recent scene and go in detail through all of the scenes to which this led, until the earliest event that was the first cause of the symptom was reached. This led to the conclusion that the trauma was most often not a single experience but the culminative effect of a series of traumata which achieved its effectiveness by summation. Each single experience might not be of adequate importance, but taken as a whole they could produce the needed traumatic force.

The concept of summation of trauma established the similarity between the "common hysterias," until then thought to be solely due to hereditary factors, and the traumatic hysterias, which were known to be acquired. This meant that the so-called common hysterias were not idiopathic but were also acquired, the result of experiences, and that as a consequence they could be treated. The common factor in both was the affect of fright (*S.E. 2* 6).

The dynamic understanding of clinical material was limited by an ignorance of infantile sexuality and the nature of unconscious mental processes. As a result Freud's concept of cure was mostly formulated in energic terms. The cathartic method involved the release of strangulated affects by means of abreaction. During the reliving of the traumatic experience, psychic energy in the form of affect could be discharged. The need for discharge was based on the constancy principle (see chapter 5). In these early formulations affects and psychic energy were considered equivalents. Mental health was thought to depend on the uninhibited discharge of energy via the expression of affects. The hypothesis of discharge through affects was only one of two possible alternatives. The other route to mental health was described as the working over of the traumatic experience until it "enters the great complex of associations . . . comes alongside other experiences, which may contradict it, and is subjected to rectification by other ideas" (*S.E. 2* 9).

This second alternative, which stresses the mastery of the trauma, was relatively neglected, and the emphasis was increasingly placed on the concept of discharge. This is known as abreaction and was the basis of the cathartic concept of therapy. The goal of treatment was the reliving of the traumatic and etiological experience and the full discharge of the appropriate affect. The therapeutic results were disappointing because the concept of mastery was ignored. In 1926 in "Inhibitions, Symptoms, and Anxiety" (*S.E. 20* 151), Freud mentions that he gave up the theory of abreaction "which had played such a large part in the cathartic method." He wrote in criticism of this early theory that: "Taken literally it implies that the more frequently and the more intensely a neurotic person reproduces the affect of anxiety the more closely will he approach to mental health—an untenable conclusion."

Freud's theoretical formulations concerning the neuropsychoses were similar to those used in understanding the actual neuroses. The neuropsychoses differed from the actual neuroses by the fact that *linkage between somatic libido and psychical libido did occur, the psychosexual group of ideas was invested, but was not maintained as a functional unit.*

In all the psychoneuroses of defense and also in normal functioning the somatic sexual excitation (somatic libido) succeeded in arousing the sexual group of ideas. This linkage resulted in an idea and an associated affect achieving psychical representation. In the normal course of events, if the sexual idea is acceptable (not conflictual), it leads to sexual action. If, however, the sexual act is inappropriate for the moment or is in conflict with other ideas, the desire is mastered by thought activity, which has the effect of a wearing away or a taming of the drive through the function of judgment and the acceptance of frustration.

In contrast to this normal way of dealing with a wish, in the neuropsychoses a conflict that could not be mastered resulted in a "splitting of the mind" which isolated the impulse from the normally functioning consciousness. Three causes for the development of this split in the mind were advanced. In the 1893 "Preliminary Communication" and in Breuer's chapter in *Studies on Hysteria*, the split was thought to be "idiopathic"—simply a consequence of a dreamy mental state characteristic of the potential hysteric. This dreamy condition, because it seemed related to the hypnotic trance, was called the hypnoid state. During this state, strong feelings and exciting trains of thought could develop that were isolated from the regular state of consciousness. The normal prototype of the hypnoid state was a reverie in which a daydream would occur. The thoughts and feelings that developed in the hypnoid state (often the consequence of autohypnosis) differed from this in that they occurred out of normal consciousness and could not be recalled (*S.E. 2* 234).

This view was favored by Breuer, and although at first Freud accepted it, he soon developed the defense concept instead and preferred it, because it fitted the facts better and provided a dynamic reason or cause for the splitting of consciousness. The hypnoid concept was based on the proposition that the idea could not be remembered, while the defense concept emphasized that the patients did not want to remember.

Breuer's hypothesis of a hypnoid state has been related to the psychical working over of the day residue in dreams and subliminal stimuli in perceptual studies.[2] The similarities, however, are more apparent than real. Both can involve altered states of consciousness and the inability to bring the material to conscious awareness. Breuer's concept relates to an isolation of *ideas and feelings* into a separate compartment of the mind, whereas the subliminal stimulus studies deal with *perceptual stimuli* that are registered outside of conscious awareness.

David Rapaport and, more recently, Martin Stein[3] have related Breuer's concept of the hypnoid state to the current ideas concerning altered states of consciousness. The hypnoid state is seen as equivalent to a reverie state during which there are modifications in the state of consciousness. These comments ignored the essential fact of that hypnoid state that involved a *split* in consciousness as a result of which two ideas could both exist out of contact with each other. Therefore, dynamically the hynoid state can best be compared with Freud's much later concept of the split in the ego (*S.E. 23* 275–278). Breuer employed the concept of the hypnoid state to explain how an idea could have an influence but exist out

[2] Holzman, "A Note on Breuer's Hypnoidal Theory of Neurosis," *Bulletin of Menninger Clinic*, **23** 4 (July 1959), 144.

[3] "States of Consciousness in the Analytic Situation: Including a Note on the Traumatic Dream," *Drives, Affects, Behavior*, vol. 2, p. 77.

of consciousness. The concept was replaced with the concept of the unconscious and the defense of repression.

Another shortlived explanation for the splitting of the mind was the "retention" hypothesis. According to this, splitting came about when an impulse developed in a setting in which its expression was impermissible. The impulse did not give rise to an intrapsychic conflict, but its expression was in conflict with the environment. In order to avoid expressing the inappropriate affect, it was isolated from normal consciousness by the development of the split. It is not made clear whether the second step in defense, repression, was also thought to occur in the retention hysterias.

Although Freud as early as 1894 had advanced the defense concept as one of the reasons for the development of a neuropsychosis, at first he saw it only as an alternative to the hypnoid and retention theories. As a result his earliest formulations, even when they rested rather firmly on the defense concept, were limited in their dynamic conceptualizations. His clinical experience led him to the idea that the split in the mind occurred only when an incompatible idea aroused "distressing affect . . . that the subject . . . had no confidence in his power to resolve . . . by means of thought activity." The patient's only solution was to put the idea out of his mind, to forget it. Freud became convinced that all of the neuropsychoses were the consequence of the type of psychical conflict around an incompatible idea which could not be mastered and which therefore set a defense into action.

The first two steps in the defense process were common to all the defense psychoneuroses. The first was the splitting of the mind which isolated the unwanted idea. The idea was now unable to enter "the great complex of associations," unable to come "alongside other experiences, which may contradict it," and therefore it was not "subjected to rectification by other ideas" (*S.E.* *2* 9).

This splitting serves only a preliminary defensive function.

During states of normal consciousness, the idea and affect would not register in awareness (amnesia). However, on occasion, since the idea and affect were still present and pressing for registration in consciousness and for gratification, they would be able to overthrow the normal state and achieve expression during dreamlike or trancelike states. This state (*condition seconde*) could also be brought about artificially by the use of hypnosis, which gave hypnosis its therapeutic value.

Because of the imperfection of the defense, a second step in defense was required. This was repression, in which the goal was to reduce the energy (affect) associated with the idea and thereby reduce its pressure to achieve consciousness and gratification.

Up to this point Freud's explanation was a dynamic one. His explanation of repression, however, paralleled his formulation of the actual neurosis and reverted to a mechanical and economic level. He stated that thememory trace of the idea an daffect could not be eradicated (i.e., it remained psychical), but much the same advantage is obtained by separating the affect from the idea. The idea is then "weak" and falls into repression (". . . the ego succeeds in *turning this powerful idea into a weak one*, in robbing it of the affect —the sum of excitation," *S.E. 3* 48 1894*a*). The repressed idea remains the nucleus of the split-off portion of the mind, but in this condition it is no longer capable of forcing its way into consciousness, nor does it press for action. It is only rearoused by a new "auxiliary" experience (*S.E. 2* 123) that is of such a nature that it threatens to unite the split-off psychical group with the normal state of consciousness.

The parallel with the actual neurosis becomes clear in the next step. After the splitting of the mind and repression via the breaking of the linkage between the idea and the affect, the affect, like the somatic libido in the actual neurosis, had to be accounted for. It was the vicissitude of this affect that varied with and explained the form of the neuropsychosis.

Freud's first formulations of the neuropsychoses were based primarily on this economic vicissitude, in which he distinguished four possible outcomes: conversion, transposition, rejection and projection.

In conversion hysteria, according to this early formulation, linkage of somatic libido and psychical libido occurs, creating an idea with its associated affect. This unit of affect and idea does not remain as a functional unit. Because the idea is unacceptable, defense occurs with a splitting of consciousness. The affect is withdrawn from the idea and converted into anxiety. This conversion renders it sufficiently similar to somatic libido so that it can be discharged through somatic channels. The affect retains enough of its quality of being mental so that the conversion symptom also expresses an idea, that is, it has a symbolic meaning. In this way it differs from the purely physiological symptoms of the actual neuroses. The pathway chosen for the discharge of the affect often follows some previous organic illness that provides it with somatic pathways already open (*S.E. 2* 175). The affect, also having been "cut off from psychical association," finds its way all the more easily along the wrong path to a somatic innervation. The once threatening idea, now robbed of its affect (energy), can be easily maintained in repression, out of consciousness, and out of communication with the rest of the mind. Freud describes it as an unstable defense with a satisfactory gain *(S.E. 1* 211).

Freud's case of Fraülein Elisabeth von R. illustrates this conversion theory. He writes (*S.E. 2* 164): "She repressed her erotic idea from consciousness and transformed the amount of its affect into physical sensations of pain." He then discusses the problem of "the peculiar situation of knowing and at the same time not knowing—a situation, that is, in which a psychical group was cut off. . . . they were cut off from any free associative connection of thought with the rest of the ideational content of her mind." (See also *S.E. 2* 117.)

Freud observed a conversion symptom in *status nascendi* in the case of Fraülein Rosalie H. *(S.E. 2* 173) and found "the energy for the conversion had been supplied, on the one hand by freshly experienced affect and, on the other hand, by recollected affect." A series of scenes created a "mnemic symbol" that could represent all the scenes at once. The formation of symptoms, like the formation of dreams, condenses experiences from both the present and the past. This observation led to the conclusion that the summation of traumas was based on associative linking of various "scenes," all of which contained similar traumas.

The retained affect accumulated in this manner until it rose above the threshold level, at which time the conversion symptom appeared. Although the final scene provided only a small increment of additional undischarged affect, in order to restore the situation to normal it was not sufficient to examine and allow discharge for it alone; instead, a total review of all the relevant memories was required. This was described as the consequence of a "facilitation" having occurred, or later, in "The Dynamics of Transference" (1912), as the necessity to liberate the libido from the "attraction of the unconscious."

The second possible fate of the affect was described as transposition, which leads to the obsessional neurosis. Here, as in conversion hysteria, linkage has occurred, and affect and idea are present. Again they do not remain as a functional unit in consciousness. Repression is effected by the detachment of the affect from the idea, but the charge of affect is then transposed or displaced onto a substitute idea. The original "incompatible" idea is shut out from recollection as in hysteria, and forms the nucleus of the second psychical group. There still remains in consciousness a highly charged substitute idea, the obsession, with which the patient continues to struggle. This is a more stable but a more disruptive method of defense than hysterical conversion. Freud describes it as achieving a permanent defense without gain.

A third vicissitude leads to hallucinatory confusion, where the idea and affect are not separated but both are rejected as being unreal, and with this, reality testing is lost. Hallucinations of a wish-fulfilling nature occur in place of reality.

The fourth vicissitude of the affect is projection, which leads to paranoia. With the development of persecutory delusions, both the idea and the affect are projected onto the outside world.

These early formulations had an admirable simplicity. Not only could the symptoms be related to the vicissitudes of the affect and the threatened recall of certain experiences ("Hysterics suffer mainly from reminiscences"), but when the incompatible idea and affect were brought to consciousness and properly expressed or felt, the symptom permanently disappeared. This formulation, because of its emphasis on the need for discharge or abreaction, is generally referred to as the theory of "strangulated affect." The first technique of cure was attributed to Breuer and was termed catharsis. The results of treatment were the disappearance of the symptoms. Freud succinctly summarized the therapeutic goal as the hope of transforming the patient's hysterical misery into common unhappiness (*S.E. 2* 305).

The limitation of these formulations was that, although they describe the mechanism of the neuropsychoses, they did not account for their cause. They left open the question of why certain sexual experiences were traumatic and required defense. Freud's further studies were a search for an answer to this basic question of etiology. He needed an explanation of why certain (sexual) experiences were the occasion for the release of unpleasure. Only when the release of unpleasure could be explained could he account for the need for pathological defense (*Origins*, Draft K, 147).

Freud's letters and drafts to Fliess are nowhere more valuable than in the understanding of this period in Freud's investigations. The letters show that after having completed the burdensome collaborative work on the *Studies on Hys-*

teria (Letters 13, 19, 22, 25), Freud began work on his second paper on the defense neuropsychoses. He was also hard at work writing the Project.

In the treatment of his patients Freud found it necessary to go further and further back into their earliest years, in the search for the traumatic experience. The trail always led back to a period earlier than the age of eight. It seemed to Freud that if there had been no trauma before eight, then experiences after the age were not pathogenic. Since the age of eight is the period of second dentition, he wondered if somehow this played some role, but it did not seem to.

As the scenes were pursued further back into the earliest years, Freud became convinced that two conditions were of prime importance in the genesis of the neuroses: the experiences had to be of a sexual nature and had to occur in infancy or early childhood. Only these scenes when recalled later could provide the necessary fresh release of unpleasure (Draft K, *S.E. 1* 221) and make their recall traumatic.

In October, 1895, Freud tells Fliess he has made a major discovery concerning the dynamics of the psychoneuroses of defense. He suspects that "hysteria is conditioned by a primary sexual experience (before puberty) accompanied by revulsion and fright and that obsessional neurosis is conditioned by the same, accompanied by pleasure" (*Origins*, Letter 29). On two occasions, after first reporting the clinical observation to Fliess, he repeats it, asking at the same time whether he has already mentioned it (Letters 30 and 38). Then during November and December, 1895, Freud alternately doubts the clinical explanation and then feels it will stand after some modification. He also grows increasingly mournful because the physiological level of explanation is not advancing as well as the clinical (Letters 38, 44, 48).

Freud's next effort to explain the neuropsychoses of defense is organized around his belief in the etiological importance of early sexual experiences. This is reported in Draft

K and Draft H on paranoia. Both drafts became the basis for his second paper on the neuropsychoses of defense (1896*b*).

In Draft K he gives an outline of the course of all the defensive neuroses. He distinguishes four stages.

(1) A sexual experience that is premature, traumatic, and is repressed. This is termed the "primary experience," and the implication is that there is a primary automatic repression.

(2) This is followed at a later date, after puberty, by an experience that threatens to call the primary experience to consciousness. This leads to defensive repression and the formation of a primary defensive symptom.

(3) Then there occurs a "stage of successful defence which resembles health except for the existence of the primary symptom." This primary symptom is an ego attitude that maintains the repression.

(4) The repressed idea continues to threaten to return in spite of the primary defensive symptom. A struggle develops in which the ego tries to ward off the return of the memory. Further secondary symptoms develop that are the evidence of the struggle. Freud then applies this new and more dynamic approach to the three neuropsychoses of defense.

In hysteria the primary experience is an early passive sexual experience associated with a large release of unpleasure. The ego is overwhelmed and responds with manifestations of fright, which is the primary symptom. No psychical defense is erected but the fright reaction discharges excitation. Along with the manifestation of fright occurs what Freud terms a "gap in the psyche." The phrase appears to refer to a split in consciousness which meant that attention could no longer be directed to the pathogenic memory and therefore no preparation could be made to ward off its traumatic impact.[4]

[4] The problem is further discussed in the Project (p. 416), where it is referred to as the hysterical *proton pseudos* (first lie). The idea also appears in *The Interpretation of Dreams* (*S.E.* 5 603) as a reference to the gap in

Repression occurs by what Freud terms the development of a "boundary idea" (Draft K, *S.E. 1* 229). Ernst Kris, one of the editors of the *Origins*, comments in a footnote that this concept does not reappear in Freud's later writings. This does not seem quite accurate. The choice of the "boundary idea" is described as being based on "displacement of attention along a series of ideas that are connected by having occurred simultaneously." The boundary idea seems similar to the concept of compromise formation, a derivative that serves both defense and discharge. It is the mechanism of symptom formation. It also seems likely that this is an early description of the screen memory idea, described more fully only three years later, in "Screen Memories" (1899).

The fright reaction in hysteria leads to the formation of the psychic gap, as a result of which the content of the traumatic experience is "retained in a segregated compartment, it is absent from consciousness; its affect [is got rid of] by conversion into the somatic sphere." (*S.E. 1* 212).

In those patients who later develop an obsessional neurosis, there is, as in hysteria, an early passive unpleasurable sexual experience. This probably occurs at an earlier age than in the hysterias. As a result there is less unpleasure and fright than in the hysterias. This first experience is then followed at a later date (around eight) by a pleasurable sexual experience, active in boys and passive in girls. This is the "primary experience" for the future obsessional patient. At the time of sexual maturity (puberty, which is often premature), the recall of the pleasurable experience now creates painful self-reproaches. The memory is repressed and the primary defensive symptom develops, consisting of conscientiousness, shame, self-distrust, and so forth. Since this succeeds in accomplishing the repression, it is, except for this conscientious-

---

the functional efficiency of our mental apparatus, and even later in "Formulations on the Two Principles of Mental Functioning" (*S.E. 12* 223).

ness, the period of apparent health. The period of illness begins with the further reactivation of the childhood memory and its threatened emergence into consciousness. Instead, displacement to a substitute idea occurs and the obsessional fears are formed. The mechanism involved is displacement, and repression occurs as a result of substitution based on a similarity of subject matter. The obsessional symptom is constructed from a mixture of the memory and the affect. The memory suffers two distortions: something current replaces the past experience (change in time), and the subject matter is altered (something nonsexual replaces the sexual content). When the symptom involves the affect, the pleasure is replaced by self-reproaches, guilt, shame, hypochondriacal anxiety, and other similar emotions. Thus, *obsessional ideas* are invariably transformed *self-reproaches* which have re-emerged from *repression,* and which always relate to some *sexual* act that was performed with pleasure *in childhood*" (1896*b* *S.E. 3* 169; see also for a later discussion *S.E. 10* 221). Further defense (secondary defense) leads to the construction of rituals, brooding, penitential measures, and other pseudo-religious activities that are affects to ward off the self-reproaches.

In paranoia the details of the primary experience are unknown. The mechanism of defense is not repression but projection. The self-reproach in relation to a sexual scene is projected to the outside. The subject matter remains unaffected but it is placed on the outside. Delusional jealousy, hypochondria, persecutory and litiginous paranoia all show this mechanism. Freud in Draft H (*Origins*) explains each on rather superficial grounds, since the underlying sexual problem was not appreciated until his analysis of the Schreber case in 1911. For example, he suggests that the alcoholic cannot admit that alcohol is the source of his impotence and prefers to blame women. The litiginous paranoiac cannot admit he has committed an injustice and the hypochondriac needs to find the cause for his illness on the outside, that is, he is being poisoned, rather than become aware that his complaints arise from his sexual practices.

Freud suggests that the delusions in megalomania deny unpleasant reality and are held to with such tenacity because "these people love *their delusions as they love themselves*. That is the secret" (Draft H, *S.E. 1* 212). This "secret" was to be developed in Freud's paper "On Narcissism," published almost twenty years later.

The defense of projection leads to the primary defense symptom of distrust. The secondary symptoms—unlike the rituals of the obsessional neurosis—in paranoia involve a deep modification of the ego and its capacity to test reality. The ego is overwhelmed, leading to the final symptoms of melancholia or protective delusions. This formulation, when compared to the earlier one, is clearly less preoccupied with a mechanical explanation of the vicissitude of the affect, and shows the beginnings of a genetic and dynamic approach.

Freud's next efforts were aimed at testing the hypothesis that the *choice of the neurosis* was determined by the age of the patient at the time of the original scene. He had at different times expressed changing views on this problem. First he attributed the specific character of the neurosis to the way in which repression was accomplished *(S.E. 1* 222). Later, in Letters 46 and 52 *(S.E. 1* 229, 233), he wrote that the time of the event was decisive and the period of repression was of no significance. Five weeks later, in Letter 57 *(S.E. 1* 242), he again favored the time of repression as more likely the determinant. A month after that (Letter 58) he was even uncertain of the time relations.

During the period when he felt the timing of the scene was the basis for determining the form of the neurosis, he worked out a detailed theory involving the relationship of the stage of sexuality to the general development of psychic structure, and particularly to the laying down of memories.

He divided the life into four sexual stages and two "transitional periods" (Letter 46, *S.E. 1* 229). The four sexual stages were: (1) the period prior to consciousness, (2) infantile, (3) prepubertal, and (4) maturity. The two transitional periods, A and B (ages 8 to 10 and ages 13 to 17), were stages in which repression could occur, based on morality and aversion to sexuality.

(1) Ages 0 to 4: *period before secondary consciousness* (i.e., preverbal). Functioning is at perceptual level.

(2) Ages 4 to 8: *infantile;* functioning includes perceptual signs and unconscious.

(A) Ages 8 to 10: *transitional period* (later latency), at which time repression can occur.

(3) Ages 10 to 14: *prepubertal;* functioning includes perceptual signs, unconscious, and preconscious signs (i.e., secondary thought consciousness via verbal representation).

(B) Ages 14 to 17. *transitional period* (later latency), at which time repression can occur.

(4) Ages 17 to x: *maturity*—same functioning as Stage 3.

Freud hypothesized that a sexual experience at an earlier stage when recalled in a later stage produced a surplus of sexuality, inhibiting thought and making it impossible to tame or inhibit the memory. Sexual experiences during Stage 1, between the ages of 0 and 4, occur at the preverbal stage of development and lay the groundwork for later conversion and somatic discharge (primary defense). Later experiences, occurring in the transitional period, arouse this memory and produce a fresh surplus of sexuality which, because of the defense, cannot be inhibited by being transformed into verbal form. The sexual excitation can only follow the earlier somatic route of discharge, that is, conversion. This accounts for conversion hysteria.

Sexual scenes occurring between ages 4 and 8, because of the greater maturity of the psychical apparatus, can be translated into words. When later experiences reawaken these repressed memories they lead to obsessional self-reproaches.

Sexual scenes in Stage 3 (ages 10 to 14), when awakened

in maturity, are defended by disbelief and projection leading to paranoia. Paranoia, depending least on infantile scenes, is the "defensive neurosis, *par excellence*."

If there are no premature sexual scenes (in Stages 1, 2, or 3), there can be no pathological consequences. The repression that occurs is normal. Alternately if there is no pause (transitional periods) during which repression can occur, there can be no defense and no later surplus of sexuality that may overwhelm the ego.

In all cases two opposing forces are at work: the strength of the sexual impulse versus the energy of attention which, involving thought, can lead to a taming of the impulse. These two factors normally function without any interfering barrier between them. Only if the intercommunication threatens to produce unpleasure is a barrier erected and associative transitions prevented (repression). This may come about either if there is an abnormal increase in the first force (for example, by early sexual experience) or a decrease in the second force (as, for example, in melancholia, exhaustion, dreaming). When the repression begins to fail, a compromise is formed, that is, a symptom "which is *irrational*, like a logical error" (later to be elaborated in *Jokes and Their Relationship to the Unconscious, S.E. 8*).

This effort to understand the determinants for the choice of the neurosis emphasized the importance of the "period during which the *event* occurs." The period during which *repression* occurs was thought to be of no importance. The *content* of the experience was considered important only "in so far as it gives rise to defense."

Freud next expanded the aspect of this theory that dealt with the laying down of memories. Whereas he had originally described Stage 1 as simply being before the existence of secondary consciousness (preverbal), he now advanced a more detailed hypothesis of the structure of the psychical apparatus. He stated (Letter 52, *S.E. 1* 233) that he was "working on the assumption that our psychical mechanism has come into being by a process of stratification: the material present in the form of memory-traces being subjected from time to time to a *re-arrangement* in accordance with fresh circumstances—to a *re-transcription.* Thus what is essentially new about my theory is the thesis that memory is present not once but several times over, that it is laid down in various species of indications."

He then describes an early form of the "picket fence" model of the psychic apparatus (*The Interpretation of Dreams,* chapter 7). Perceptions, he states, are automatically conscious, but remain conscious only while in the perceptual field. The memory of these perceptions has a different fate. They are registered as "perceptual signs" (memory traces). These are incapable of becoming conscious and are *organized according to causal relations.*

A third registration occurs in the preconsciousness, *is attached to verbal images* (allowing recall), and can achieve a *secondary thought consciousness* as a result of hypercathexis by attention cathexis.

Certain fundamental assumptions governing the function of this mental apparatus were made.

(1) Each successive transcript represents a psychical achievement, related to maturation.

(2) Each transcript is governed by its own psychological laws (simultaneity, causality, verbal association).

(3) Each transcript as it develops inhibits the previous transcript and takes over its psychic energy.

(4) A lack of transcription to a new level is the equivalent of repression, since it interferes with its achieving "secondary thought consciousness."

The timing of the traumatic sexual experience could be related to this developmental and maturational picture of the psychic apparatus as follows:

The earliest traumatic scene, occurring before verbal transcription (i.e., the psychic apparatus had available only percept signs), led to somatic discharge, that is, hysteria.

When the psychic apparatus included unconscious transcriptions as well as percept signs, the obsessional neurosis could develop. Paranoia resulted if the traumatic sexual event occurred between the ages of eight and fourteen, by which time perceptual, unconscious and preconscious transcriptions had occurred (see chart, *S.E. 1* 237). Perversions appeared to result when sexual experiences occurred without interruption during all phases of sexual maturation.

Freud's preoccupation with the problem of the choice of the neurosis was based on his wish to nail down the specific etiology in each neuropsychosis. Precocious sexual experience was a prerequisite to all the neuropsychoses of defense. The medical mind then, as now, searched for the specific factor. A breakthrough of knowledge in this area would help substantiate the entire sexual theory and could lead to further advances in therapy and prophylaxis.

These early efforts concerning specific etiology reflect Freud's struggle toward a *developmental* view of psychical functioning. The goal was partially reached with the formulation of the libido theory and even more fully when to this was added the concept of the development of the ego.

Freud reports his first real success in a gay and triumphant letter to Fliess written on November 14, 1897 (Letter 75, *S.E. 1* 268). There, after describing the developmental shift in erotogenic zones, he writes: "The choice of neurosis (the decision whether hysteria, obsessional neurosis or paranoia emerges) depends on the nature of the wave of development (that is to say its chronological placing) which enables repression to occur, i.e., which transforms a source of internal pleasure into one of internal disgust."

The more detailed elaboration of this discovery led to the libido theory, but the problem was still not satisfactorily resolved. Freud returned to it in his 1911 paper, "Formulations on the Two Principles of Mental Functioning," where he wrote that the choice of neurosis "will depend on the particular phase of the development of the ego and of the libido in which the dispositional inhibition of development has occurred. Thus unexpected significance attaches to the chronological features of the two developments (which have not yet been studied), and to possible variations in their synchronization" (*S.E. 12* 224–225).

A later paper (1913), "The Disposition to Obsessional Neurosis," subtitled "A Contribution to the Problem of Choice of Neurosis" (*S.E. 12* 317–326), represents another effort to define the principal factors that determine the choice of obsessional neurosis.

Another problem that Freud attempted to deal with in this early period was the metapsychological explanation for repression. The earlier explanation that assumed a split in the consciousness during the hypnoid state was inadequate even at a descriptive level and was neither dynamic nor economic. His solution began with the assumption that painful memories were painful because they tended to lead to the release of unpleasure. Unpleasure was defined as one of the endogenous stimuli and, like libido, was probably a chemical substance. The release of this endogenous substance added energy to the system and raised the tension level. This, as a result, produced the sensation of unpleasure.

Freud states his reasons for feeling that the fresh release of energy is a necessary postulate. He points out (Project 320) that in response to painful stimuli from the external world, the "erupting external quantity" was responsible for the rise in the energy level. But when a painful experience is recalled, the quantity of energy involved is the same as in the recall of any other memory and therefore would not produce the energy increase needed to explain unpleasure. He writes:

> It only remains to assume, therefore, that owing to the cathexis of memories unpleasure is *released* from the interior of the body and freshly conveyed up. The mechanism of this release can only be pictured as follows. Just as there are motor neurones which, when they are filled to a certain amount, conduct $Q\acute{\eta}$ into the muscles and accordingly discharge it, so there

must be "secretory" neurones which, when they are excited, cause the generation in the interior of the body of something which operates as a stimulus upon the endogenous paths of conduction to ψ–neurones [for an explanation of these symbols, see chapter 7] which thus influence the production of endogenous $Q\acute{\eta}$, and accordingly do not discharge $Q\acute{\eta}$ but supply it in roundabout ways. We will call these [secretory][5] neurones "key neurones." Evidently they are only excited when a certain level in ψ has been reached. As a result of the experience of pain the mnemic image of the hostile object has acquired an excellent facilitation to these key neurones, in virtue of which [facilitation] unpleasure is now released in the affect.

Support is lent to this puzzling but indispensable hypothesis by what happens in the case of sexual release. At the same time a suspicion forces itself on us that in both instances the endogenous stimuli consist of *chemical products*, of which there may be a considerable number. Since the release of unpleasure can be an extremely big one when there is quite a trivial cathexis of the hostile memory, we may conclude that pain leaves behind specially abundant facilitations. In this connection we may guess that facilitation depends entirely on the $Q\acute{\eta}$ reached; so that the facilitating effect of $3Q\acute{\eta}$ may be far superior to that of $3 \times Q\acute{\eta}$.

The second and essential part of the repression hypothesis was based on the concept of a *delayed reaction* to an infantile sexual scene.[6] This delayed response was both the center of Freud's explanation of repression and was at this time thought to be the precondition for the development of the

[5] The editors have supplied a footnote at this point which reads, "The manuscript reads 'motor'—evidently a slip of the pen." The term motor does not appear to be an error—the secretory neurones are of course motor neurones. In *The Interpretation of Dreams* (S.E. *5* 468), affects are the result "of motor and secretory innervation." The term innervation is described by the editors as meaning the "transmission of energy into a system of nerves . . . specifically into an efferent system, to indicate . . . a process tending towards discharge" (*ibid.*, p. 537). See also *S.E. 5* 582, where affects are "viewed as a motor or secretory function," and also footnote 1, *S.E. 14* 179.

[6] Since infantile sexuality was not yet known to be a regular part of the drive endowment, it was considered to occur only as a reaction to an external experience, a seduction.

psychoneuroses of defense. Nonsexual painful memories did not arouse defense (repression), although they too could release unpleasure.

Freud realized repression was not correlated directly with the amount of unpleasure a memory produced. He wrote (*S.E. 1* 235–236):

> It cannot be due to the *magnitude* of the release of unpleasure if the defence succeeds in bringing about repression. We often struggle in vain precisely against memories involving the greatest unpleasure. So we arrive at the following account. If an event A, when it was a current one, aroused a certain amount of unpleasure, then the mnemic registration of it, A I or A II, possesses a means of inhibiting the release of unpleasure when the memory is re-awakened. The more often the memory recurs, the more inhibited does the release finally become.

This paragraph describes the taming of a memory. When first recalled the painful memory could arouse distress, but since the memory had been transcribed (that is, not repressed), it was subject to attention and being brought to consciousness. As a result the ego, being alerted, could defend itself against the unpleasure and progressively learn to master this release until the memory was no longer painful.

From this it can be seen that defense is a normal reaction which is directed toward memories or thoughts. Only in connection with certain sexual memories is the defense pathological.

Freud describes the mechanism as follows:

> There is *one* case, however, in which the inhibition is insufficient. If A, when it was current, released a particular unpleasure and if, when it is re-awakened, it releases fresh unpleasure, then this cannot be inhibited. If so, the memory is behaving as though it were some current event. This case can only occur with sexual events, because the magnitudes of the excitations which these release increase of themselves with time (with sexual development). [See also Pathological Defense, Project 351–352 and *S.E. 3* 154 (1896*a*), 167 (1896*b*).]

This deferred response to a sexual scene in childhood was the weakness in the functioning of the apparatus. Each recall of the scene was sure to result in the release of unpleasure which could not be mastered; normal defense could not be successful and repression had to occur.

Freud described the relationship of defense to sexual memories when he wrote (Draft K, *S.E. 1* 221):

> There is a normal trend towards defence—that is, an aversion to directing psychical energy in such a way that unpleasure results. This trend, which is linked to the most fundamental conditions of the psychical mechanism (the law of constancy), cannot be employed against perceptions, for these are able to compel attention (as is evidenced by their consciousness); it only comes in question against memories and thoughts. It is innocuous where it is a matter of ideas to which unpleasure was at one time attached but which are unable to acquire any contemporary unpleasure (other than remembered unpleasure), and in such cases too it can be over-ridden by psychical interest.
>
> The trend towards defence becomes detrimental, however, if it is directed against ideas which are also able, in the form of memories, to release fresh unpleasure—as is the case with sexual ideas. Here, indeed, the one possibility is realized of a memory having a greater releasing power subsequently than had been produced by the experience corresponding to it. Only one thing is necessary for this: that puberty should be interpolated between the experience and its repetition in memory—an event which so greatly increases the effect of the revival. The psychical mechanism seems unprepared for this exception, and it is for that reason a necessary precondition of freedom from neuroses of defence that no considerable sexual irritation should occur before puberty, though it is true that the effect of such an experience must be increased by hereditary disposition before it can reach a pitch capable of causing illness.
>
> We shall be plunged deep into psychological riddles if we enquire into the origin of the unpleasure which seems to be released by premature sexual stimulation and without which, after all, a repression cannot be explained.

The inclination toward defense is the result of regulation by the Pleasure Principle. The aim is not only a reduction of tension by discharge, but also an active goal of inhibiting the further fresh release of unpleasure. A sexual experience in childhood could be mildly pleasurable or not have much meaning. Since it did not provoke sexual tension (unpleasure), it did not arouse the need for defense (binding of the energy). After puberty, however, the memory took on meaning and its recall was the occasion for the release of much greater amounts of endogenous stimuli that would be experienced as unpleasure. Since there was no expectation of this fresh release of tension, it could have a damaging (traumatic) effect before the ego was alerted to the need for defense.

A clinical illustration of this hypothesis is described in the Project *(S.E. 1* 358): a sexual assault did not, when it occurred, prove traumatic, but only later, after puberty. "Here we have an instance of a memory exciting an affect which it had not excited as an experience." Normally,

> . . . the release of unpleasure was quantitatively restricted, and its start was precisely a signal for the ego to set normal defence in action. . . .
>
> Thus it is the ego's business not to permit any release of affect, because this at the same time permits a primary process. Its best instrument for this purpose is the mechanism of attention. . . . Attention is [normally] adjusted towards perceptions, which are what ordinarily give occasion for a release of unpleasure. Here, [however, what has appeared] is no perception but a memory, which unexpectedly releases unpleasure, and the ego only discovers this too late.

In Letter 75, written November 14, 1897 *(S.E. 1* 268), Freud elaborates on this theory. He suggests that the source of normal sexual repression is a turning against the abandoned sexual zones (mouth and anus). This comes about because man adopts an upright carriage and stimuli associated with the sense of smell become repellent. Early seductions that involve only the genitals do not produce neurosis, but later on the recall of the experience produces a fresh release of libido which leads to compulsive masturbation. Only when the early experiences involve stimulation of the mouth or anus, will the later recall lead to unpleasure instead of libido and to pathological defense (repression).

Freud now had a theory concerning the pathogenesis of the neuropsychoses that rested on three closely interwoven and mutually supporting parts. His clinical material repeatedly showed him that a prerequisite was an infantile sexual experience, *a seduction,* which was the traumatic scene. The next proposition was that the timing of this scene, or possibly the timing of repression, was the determinant of the form of the neurosis. Finally he could account for the need for pathological defense on the basis of the delayed response to the precocious sexual experience. This and this alone provided an occasion for a fresh release of unpleasure, greater in the memory than in the original experience, and accounted for the great enigma, the fact that only sexual impulses could be the cause of pathological defense. Each new clinical example seemed to confirm this intricate, interlocking explanation of the neuropsychoses, and Freud, despite some doubts, decided to publish his results. This he did in three papers, all of similar content, and published in early 1896 within a few months of each other.

The purpose of the first paper, "Heredity and the Aetiology of the Neuroses" (*S.E. 3* 143–156 1896*a*), was to combat the French view (Charcot and Pierre Janet) that heredity was the specific and indispensable factor in the etiology of the neuropsychoses. Freud's position was that heredity only acted as a multiplier in an electric circuit. He argued that a precocious sexual experience and not "nervous heredity" was the specific etiological factor. This precocious sexual experience consisted of "*actual excitement of the genitals, resulting from sexual abuse committed by another person*"

(*S.E. 3* 152). The time of the experience was in "earliest youth," always before eight to ten and therefore before the child reached sexual maturity. The sexual activity could even occur as early as the age of two. Most frequently the trauma occurred between the ages of four and five. The *specific cause* of hysteria was the memory of the sexual experience, which must have two important characteristics: it must be unconscious and it must have been passively experienced. Obsessional symptoms were similarly due to early sexual experiences, but in these cases after a passively experienced seduction, the child repeated the experience but was active and the experience was pleasurable. The obsessional symptoms were "*reproaches addressed by the subject to himself on account of this anticipated sexual enjoyment*" (*S.E. 3* 155).

Freud stresses the fact that the experience at the time of its occurrence, because of the child's sexual immaturity, produces little or no effect and that later, at the time when changes due to puberty occur, the memory takes on new and traumatic force. He writes, "*The memory will operate as though it were a contemporary event.* What happens is, as it were, *a posthumous action by a sexual trauma*" [*S.E. 3* 154]. It is the only situation in which a memory can be more traumatic than an experience. It reflects the weak side of the psychical apparatus, and is the reason for a memory remaining unconscious (i.e., repressed).

The second paper, "Further Remarks on the Neuro-Psychoses of Defence" (*S.E. 3* 162–185 1896*b*) also sent to a publisher on February 5, but published in May, six weeks after the French paper, repeats the theme that the specific etiology of hysteria is a childhood sexual trauma. Later, postpubertal sexual experiences, at the time of which the illness may become apparent, have an effect only because of the earlier sexual experience.

Freud makes quite explicit (*S.E. 3* 152) his belief in the actuality of the sexual seduction. He also expects his announcement to arouse skepticism. He repeats in much the same words as in the French paper his belief in the seduction with "actual irritation of the genitals (of processes resembling copulation)" (*S.E. 3* 163). The deferred operation of this early trauma is stressed, and in a footnote (*S.E. 3* 167) Freud points out again the importance of this fact for the occurrence of repression. He writes: "An inverted relation of this sort between real experience and memory seems to contain the psychological precondition for the occurrence of a repression" (*S.E. 3* 166fn. 1896*b*; see also *S.E. 3* 212, 219, 281).

Freud names (*S.E. 3* 164) as "Foremost among those guilty of abuses like these, with their momentous consequences, are nursemaids, governesses and domestic servants . . ." Teachers are also implicated, as are siblings who had previously been seduced by an adult. As the editors of the *Standard Edition* mention, the role of fathers as seducers of daughters who later developed hysteria is intentionally omitted and had been suppressed in the case histories of Katarina and Rosalie. But it is not clear that he yet felt that it was *always* the father who was involved.

The third paper, based on a lecture given April 21 or May 2, 1896,[7] was published May 31, 1896 with the title, "The Aetiology of Hysteria" (*S.E. 3* 191–221). Freud mentions to Fliess in Letter 46 (*Origins* 166) that he wrote it out in defiance of his colleagues, who had given it an icy reception.

This paper is of particular interest because it emphasizes the genetic point of view in tracing the hysterical symptom to its origin. The traumatic scene to be suitable as a determinant of the symptom must fulfill two conditions: it must explain the content of the symptom and it must have been sufficiently *traumatic* to provide the necessary impact or force to justify symptom formation. Breuer's concept of

[7] Jones, *Life and Work of Sigmund Freud*, vol. 1, p. 263.

the hypnoid state is criticized because it avoids the problem of the suitability of the scene as a determinant (content) of the symptom and substitutes the uncritical idea of a "special psychical condition" for the more demanding historical (genetic) view.

Even when the remembered events by which the patients explain to themselves the origin of their symptoms appear suitable in both content and force, further inquiry shows that other earlier and forgotten memories (scenes) lie at the root of the illness. Freud writes, ". . . hysterical symptoms can only arise with the co-operation of memories," and ". . . *in the end we infallibly come to the field of sexual experience*" (*S.E. 3* 197–199).

First Freud considers that repressed sexual experiences dating from puberty may be the origin, but this expectation is not fulfilled and the memories must be traced even further back to a premature sexual experience of the earliest years. The supposed fact of childhood seduction seemed fully confirmed in the eighteen cases Freud had treated. The case material, however, was not entirely supportive. Many of the patients could recall the sexual experiences and their actual occurrence could be confirmed, but with others the scenes could be arrived at only "by way of phantasies set up in front of them." These latter examples Freud mistakenly believed were genuine (Letter 61, *S.E. 1* 247).

Finally Freud played his trump card. He pointed out that for the first time he could explain the reason for repression of the incompatible idea and why the incompatible idea was a sexual one. Referring to his first paper on the defense neuropsychoses (1894), he wrote (*S.E. 3* 211): "What the circumstances are in which a defensive endeavour of this kind has the pathological effect of actually thrusting the memory which is distressing to the ego into the unconscious and of creating a hysterical symptom in its place I was not able to say at that time. But today I can repair the omission. *The defence achieves its purpose of thrusting the incompatible idea out of consciousness if there are infantile sexual scenes present in the (hitherto normal) subject in the form of unconscious memories, and if the idea that is to be repressed can be brought into logical or associative connection with an infantile experience of that kind.*"

After this sudden rush into print of three very similar papers, all concerned with what has come to be known as the seduction theory, there came a long period of analytic silence. The next paper, "Sexuality in the Aetiology of the Neuroses," was not published until two years later (1898) and was spoken of contemptuously by Freud as "Gartenlaube," and as a "tittle-tattle article." By this time he had discovered the fact of infantile sexuality. As Jones states, the paper is remarkable *in that it doesn't mention the seduction theory*.[8] The published papers are, as one might expect, less speculative than the letters and drafts. What is omitted is perhaps the most valuable aspect of Freud's work, the development of a genetic and dynamic view and his first formulations of a general psychology, the functioning of the psychic apparatus. The papers instead labor to drive home the reality of the seduction experience, which is all the more remarkable because it was precisely about this that Freud had some doubts.

The seduction hypothesis, as it has come to be known, originally involved the intricate concepts summarized above. In recent years the term "seduction hypothesis" has come to mean the narrower thesis involving the father's role as seducer. The term should refer to the larger argument, based on considerable clinical observation, and involving the timing of the event, the limitations of the immature psychic apparatus, and the delayed response, resulting in the fresh release of unmasterable unpleasure that led to the need for pathological defense. Freud developed this more general theory over a number of years, but was increasingly forced by his clinical observations to accept the less and less tenable formulation that the father was almost invariably the seducer.

[8] *Ibid.*, p. 265.

Even this original and wider definition of the seduction hypothesis has led to some misunderstanding. The earliest reference to the seduction theory is said to occur in Letter 12 (May 30, 1893). A footnote to the letter states that it is "the first hint of the theory of sexual seduction (in the broadest sense) in the aetiology of the neurosis." Jones also refers to this letter as containing the first reference to the seduction theory and says that "For more than four years he maintained this conviction . . ."[9]

This appears to be incorrect. The paragraph in the letter refers to the etiology of the *actual* neurosis in "*virgins with no history of sexual abuse*" (italics added). The use of this phrase, "no history of sexual abuse," clearly rules out any suggestion of seduction. The patients described are children (young people) who have the anxiety form of the actual neurosis. The problem is more clearly stated in Draft E, where the occurrence of anxiety in *virginal* subjects (children) can *still* be understood as having a sexual origin, because "sexual observations have been made or sexual information received, or where there are foreshadowings of sexual life" (see also *S.E. 3* 99 1895*b*).

Only with this formulation could anxiety in "young people" with no history of sexual activity be understood. The "apprehensive terror of sexuality" had to be the result of "things they had seen or heard and only half understood."

It appears then that Letter 12 is not a reference to the seduction theory, but seems rather to be a very early reference to infantile sexuality. The phrase "things they had seen or heard and only half understood," used in Letter 12, is repeated in Letter 59 (*S.E. 1* 244), where in a footnote in the *Origins* it is taken as a "hint of the significance of phantasy life." The phrase occurs again in Letter 61 and Draft L where the role of fantasy is explicitly developed.

Since this study of the context in which Letter 12 was

[9] *Ibid.*, p. 321.

written does not support the interpretation given it previously as an early reference to the seduction theory, but rather shows it to be an early reference to the importance of fantasy life in the formation of symptoms, the earliest reference to the seduction theory appears to occur in Letter 29 (October 8, 1895). The fact of seduction is not specifically mentioned, but Freud suspects "that hysteria is conditioned by a primary sexual experience (before puberty) accompanied by revulsion and fright, and that obsessional neurosis is conditioned by the same accompanied by pleasure."

In Letter 30 a week later Freud repeats this formulation, stating that "hysteria is the consequence of presexual *sexual shock*. Obsessional neurosis is the consequence of presexual *sexual pleasure*, later transformed into guilt. 'Presexual' means before puberty, before the production of the sexual substance: the relevant events become effective only as *memories*." This he describes as his "clinical secret." Fliess apparently approved of this formulation (Letter 32, October 20, 1895). From this time on the growing implication is that the "prehistoric unforgettable other person who is never equalled by anyone later" (the father) is involved (Letter 52, *S.E. 1* 239).

In Letter 31, Freud feels at "sixes and sevens," but is "practically sure" he has "solved the riddle of hysteria and obsessional neurosis with the formula of infantile sexual shock and sexual pleasure." His doubts quickly appeared, however, and by October 31, 1895 (Letter 33), he begins to question this "pleasure-pain explanation of hysteria and obsessional neurosis."

A case referred to in Letter 34 (November 2, 1895) seems to confirm the hypothesis of infantile sexual abuse as the specific etiological factor. In Letter 36 (November 29, 1895), he feels the "clinical explanation of the two neuroses will probably stand, after some modifications." (See also Letter 38.)

This "*clinical*" explanation seems to stand even though the psychological (theoretical) formulations are uncertain. Freud refers in Draft K (January 1, 1896) to early sexual experience (primary experience) as the etiological factor in obsessions and hysteria. Seduction by the father is explicitly mentioned in Letter 52 (December 6, 1896) as the "essential point" (*S.E. 1* 238). In Letter 54 (January 3, 1897), Freud mentions a case in which the seduction was confirmed. He also mentions that "everything now points more and more to the first three years of life." The seduction theory seems fully confirmed by the case material, and explains what has been regarded as "degeneracy."

A sudden change of interest occurs in Letter 56 (January 17, 1897) when Freud reemphasizes the similarity between the medieval theory of possession and what his patients tell him. This begins his interest in the role of fantasy and is to free him from the seduction theory and lead him to the discovery of infantile sexuality. In spite of this, the theory of seduction reaches its apogee in Letter 58 (February 8 and 11, 1897), where, according to Jones, Freud expressed the belief that since his sisters were neurotic, his own father must be implicated in some seduction.[10] (This passage is unfortunately but understandably omitted in the reproduction of the letter.)

Letters 59 and 61 tend to emphasize the fantasy life and even specifically mention masturbation fantasies. Letter 62 (May 16, 1897) suggests that a new surge forward is expected and Freud is reluctant to do any provisional summing up. Again he emphasizes fantasies and that in hysteria it is a question of things "heard but only understood *subsequently*."

In Letter 64 (May 31, 1897) Freud reports a dream in which he was feeling overaffectionate to his daughter Mathilde. He believes the dream fulfills his wish "to catch a father as the originator of neurosis, and so to put an end to my doubts about this which still persists."

[10] Jones, *Life and Work of Freud*, vol. 1, 322.

Jones incorrectly reports that in this letter Freud did put an end to his doubts: quite the reverse seems true; the doubts could not be silenced, except in a dream.[11]

The last reference to the seduction theory before it is given up in Letter 69 (September 21, 1897) occurs in Letter 65 (June 12, 1897), written before Freud's summer vacation (and the continuation of his self-analysis). He mentions a new case, "a girl of nineteen with almost pure obsessional ideas." Since obsessional ideas were related to seduction at a later age, the father would not be likely to be implicated. In this case the father had died when the patient was eleven months old. The brothers seem to be implicated instead, and the case seems to support the belief that seduction was the essential etiological factor, and seduction by the father was the usual case in hysteria.

From this review it seems likely that the belief in the seduction theory can be dated to October 8, 1895 (Letter 29) at the earliest. The specific involvement of the father seemed increasingly clear until the whole concept became untenable (Letter 34, November 2, 1895, and Draft K, January 1, 1896). Therefore the entire time of Freud's belief in the theory appears to cover twenty-three months (October 8, 1895 [Letter 29] to September, 1897 [Letter 69]). This is a generous estimate of the time during which Freud believed in the role of actual seduction as an etiological factor and is considerably less than the four years that Jones ascribes to Freud.[12]

After the beginning of Freud's self-analysis and a number of months of anxiety, "cloudy thoughts and veiled doubts," Freud wrote to Fliess in September, 1897 (Letter 69, *S.E. 1* 259), that he no longer believed in the actuality of the precocious sexual experience which had been such a cornerstone in his theory of etiology. He was persuaded of his

[11] *Ibid.*, pp. 322, 324.
[12] *Ibid.*, p. 321.

error because of his lack of success with his patients and because too often the father was blamed for perverse acts. Also he had come to realize that in the unconscious no distinction was made between "truth and emotionally-charged fiction." Finally since even in the psychoses the unconscious does not dominate the conscious system, so one cannot expect in treatment a total domination by consciousness of the unconscious.

The complex interlocking theoretical scaffolding that Freud had painstakingly developed turned out to be based not on fact but on the patients' fantasies. He later wrote of this moment (*S.E. 14* 17): "Analysis had led back to these infantile sexual traumas by the right path and yet they were not true. The firm ground of reality was gone. At that time I would gladly have given up the whole work. . . . Perhaps I persevered only because I no longer had any choice and could not then begin again at anything else."

Letter 69 written to Fliess at the time gives a quite different picture. Freud tells Fliess that he no longer believes in his *neurotica*, and then explains the reasons for giving up the seduction theory. He then writes: "If I were depressed, confused, or exhausted, doubts of this kind would no doubt have to be interpreted as signs of weakness. Since I am in an opposite state, I must recognize them as the result of honest and forcible intellectual work and must be proud that after going so deep I am still capable of such criticism. Can it be that this doubt merely represents an episode in advance towards further knowledge?"

To fully appreciate Freud's courage in this moment of self-criticism we should remind ourselves that he was attempting to understand total mental functioning and his only tool was his own mind. Formulations of psychological systems have only too often been the product of madness, in which the theories turn out to be efforts toward self-cure. Freud recognized this danger. After a careful analysis of the paranoid fantasies of Senatspräsident Schreber, he commented on the close parallel between the psychotic fantasies and his libido theory. He wrote: "It remains for the future to decide whether there is more delusion in my theory than I should like to admit, or whether there is more truth in Schreber's delusion than other people are as yet prepared to believe" (*S.E. 12* 79).

This quotation reflects Freud's remarkable capacity for self-criticism. It was never more apparent than in his correction of the seduction hypothesis. He not only corrected a belief to which he had already committed himself in print, but this correction also destroyed the basis for his theoretical understanding. The giving up of the seduction theory required almost an entirely new beginning. The collapse of the seduction theory meant that the concept of the deferred action of an early sexual experience could no longer be the basis for repression. This had been the sole explanation for later repression of relatively innocuous experiences. The earliest sexual traumas were automatically unconscious in the sense that they had no meaning, did not arouse affect and were not defended against. Later scenes that could be associated with the earlier traumatic scene were subject to repression because of this relationship (after repression).

In later psychoanalytic formulations, in *The Interpretation of Dreams* (1900) and in "Repression" (1915), the explanation of the problem of repression was similar in many ways to this early theory. There was still a primal repression, which permitted later secondary repression. The cause was no longer an early seduction experience, however, but was explained as a consequence of the belated appearance of the secondary processes (*S.E. 5* 547, 603; *14* 148). The earlier primary process functioning formed the core of the nonrepressed id and was then overlaid by the secondary process creating the infantile amnesia. Later experiences that became associated with this nonrepressed core were subject to secondary repression.

Some of Freud's concepts from this ten-year period of

1888 to 1898 remain as unexamined *revenants* in our current psychoanalytic theories. The concept of a specific traumatic scene or memory still influences the popular conception of psychoanalytic therapy, and even practicing analysts are likely to place an overevaluation on the uncovering of traumatic childhood memories.[13] The timing of the traumatic scene, which was in this early period related to the problem of etiology and the choice of the neurosis, has taken on a different meaning in current theory. Today it finds expression in the concept of phase-specific trauma. For example a surgical procedure, such as a tonsillectomy, will have an entirely different meaning to a child in the oral phase than it will if it occurs later, in the phallic phase of development. In the oral phase of libidinal development the tonsillectomy will be seen as a talion punishment for oral (cannibalistic) impulses, whereas in the phallic phase it will be conceived of as a threat of castration for sexual impulses.

The erroneous concept of the delayed response to an early sexual trauma as a source for the release of fresh unpleasure and a motive for repression has had one of the longest careers of any idea in psychoanalysis. It was offered originally as a purely physiological concept of both sexuality and anxiety and was presented most fully in the paragraph already quoted that describes the "secretory neurones" in the Project (p. 320). It is described again in detail in Letter 52 (December 6, 1896) and Letter 75 (November 14, 1897), where an attempt is made to relate it to Fliess's concept of a twenty-three- and twenty-eight-day cycle that also had a presumably chemical basis. Only as late as Letter 75 did Freud state that he decided to "regard as separate factors what causes libido and what causes anxiety." The editors of the *Standard Edition,* in their introduction to "Inhibition, Symptoms, and Anxiety" (*S.E. 20* 79), comment about this phrase that, "No

[13] See, however, Greenacre, "Re-Evaluation of the Process of Working Through," *International Journal of Psycho-Analysis,* 37 6 (November-December 1956), 439–444.

further evidence is anywhere to be found of this isolated recantation."

Although Freud corrected some implications of the seduction theory, he had no reason to abandon others of them. He commented in a footnote written in 1924 (*S.E. 3* 168 1896*b*) that he had "attributed to the aetiological factor of seduction a significance and universality which it does not possess," but he warns against rejecting everything about it. This brief summary of Freud's thoughts at this time illustrates the disadvantages of referring to his formulations simply as the seduction theory. The term emphasizes the concretistic error and ignores the problems that were being faced. These include the determining factors for the choice of the psychoneuroses, the origin of unpleasure and the consequent need for defense, and the disruptive influence of out-of-phase stimulation.

The seduction theory reappears in a more attenuated form later in Freud's writing. In his 1937 paper, "Construction in Analysis," in which he discusses delusions, Freud suggests that they can best be approached therapeutically by recognizing the "kernel of truth" on which they are based. It is a fair warning to those who see seduction as only and always a fantasy.

As if waiting for this correction, Freud's self-analysis moved ahead, and the universality of the oedipal impulses became apparent. The groundwork for these advances, however, was already laid as early as in May of 1897. Although he then believed in the genuineness of the seduction stories, he already recognized the importance of masturbation fantasies. Most important of all, he writes (*S.E. 1* 247), "the psychical structures which, in hysteria, are affected by repression are not in reality memories—since no one indulges in mnemic activity without a motive—but impulses which arise from the primal scenes" (see also *S.E. 14* 177 1896*b*). Jones describes this sentence as the beginning of the id concept,[14] and Kris in a footnote to Letter 61 comments that it

[14] Jones, *Life and Work of Freud*, vol. 1, p. 283.

"subsequently led to a complete revision of his psycho-analytic hypotheses and turned psycho-analysis into a psychology of the instincts." After this change in his beliefs, the role of fantasy, symbolism, the compromise structure of symptoms, and the similarity of dreams and neurosis, even the dynamics of forgetting, all became part of Freud's increasing understanding.

Perhaps our entire history of scientific thought does not offer a comparable example of creativeness and discipline. Freud's recognition of his error led to his awareness that he was dealing not with accurately recalled memories but with early "memory fragments" and that the child's impulses and wishes had molded these into "defensive fictions." The realization that his patients' stories were not true but were fantasies was a small difference from the first formulations, but this small difference made all the difference. It led to the discovery of the biogenetic unfolding of the sexual impulse, which in turn made possible the understanding of the psychoneuroses, the perversions, and character formation.

5. The Economic Formulations

THE ASSUMPTION of the existence of a psychic energy is as old as man's attempt to understand himself. It stems from a subjective and "common sense" point of view as well as from the observation of the workings of the outside world. In describing any dynamic system we think almost unavoidably in terms of structure, function, and energy. The goal of describing mental function as a machine, involving structure and function, makes the assumption of an energy as a driving force inescapable. Nevertheless the psychoanalytic concept of a psychic energy has been criticized as being a return to a vitalistic theory in which there is an assumption that a mysterious life force exists.[1]

It is claimed that the energy concept in psychoanalysis is only pseudoscientific and is similar to religious formulations. Religious explanations invoke the existence of a prime mover who is the ultimate determiner of all events, the original cause from which all effects result. This is generally a God

[1] Holt, "Beyond Vitalism and Mechanism: Freud's Concept of Psychic Energy," *Science and Psychoanalysis*, edited by J. H. Masserman (New York: Grune and Stratton, Inc., 1967), vol. 11, pp. 1–41: Apfelbaum, "Ego Psychology, Psychic Energy, and the Hazards of Quantitative Explanation in Psycho-Analytic Theory," *International Journal of Psycho-Analysis, 46* 168–182; and for a general discussion, Modell, "The Concept of Psychic Energy," *Journal of the American Psychoanalytic Association*, **11** 3 (July 1963), 605.

to whose will all consequences can be related. The formulations that follow the basic assumption of a prime source can have great inner consistency, but they have what Einstein has described as no rigidity; any or all explanations can follow from the original assumption; nothing remains to be explained. Scientific explanations are often thought of as requiring experimental verification and quantification. Although these are often desirable, they are not essential. More essential is that the theory should have some limitation in flexibility so that all possible new observations do not automatically fit into the concept.

Vitalistic theories suffer from this lack of rigidity, and the energy concept in psychoanalysis has been said to have a similar fault. Psychic energy is described as onl yan abstraction, since it refers to an energy that is not real in the sense of being measurable in the usual physical terms. It also does not obey the laws governing energy described in Newtonian physics. For example, in analytic theory energy is said to have an aim. It is described as aggressive or sexual and the latter subdivided into oral, anal, and phallic. As we know through pure science, energy by itself can have no aim. When energy has direction it is described as a force, and force times distance is the definition of work.

Finally, numerous examples of the misapplication of the energy concept are quoted as proof of its unscientific nature. To the extent that these criticisms are justified, they point only to the abuse of the energy concept, and are not valid criticisms of the theory itself.

Criticisms of the basic concept do not stand up on careful examination. The goal in psychoanalysis, as it is in the sciences generally, is to find theoretical concepts that help order the observations in terms of cause and effect. The concept of psychic energy is only one of these basic concepts and its value cannot be judged in isolation. The assumption of a psychic energy is neither remarkable nor particularly enlightening by itself. The criticism that psychic energy is a theoretical abstraction ignores the fact that all energy concepts are abstractions. The useful application of an energy concept in psychoanalysis is termed the economic view. It is only meaningful when coordinated with the genetic, dynamic, and structural views. These coordinated views in their totality are defined as the metapsychological level, which is the most abstract level of psychoanalytic theory formation. The metapsychological view serves to organize clinical observations in a fruitful manner. Consistency and unification are its goals and it is neither validated nor invalidated by clinical observations.

The economic point of view serves to relate one drive schema to another and to follow these until gratification (discharge of the energies) occurs. Drive schema are defined by Kenneth Colby in his book, *Energy and Structure in Psychoanalysis*, as structural components of the psychic apparatus containing specific concept meanings referable to drive source, drive aim, drive object, and drive space-time considerations. It is this association of psychic energy with a drive schema that gives the energy a direction—that is, makes it a force—and that is the essential aspect of the economic approach.

This view was implicit in Freud's discussion of psychic energy, as when he spoke of the distinction between somatic libido and psychical libido. Later, when this distinction was dropped, he still referred to drives as the "psychical representative of organic forces" and stated that "An instinct can never become an object of consciousness—only the idea that represents the instinct can" (*S.E. 14* 177). In "Repression," he described an instinctual representative as "an idea or group of ideas which is cathected with a definite quota of psychical energy coming from an instinct" (*S.E. 14* 152). In these quotations we see Freud's insistence on dealing with psychic energy only in terms of its relationship to structure, and never in isolation.

The criticism that psychic energy is nonphysiologicalanatomical reflects a confusion in the level of abstraction at which the problem is being discussed. The concept of psychic energy is clearly modeled on physical energy and originally there was some hope that it referred to the physiological energy which operates in brain functioning.[2] It soon became apparent that restricting analytic theory to the physiological level was a great and unrewarding limitation. Psychic energy as a concept became independent and only analogous to physical energy. The parallel between the two did not have to be maintained and it became important not to confuse them. In this connection Freud wrote in *An Outline of Psycho-Analysis* (*S.E. 23* 163): "We assume, as other natural sciences have led us to expect, that in mental life some kind of energy is at work; but we have nothing to go upon which will enable us to come nearer to a knowledge of it by analogues with other forms of energy." Psychic energy as a concept clearly has an independent status and is valuable in its own way as an organizing concept at a metapsychological level, the highest level of theoretical abstraction.

Since economic formulations are entirely theoretical, they are outside any subjective frame of reference. Subjective awareness of feeling "peppy" and "emotionally exhausted" can be understood only in psychodynamic terms and are not examples of, and certainly not validations of, an economic approach. Although the purpose of the concept is to bring order into clinical observations, it is not provable nor disprovable at a clinical level.

A variety of different energy formulations is possible, two of which are contained in Freud's writings; these are the assumption of a mechanical model and, alternatively, a field theory approach. In the mechanical model, drive energy and structure are considered as separate units; the structure exists independently and is driven by the energy. The alternative model involves field theory concepts in which energy

[2] For a recent imaginative approach to the problem of brain energy, see Donald Hatch Andrews, *The Symphony of Life*, particularly pp. 234–239.

and structure are less easily separated. In field theory, energy exists in a field that obtains its structure through the arrangement of the energy, and in a field theory approach, the ego and/or superego "structures" would be conceptualized as different organizations of energy. Order and rhythm are essential to field theory concepts, whereas energy that makes a machine "go" is the basic aspect of the structure-drive theory.

Freud's approach was essentially of the structure-drive type, although his ego concept as presented in the Project ("a group of neurones which is constantly cathected"—*S.E. 1* 323) is essentially a fiel dtheory approach. Breuer's concept of a resting tension in the neuronal network is a field theory. The discussion in the opening paragraph of section F of chapter 7 of *The Interpretation of Dreams* (*S.E. 5* 610–611), which was later expanded in the paper on "The Unconscious," shows that Freud conceived of a field theory approach and otherwise only wrote as a type of shorthand.[3]

Even before Freud's psychoanalytic discoveries the pathology of hysteria was understood in terms of the discharge of cerebral excitation. Charcot, in his description of the typical hysterical attack, had designated the first phase as epileptoid. His implication was that, as in epilepsy, there was a motor discharge of cerebral energies. Freud (*S.E. 1* 151), after criticizing Charcot's lack of a dynamic approach, wrote in a somewhat supercilious manner: "Perhaps we shall not be wrong in supposing that the majority of physicians are inclined to regard the hysterical attack as 'a periodic discharge of the motor and psychical centers of the cerebral cortex.' "

In spite of these critical comments, Freud's own early

[3] Pumpian-Midlin, "Propositions Concerning Energetic-Economic Aspects of Libido Theory. . . ," *Annals of the New York Academy of Science,* 74 4 (January 23, 1959), 1038–1051, and Erikson, "Freud's 'The Origins of Psycho-Analysis,' " *International Journal of Psycho-Analysis,* **36** I (January–February 1955), 1.

efforts to understand hysterical attacks also stressed the concept of discharge and bore considerable resemblance to the then current neurological orientation. Although the theoretical basis for Freud's discharge concept was always described as the reflex arc, the imagery is clearly taken from the grand mal attack of epilepsy. This is particularly clear in Freud's discussion of epilepsy in his paper, "Dostoevsky and Parricide" (*S.E. 21* 180–182).

The earliest therapeutic formulations were based on the abreaction theory, in which the discharge of "strangulated affects" was the goal, and for almost seventy-five years this has remained the major tenet of the economic concept in psychoanalysis. It states that the function of the psychic apparatus is the discharge of excitation (quantity), with the goal of avoiding a state of overstimulation. This economic formulation is not only the earliest, but is also one of the most essential, most ambiguous, most criticized, and least altered of all Freud's theories.

In order to clarify our discussion of Freud's economic concepts, it is desirable to distinguish two aspects. One aspect can be termed the "cathexis hypothesis," which refers to the displacement of energies from one drive schema to another *inside* the mental apparatus; the other, which involves the unburdening of the apparatus by the discharge of energy, can appropriately be designated the "discharge hypothesis."

Freud's earliest economic formulations dealt primarily with the discharge hypothesis. These first references are contained in three posthumously published notes, which were early drafts of the 1893 paper, "Preliminary Communication."

Because of Freud's success with the case of Frau Cäcilie M., Breuer had reluctantly agreed to a joint publication of the abreaction theory and other works on hysteria. Freud promptly sent him a "few pages" in which he made suggestions for their first paper. We know of these pages only because of a reference to them in a letter Freud wrote to

Fliess (*Origins*, Letter 9, 62), and because of his next communication to Breuer. In a letter to Fliess, Freud reported Breuer's agreement to publication and wrote that in other circumstances he would have sent a copy of the "few pages" on to Fliess. Apparently because it was to be a joint authorship he felt inhibited from following this impulse, and as a result no copy of these notes has survived. In the letter to Fliess, Freud also reported that he would have preferred to do the writing alone—a strange beginning for a collaborative effort that Freud later described (*Origins*, Letter 11, 64) as a "long battle."

The day after sending his notes to Breuer and the letter to Fliess, Freud wrote to Breuer. This letter, the first of the three posthumously published ones, begins with an expression of concern about the earlier notes. He writes, "The satisfaction with which I innocently handed you over those few pages of mine has given way to the uneasiness which is so apt to go along with the unremitting pains of thinking" (*S.E. 1* 147). He then proposes a new outline of their joint work. This outline has been accurately described by the editors of the *Collected Papers* as "exceedingly condensed jottings." The first theorem is to deal "with the constancy of the sums of excitation." The outline then describes the etiological role of trauma which increases the need for energy discharge. The hysterical attack is an attempt at reaction and discharge by means of recollection, but it involves abnormal displacements of the sums of excitation that have not been released. The abnormality consists of conversion of the energy and discharge through somatic channels.

The second note (*S.E. 1* 149) is titled "III," which refers to the third section in the "Preliminary Communication" (*S.E. 2* 11) for which it is an early draft. The content of this fragment deals primarily with the hypnoid concept, but also mentions the therapeutic goal of reviving the trauma and abreacting it.

The longest note (*S.E. 1* 151–154) is dated the end of

November, 1892, and is in Freud's handwriting, but was presumably composed by both Breuer and Freud. It bears the title "On the Theory of Hysterical Attacks." The material, much modified, forms part four of the "Preliminary Communication." In the closing paragraphs Freud deals with the energy problem, and defines psychical trauma as "any impression which the nervous system has difficulty in disposing of by means of associative thinking or of motor reaction." This leads to the early dynamic and economic theorem that the content of all hysterical attacks is those impressions which have failed to find an adequate discharge. Freud writes, "*The nervous system endeavours to keep constant something in its functional relations that we may describe as the 'sum of excitation.' It puts this precondition of health into effect by disposing associatively of every sensible accretion of excitation or by discharging it by an appropriate motor reaction.*"

Freud's theory that affects, which at this time he equated with psychic energy, needed to be discharged appeared in a footnote to his German translation (*Poliklinishe Vorträge* 1892–93*a*) of Charcot's *Leçons du mardi.* There Freud commented that "*A trauma would have to be defined as an accretion of excitation in the nervous system, which the latter has been unable to dispose of adequately by motor reaction.* The hysterical attack is *perhaps* to be regarded as an attempt to complete the reaction to the trauma" (*S.E. 1* 137).

This formulation emphasizes discharge, and although it is similar to the idea of a "periodic discharge of the motor and psychical centers of the cerebral cortex," it is, in fact, fundamentally different. The difference lies in the emphasis on the etiological role of a specific emotionally charged experience that has not been fully reacted to.

The early notes emphasize the discharge hypothesis but leave unstated the reason why discharge must occur. The assumption that justifies the discharge hypothesis is known as the "constancy principle." Freud felt that the concept of the constancy principle was of major importance, just as previously he had attached great importance to the etiological formula. His letters to Fliess show the great store he set on the idea of constancy, and in Letter 36 (*Origins*, 135) he is upset that Heinrich Sachs has put forth "the principle of the constancy of psychological energy." He was told by Fliess not to worry about the copyright and was reassured since "the most various things might be understood by it" (*Origins*, Letter 38, 137). This was only too true, and although Freud believed the idea to be of the greatest significance, he never defined its meaning in a clear and unambiguous way.

For example, it is puzzling in light of the emphasis on the constancy principle, that it is not mentioned in the first analytic publication, the "Preliminary Communication," published jointly by Breuer and Freud. This paper was published in two installments, the first appearing on January 1, 1893, and the second two weeks later. It subsequently became the introductory chapter to the 1895 joint monograph, *Studies on Hysteria* (*S.E. 2* 3). Instead of a mention of the constancy principle, the emphasis in the paper is on the role of frightening experiences and the individual's need for an energetic reaction to them, "in which as experience shows us, the affects are discharged." An alternative is also mentioned; that the affects may be "disposed of . . . by being worked over by means of association."

In 1894 Freud sent Fliess an outline of an ambitious paper that he was contemplating publishing (*Origins*, Draft D, 84). The theory of constancy was of central importance, but it was neither developed in any detail in his notes nor emphasized in the publication that followed. This oddity becomes even greater when, as it turns out, the first published reference to the principle is made not by Freud, but by Breuer, who then credits Freud with the idea. This reference appears in Breuer's theoretical chapter in the *Studies on Hysteria*

(*S.E. 2* 197), where he writes: "... feelings are always generated when one of the organism's needs fails to find satisfaction. Since these feelings disappear when the surplus quantity of energy which has been liberated is employed functionally, we can conclude that the removal of such surplus excitation is a need of the organism. And here for the first time we meet the fact that there exists in the organism a '*tendency to keep intracerebral excitation constant*' (Freud)."

One of the meanings attributed to the poorly defined constancy principle is that the total sum of energy in the psychical apparatus stays constant in amount over a given period of time. Psychic energy, like other forms of energy, is not to materialize suddenly nor disappear mysteriously. It means that energy will either be displaced from one investment to another (cathexis hypothesis) or be discharged from the system (discharge hypothesis). When defined in this manner the constancy principle is another name for the principle of the conservation of energy, the first law of thermodynamics. This is the interpretation given to the principle of constancy by Jones.[4]

From a historical point of view, Freud's application of the principle of the conservation of energy to psychoanalysis was probably the consequence of his working under Brücke, who in turn had been influenced by Helmholtz, who had given a lecture on his principle of the conservation of energy to a group that included Brücke.[5]

The historical view is of less significance than the dynamic implication for the theory of psychoanalytic metapsychology. The significance of this interpretation of the constancy principle was that for a given period of time the psychical apparatus could be considered to be a closed system; that is, it had a constant amount of energy. As a consequence the

[4] *Life and Work of Freud*, vol. 1, p. 396.

[5] Bernfeld, "Freud's Earliest Theories and the School of Helmholtz," *Psychoanalytic Quarterly*, **13** 3 (1944), 341.

vicissitudes of the energy could be followed through the apparatus, and the laws of causality applied to any energic formulation.

There are many reasons why the constancy principle, when seen as the equivalent of the conservation of energy, should be viewed as a useful fiction. For one thing, it obviously cannot be applied in analytic theory with the precision possible in mechanical physics. First, the psychic apparatus is not a closed system; energy can be added or be removed. Second, and even more significant, is the fact that the concept of the binding of energy, in which energy is modified so that it loses its pressure for discharge, is the equivalent of its disappearance from the system.

This change is currently conceptualized as being the result of energy in the form of an anticathexis employed in opposing the discharge of drive energy. A consequence of these opposing energies is that a new level of organization comes about which in field theory terms can be described as the formation of structure.

Much as the undefinable variables in the overvalued etiological equation made it impossible to apply it quantitatively, so also the economic point of view must not be too concretistically applied. It is valuable as an explanatory device and should not be taken as a literal description.[6]

However, implications of the constancy principle when defined as the conservation of energy are of the greatest significance. Without the conservation assumption, it would be impossible to describe behavior in economic terms. *The conservation principle is to the economic point of view what psychic determination is to dynamic formulations.* Both are essential axiomatic assumptions without which there would be no possibility of explanations based on causality.

Freud's early application of the conservation of energy

[6] Hartmann, "The Development of the Ego Concept in Freud's Work," *International Journal of Psycho-Analysis,* 37 6 (November-December 1956), 436.

was combined with his concept of the actual neurosis, particularly the transformation of libido into anxiety. This simplistic application is illustrated in a paragraph from his first paper (1894*a*) on the defense neuropsychoses. There he writes (*S.E. 3* 48–49) that the removal from an idea of its sum of excitation results in "*turning this powerful idea into a weak one.*" He then goes on to say, "the *sum of excitation which has been detached from it must be put to another use.*" He then concludes that the energy is transformed into anxiety and discharged in the anxiety attack. Although this conclusion turned out to be incorrect, the belief in causality is of central importance to an economic view.

Since the assumption of some form of energy is unavoidable, and the conservation of energy is an axiomatic assumption, any critical review of economic formulations in psychoanalysis can profitably focus only on the application of these fundamental assumptions. This leads to a second, and the most frequent, meaning given to the concept of the constancy principle. It has been interpreted as referring to a regulatory mechanism, the aim of which was to keep the tension in the system at a *constant* level. Defined in this manner, the constancy principle is the theoretical assumption that justifies the discharge hypothesis. Basically it describes an input-output concept in which the constancy of the excitation in the apparatus is a result of the fact that any increase in excitation above a given threshold will lead to discharge.

Freud stated this aspect of the principle most clearly in a lecture (*S.E. 3* 27) given at the same time as the publication of "Preliminary Communication." In his report on the lecture, he writes (*S.E. 3* 36): "If a person experiences a psychical impression, something in his nervous system which we will for the moment call the sum of excitation is increased. Now in every individual there exists a tendency to diminish this sum of excitation once more, in order to preserve his health." When stated in this way the constancy principle is similar to G. T. Fechner's principle of stability, to which Freud compared it (*S.E. 18* 8). It has been compared to Walter Cannon's homeostatic principle,[7] but differs from the homeostatic principle in that although the increase in tension leads to discharge, there is no regulation of the lower level of tension.

All three principles, Freud's, Fechner's, and Cannon's, describe biological tendencies but only the last two describe a system aimed toward maintaining a dynamic equilibrium at an optimum point in a steady state. Thus the constancy principle turns out to be mainly a justification for the discharge hypothesis, and states that the psychical apparatus serves to discharge endogenous tension. Why does it do this? Because this is its function, and if it did not, energies would accumulate. The implication is that it is not the energy which runs the model, but that the energy makes it necessary for the model to run. In a similar fashion we could say it is not the steam that runs the steam engine: the steam engine runs "to let off steam." The formula changes causality into motivation. This view of the constancy principle gave a function to the psychical apparatus, but more importantly it slowly focused attention on the essential issue of the appetitive needs or drives.

At first the input of energy that increased the "sums of excitation" was conceived of as coming from the outside, and the function of the apparatus was to discharge these external stimuli that impinged on it. This simple energic formulation was limited because it could not be related to any dynamic considerations, and ignored the internal sources of stimulation.

This aspect of the input-output view is presented in its simplest and most mechanical form in the opening paragraphs of the Project, where Freud writes, "Here in general there is a proportion between the Q [quantity] of excitation and the effort necessary for the flight from the stimulus, so

[7] Cannon, *The Wisdom of the Body*.

that the principle of *inertia* is not upset by this." This statement suggests that an unknown amount of hypothetical energy produced by incoming stimuli is exactly equal to the unmeasurable amount of energy consumed in flight. In this statement Freud made the mistake of applying the energy concept too literally.

Breuer also made the same mistake. He had explained the hysterical attack as being the result of a rise in excitation that could not be discharged along normal pathways because these were blocked by a split in consciousness, which he called the hypnoid state. If this were true, any tension increase that could not find an outlet should lead to an hysterical attack. For example, the unsuccessful search for a solution to a problem should build up tension and since it involved delay and frustration should lead to discharge along abnormal pathways. Obviously this did not occur and he explained his way out of this dilemma by writing, in *Studies on Hysteria*, that "since . . . the search . . . involves a large amount of work, though it may be to no purpose, even a powerful excitation finds employment and does not press for discharge . . ." (*S.E. 2* 209).

Although this early primitive energy formulation that I have termed the input-output view has decreased in significance, it represented an effort to describe the economic aspect of defense (flight or fight). Freud later (*S.E. 14* 180) conceptualized psychic flight (repression) as the withdrawal of libidinal investment from the wish and the further use of the energy to maintain repression. Hartmann more recently has suggested that the aggressive drive plays an essential part.[8] If aggression is not used for flight, the aggressive energy may be employed intrapsychically to hold the original impulse in repression (anticathexis). The absolute quantities of energy are no longer the essential point but the nature and the employment of the energies remain important.

Freud soon came to realize that this input-output theory

[8] Hartmann, *Essays on Ego Psychology*.

was too great a simplification. This followed his increasing awareness of the importance of internal stimulation, from which there could be no flight and which required specific action for relief. As Freud realized the importance of internal excitation as the principal source of energy, the term "sums of excitation" as the principal source of energy came to refer to endogenous stimuli that steadily increased by summation and became a burden to the psychic apparatus.

In spite of the increasing emphasis on internal stimulation as the source of energy, Breuer's formulations remained static and illustrate the limitations of an energy view which is not directly related to dynamic considerations. A summary of his views as they were formulated in his theoretical chapter in *Studies on Hysteria* illustrates this point.

He described the energy, which he considered to be physiological, as having three sources. It could originate from the brain cells, from the physiological needs of the body, and from perceptions of the outside world.

The energy level could fluctuate in two significant ways. There could be variations in the general level of intracerebral excitation[9] and there could be focal increases in excitation. These focal increases meant an uneven distribution of the energy with peaks of energy in certain areas, surrounded by and cut off from areas of lower energy level.

In discussing the general variation in intracerebral excitation, Breuer pointed out that a *decrease* below a certain threshold of tonic excitation would lead to sleep. An *increase* would first lead to wakefulness, which Breuer called encitement, and stimulation. A further general increase in the level of intracerebral excitation would produce restlessness and distress and finally agitation and excitement. This general (nonfocal) energy could be discharged by nonspecific or aimless motor action.

[9] As Bernfeld has pointed out in "Freud's Earliest Theories . . . ," the term "intra-cerebral excitation" was a cautious way, consistent with then current scientific tradition, of referring to an energy concept conceived of in a very physical way.

Breuer then described the consequences of focal increases in intracerebral excitation. These led to the investment of a psychical representative subjectively experienced as an affectively charged idea. This, in contrast to a general increase of tension, could only be discharged by a specific act leading to gratification. According to Breuer, when this specific act was not possible for any one of three reasons (suppression, defense, or the hypnoid state), the resultant accumulation of energy (sums of excitation), after passing a critical threshold, resulted in a breakdown of resistances, a short-circuiting (conversion), and an abnormal discharge through inappropriate (somatic) pathways. Sudden increases of energy, since they did not allow time for associative elaboration, decreased the likelihood of normal discharge and promoted the use of abnormal pathways. Once the abnormal pathway of discharge was employed, its further use became facilitated, and because of its associative isolation ("withdrawn from 'associative contact'," *S.E. 2* 214), the threatened recall of the traumatic memory and its affect again and again discharged through this abnormal, somatic, peripheral pathway *without the affect's reaching consciousness.*

The pathogenic consequences of the hypnoid state could be easily understood in economic terms: in the state of reverie characteristic of the hypnoid state "intracerebral excitation sinks below its clear waking level." If during this state "a group of affectively colored ideas is active, it creates a high level of intracerebral excitation which is not used up by mental work and is at the disposal of abnormal functioning such as conversion" (*S.E. 2* 218).

Breuer pointed out that even the innate disposition for hysterical illness could be described in economic terms. People who were lively, restless, and craved sensations and who could not tolerate monotony and boredom were simply people "whose nervous system while it is at rest liberates excess of excitation . . ." (*S.E. 2* 240).

The limitation of Breuer's theoretical formulation lies in the fact that it is almost entirely explanation by analogy.

This is seen in his mechanical explanation of conversion, which by analogy he compares with an electrical short circuit. It creates a sense of understanding, when in fact nothing new has been added.

In spite of the concretistic simplicity of Breuer's views, recent neurophysiological studies of the limbic brain are surprisingly reminiscent of Breuer's early formulations. These include Magoun's study of the ascending reticular system, Jouvet's description of the role of the pontine nucleus in the regulation of sleep patterns, and Maruzzi's report of brain stem activity during both the synchronized and desynchronized phases of sleep.[10]

Freud's earlier (1894*a*) formulation of his "working hypothesis" is superior to Breuer's views because of its tentative quality, and his expectation of relating it to dynamic (defensive) goals. He wrote: ". . . in mental functions something is to be distinguished—a quota of affect or sum of excitation—which possesses all the characteristics of a quantity (though we have no means of measuring it) which is capable of increase, diminution, displacement, and discharge, and which is spread over the memory-traces of ideas somewhat as an electric charge is spread over the surface of a body." He believed that the hypothesis is "provisionally justified by its utility in co-ordinating and explaining a great variety of psychical states" (*S.E. 3* 60).

The paragraph clearly states the purpose of the economic view; it is an explanatory concept and not a descriptive one. In retrospect one can see Freud's hesitancy in committing himself to an energy view that explained everything too easily and was not associated with a dynamic understanding.

This difference in attitude between Breuer and Freud is illustrated again in Freud's rejection of the concept of the

[10] Magoun, "An Ascending Reticular Activating System in the Brain Stem," *The Harvey Lectures;* Jouvet, "Telencephalic and rhombencephalic sleep in the cat," *The Nature of Sleep*, ed. by Wolstenholme and O'Connor; and Maruzzi, "Active Processes in the Brain Stem During Sleep," *The Harvey Lectures.*

hypnoid state and his preference for the defense hypothesis. The former was static and circular in reasoning, whereas the concept of defense as the cause for pathology was dynamic and open-ended.

Freud's own early economic theories were worked out in great detail in the Project. This was written in 1895 and was not meant for publication. Many of the same ideas, less burdened by the wish for mechanical formulations, appeared in the seventh chapter of *The Interpretation of Dreams* (1900) and were further elaborated in his 1920 monograph, *Beyond the Pleasure Principle* (*S.E. 18* 7).

In the Project Freud begins by comparing the most primitive form of the psychic apparatus to a reflex arc in which there is only a sensory and motor component. The function of the apparatus is the immediate discharge of any stimulus. The apparatus is described as operating under the principle of neuronic inertia, which asserts that the neurones tend to divest themselves of quantity. This immediate discharge is described as the primary function of the apparatus.

In the first few sentences of the Project, the structure, function, and regulatory principle of the most primitive theoretical model are described. The term regulatory principle is somewhat paradoxical, since there is no true regulation at this level. The only vicissitude of any energy input is its immediate discharge and the trend is toward a zero tension in the apparatus (neuronic inertia and later the Nirvana principle). The image of the reflex arc is also used in *The Interpretation of Dreams* (*S.E. 5* 565). Freud later refers to it as a "fiction" (*S.E. 5* 598). Recently this stage of reflex response to stimuli has received clinical support and has been elaborated by the studies of Réné Spitz, Willi Hoffer, and Max Schur.[11] The work of Konrad Lorenz and

[11] Spitz, "A Genetic Field Theory of Ego Formation"; Hoffer, "Mouth, Hand and Ego-Integration," *Psychoanalytic Study of the Child*, 3–4 49–56; and Schur, "Phylogenesis and Ontogenesis of Affect- and Structure-Formation and the Phenomenon of Repetition Compulsion," *International Journal of Psycho-Analysis*, 41 4–5 (July–October 1960), 275–287.

N. Tinbergen on instinctual behavior of animals, which is governed by innate releasing mechanisms and imprinting, has also enlarged our understanding of this phase in development and maturation.[12]

This most primitive apparatus must immediately be elaborated. Although it is adequate to deal with stimuli that originate from the outside world, since random activity can discharge these energies, it cannot discharge stimuli which arise from the inside, the appetitive needs. These require specific action (the need satisfying object) for relief.

The necessary change comes about by the gradual addition of two modifications to the apparatus. The first change consists of the insertion of resistances in the conduction pathways, as a result of which the threshold of tension is increased before discharge occurs. The second modification consists of the development of a greater complexity in the structure. This means that the energy being transmitted can follow one or another pathway. As a result of these two modifications the endogenous stimuli can accumulate in small increments (via "sums of excitation"), slowly filling the conduction pathways as the energy progressively overcomes the resistances. At some point the gradually increasing tension produces a signal of rising need, registered as "unpleasure." As the increase continues, the signal becomes more imperative until some action is focused on the apparatus. The increased complexity of the structure, which now provides alternative pathways along which the excitation can pass, permits a flexibility of response not present in the true reflex arc model. As a result of these changes, the model functions in a quite different manner. At the time of increase in tension (need), random activity or outside help will lead to an experience of satisfaction. A memory trace will be laid down in which a link (facilitation) is formed between the need and the perception at the time of satisfaction. At the

[12] Lorenz, "The Nature of Instincts," *Instinctive Behavior*, ed. by Schiller, and Tinbergen, *The Study of Instinct.*

next arousal of the same need there will also be a revival of the memory of this perception. The impulse to search out and reevoke this remembered perception that was associated with gratification is defined as a wish. The governing or regulatory mechanism of this still quite primitive apparatus is only the striving for pleasure and the avoidance of unpleasure. Freud states (*S.E. 5* 598), "A current of this kind in the apparatus, starting from unpleasure and aiming at pleasure, we have termed a 'wish'; and we have asserted that only a wish is able to set the apparatus in motion *and that the course of the excitation in it is automatically regulated by feelings of pleasure and unpleasure*" (italics added).

In this manner past experiences of satisfaction, associated with pleasure, or of frustration, associated with unpleasure, leave behind them a motive force (Project 322, 327). Freud's use of the term motive does not imply a cause for the initiation of action, but describes the means by which pathways for the discharge of energy are determined (Project 301). The pathways that result in unpleasure have the value of directing flow away from themselves (Project 330). Those pathways that lead toward pleasurable discharge are "facilitated" in the sense that the resistances are low. Dreams are described as examples of uninhibited flow (primary process) along pleasurable pathways (Project 340).

The regulatory principle that governs the operation of this more advanced model[13] is termed the pleasure-unpleasure principle or more simply the pleasure principle.

Freud describes this form of regulation (Draft K, *S.E. 1* 221) when he writes, "There is a normal trend towards defence–that is, an aversion to directing psychical energy in such a way that unpleasure results." In the Project (*Origins* 373) he writes: "Since we have certain knowledge of a trend in psychical life towards *avoiding unpleasure*, we are tempted to identify that trend with the primary trend

[13] Freud also referred to this model as a "fiction" (*S.E. 12* 220), by which he meant a theoretical construct.

towards inertia. In that case *unpleasure* would have to be regarded as coinciding with a raising of the level of Q$\acute{\eta}$ or an increasing quantitative pressure: it would be the *W* sensation when there is an increase of Q$\acute{\eta}$ in ψ. Pleasure would be the sensation of discharge."

In 1920 Freud defined the pleasure principle in much the same terms. He wrote in *Beyond the Pleasure Principle:* "In the theory of psychoanalysis we have no hesitation in assuming that the course taken by mental events is automatically regulated by the pleasure principle. We believe, that is to say, that the course of these events is invariably set in motion by an unpleasurable tension, and that it takes a direction such that its final outcome coincides with a lowering of that tension—that is, with an avoidance of unpleasure or a production of pleasure." Freud later states it is more accurate to say that "there exists in the mind a strong *tendency* towards the pleasure principle" (*S.E. 18* 7).

It seems desirable for the sake of clarity to make a distinction between the pleasure principle and the pleasure-unpleasure series. Both terms are used in Freud's writings without much effort to distinguish them. I should like to reserve the term pleasure principle to describe the "general trend in psychical life." It describes an *affect level of functioning*, where behavior is governed not, as in the reflex arc, by a need, but by its psychological representative, a wish. The term pleasure-unpleasure series I shall employ to refer to the means (signals) by which the principle operates. Freud may have had some such distinction in mind, since he spoke of the mental apparatus as "subject to the pleasure principle, i.e., (it) is automatically regulated by feelings belonging to the pleasure-unpleasure series . . ." (*S.E. 14* 120).

The operation of the psychical apparatus under the pleasure principle can be described in dynamic and economic terms. Of central importance to the dynamic view is the role of the wish. Freud points out that in all mental functioning "nothing but a wish can set our mental apparatus at work" (*S.E.* *5* 567). The reappearance of the perception associated with the original satisfaction is the fulfillment of the wish and the aim of the activity is to produce this "perceptual identity" (*S.E.* *5* 566).

The psychical apparatus at this level of development can do "nothing but wish, work for a yield of pleasure and avoid unpleasure . . ." (*S.E.* *12* 223).

From an economic point of view, two facts are significant in the functioning under the pleasure principle. The first is that pleasure is defined as a decrease of quantity and unpleasure as an increase of quantity. These affects automatically regulate the course of the energy discharge. Freud speaks of this signal aspect of the pleasure-unpleasure series when he describes it as providing signals for defense (Project 324, 330). Thirty-five years later (*S.E.* *18* 29) he describes it as "an index to what is happening in the interior of the apparatus." These signals, being biological regulators, are not necessarily conscious and Freud describes them as "taking place between quotas of energy in some unimaginable substratum" (*S.E.* *22* 90). There are alternate pathways along which the energy may travel, and the regulatory function is carried out automatically through changes in the resistance barriers, the facilitations, the cathexis of adjacent neurones and by affect signals. These signals probably consist of vague and rudimentary drive-organized memory traces. They signal the tension state (wish), the pathways toward gratification and the fact that gratification or frustration has occurred.

The second important fact is that the energy involved in the system, while it operates under the pleasure principle, is mobile and presses for quick discharge. There is rapid total flow of energy from one neurone to another (from one idea to another with which it is loosely associated). Energy moves through the system "en masse" and delay is minimal. Also, the energy can accumulate around one idea that stands as a representative for numerous others even if they are only loosely associated and even contradictory. This mechanism is termed displacement and condensation. This form of mental functioning was called by Freud the primary process (Project 326; *S.E.* 5 601).

The fundamental improvement of this model over the reflex model is the capacity to recall past experiences of satisfaction, to wish, and to regulate the pathway of discharge in terms of these wishes. This is also the weakness of the mode of functioning. If, as is likely, delay in gratification occurs, the memory because of condensation can achieve great intensity and be recalled with hallucinatory vividness. This is termed hallucinatory wish fulfillment: memory and perception cannot be distinguished, and the memory is treated as a reality. The apparatus is limited to striving toward a "perceptual identity," the reevocation of the identical perception associated with the experience of satisfaction, and confuses memory with actual perception. It is led astray by the *intensities* of the ideas (*S.E.* 5 602), which occur as a result of the massive shifts in their energic investment.

This hallucinatory revival of the memory occurs when the level of tension overcomes the resistances and when external delay (the exigencies of life) imposes frustration instead of immediate gratification. Like a dam breaking, the total amount of drive energy pursues its way through the apparatus, following the pathways of least resistance, which have been facilitated by previous experiences of gratification. There is a massive investment of the memory trace associated with gratification. This brings about the hallucinatory vividness, which in turn creates the expectation of satisfactory total discharge and the return of the level of tension to zero. Thus even this "improved" model still operates with the goal of fulfilling the primary function of the apparatus (i.e., to rid itself of all tension), and the manner of functioning is still the primary process.

As a result of the hallucination of the wished-for object the apparatus is given a false signal for discharge and expects gratification. Instead of experiencing a reduction in tension (pleasure or gratification), the discharge through the apparatus leads to frustration and disappointment (unpleasure).

From an economic view the essential factor is that the energic discharge is all or none. The weakness in this form of functioning is the inability to delay or control the massive shifts in energy and the consequent failure to distinguish memory from perception. In addition there is a limitation in the range of memories available to the apparatus. There is a search for memories associated with gratification (pleasure) and an avoidance of memories associated with painful frustration (unpleasure). The apparatus *must* avoid any unpleasurable memory. Freud (*S.E.* 5 600) describes the functioning of the apparatus as being governed by an "effortless and regular avoidance . . . of anything that had once been distressing." He states that the apparatus at this stage of development is "totally incapable of bringing anything disagreeable into the context of its thoughts. It is unable to do anything but wish" (see also Project 322, 357).

This defect in the functioning under the pleasure principle (affect regulation) requires another modification in the apparatus. Since the need-satisfying object is not always present in the outside world and yet is essential for the specific action that can lead to gratification, some delay in discharge is required. During this delay an accurate knowledge of the outside world can be acquired. Massive total shifts of energy must be restrained to allow for exploratory investigation of external circumstances. During this exploration, which is a search aimed at a refinding of the circumstances of gratification, memory must be distinguishable from perception. Drive energy must not be allowed to romp through the apparatus, pursuing the path of least resistance, following previously facilitated pathways with no regard for the outside, but unimpededly aiming toward discharge. A capacity for delay or impedence of drive energy must develop. If in error wrong pathways are followed that release unpleasure, there must be a way of diminishing the effect of this unpleasure on the apparatus so that it will not produce a total response of pain, but instead a muted "signal response." To accomplish this double inhibition—a delay in drive discharge and a reduction of the traumatic effect of unpleasure—the apparatus must have a storage capacity that can absorb or bind drive energy, delaying its passage, and which can also absorb or bind unpleasurable tension, which is always released when the discharge threatens to go along the wrong pathways.

Freud described the required modification of the apparatus when he wrote (*S.E. 1* 297): "In consequence, the nervous system is obliged to abandon its original trend to inertia (that is, to bringing the level [of Qή] to zero). It must put up with [maintaining] a store of Qή sufficient to meet the demands for a specific action. Nevertheless, the manner in which it does this shows that the same trend persists, modified into an endeavour at least to keep the Qή as low as possible and to guard against any increase of it—that is, to keep it constant."

The paragraph is, to say the least, confusing. The situation is not helped by Freud's other references to the pleasure principle and to the constancy principle, which are also ambiguous. He wrote in 1915, in "Instincts and Their Vicissitudes" (*S.E. 14* 120), "The nervous system is an apparatus which has the function of getting rid of the stimuli that reach it, or of reducing them to the lowest possible level; or which, if it were feasible would maintain itself in an altogether unstimulated condition." Not fully satisfied with this description, he returned to the problem at a later date in *Beyond the Pleasure Principle*, 1920 (*S.E. 18* 9):

> The facts which have caused us to believe in the dominance of the pleasure principle in mental life also find expression in the hypothesis that the mental apparatus endeavors to keep the quantity of excitation present in it as low as possible or at least to keep it constant. This latter hypothesis is only another way of stating the pleasure principle; for if the work of the mental apparatus is directed towards keeping the quantity of excitation low, then

anything that is calculated to increase that quantity is bound to be felt as adverse to the functioning of the apparatus, that is as unpleasurable. The pleasure principle follows from the principle of constancy: actually the latter principle was inferred from the facts which forced us to adopt the pleasure principle.

In another attempt toward a more precise definition of the relationship between the pleasure principle and the constancy principle (*S.E. 18* 62), Freud describes the pleasure principle as "a tendency operating in the service of a function whose business it is to free the mental apparatus entirely from excitation or to keep the amount of excitation in it constant or to keep it as low as possible. We cannot yet decide with certainty in favour of any of these ways of putting it . . ."

Each time Freud deals with the problem of constancy, he proposes three ways in which the problem can be stated. The first proposes that the goal of the psychical apparatus is to achieve zero tension or an "altogether unstimulated condition" or freeing "the mental apparatus entirely from excitation." This is clearly the principle of inertia that later became the Nirvana principle when it was linked to the concept of the death instinct.

The neuronic system is obliged to abandon this goal because of the "exigencies of life." This phrase refers to two factors that require delay in drive discharge. The first is enforced external delay that results from the need for specific action. The second refers to the fact that instinctual stimuli must be dealt with. As a result of these internal stimuli the nervous system is obliged to "renounce its ideal intention of keeping off stimuli, for they maintain an incessant and unavoidable afflux of stimulation" (*S.E. 14* 120).

This leads to the second way of describing the constancy principle. Its goal is to keep the "quantity down, or avoid any increase"; "to keep the excitation present in it as low as possible." This description follows directly from the nature of instinctual reflex. The only way in which quantity can be "kept down" is by discharge; drive energy accumulates steadily by summation and the rate of production, except in unusual circumstances, is not alterable. The same argument applies to keeping quantity as low as possible or avoiding any increase in it. This formulation is simply a restatement of the discharge hypothesis, modified by the fact that zero tension is, because of the instincts, not possible. The need for discharge has been inaccurately equated with the pleasure principle. The pleasure principle is a form of regulation, based on affect signals, either conscious or unconscious. The fact of tension reduction that cannot obtain zero level is an unavoidable fact of the existence of and pressure from the instincts.

Finally, the goal of the constancy principle is stated (in parentheses!) as ". . . to keep its level of tension constant" or "to keep it [quantity of excitation] constant" or "to keep the amount of excitation in it [the mental apparatus] constant."

To interpret this to mean that the goal of the psychical apparatus is to keep a constant amount of drive energy present makes little sense. According to this the term constancy (as opposed to the constancy principle) would in effect state that the goal of the apparatus under the domination of secondary process functioning is partial discharge of drive energy (i.e., partial gratification of hunger or of the sexual impulse), with some residue of drive energy being retained. This is clearly not the case. These phrases describing the third alternative could be understood as stating that the accumulation of drive energy will occur until a threshold level has been reached. Any further accumulation would be discharged, but the subthreshold amount would always be present. Discharge here would represent an overflow after the level had passed the threshold. This dribbling off of the surplus energy does not represent an accurate view of Freud's concept of tension build-up and discharge.

The most meaningful interpretation of the phrases comes

about if the emphasis is placed not on the absolute quantity of excitation in the apparatus but (as stated in the Project) on the *level* of tension. The goal then is not to keep the quantity of excitation constant, but the level of tension constant *and below a threshold level.*

The absolute quantity is not kept down, but is altered in its mode from an energy that is mobile to an energy that is bound. By this alteration in the mode of the energy (binding), the *tension level* of drive energy as defined in terms of its push for discharge can be kept almost constant. Even though the absolute amount of drive energy in the apparatus increases, the binding keeps the pressure for discharge below the threshold level. The constancy principle would then state that the neuronic apparatus, because of the need for delay, manages to maintain a *constant level of drive discharge tension* by its binding capacity.

This leaves next the question of the means by which binding can occur. Freud's paragraph states that the function of the store of quantity which the system must learn to tolerate is to meet the demands for "specific action." Specific action is the action that will bring about certain definite conditions in the external world—that is, the situation in which gratification can occur. The required action must be performed independently of endogenous energy, because of the difference in aims; the action also requires more energy than can be obtained from the endogenous energies (Project 297).

The stored energy that the system must learn to tolerate does not therefore refer only to drive energy, but also to energy which is invested in the neurones forming the ego. The role of internal stimuli makes it impractical and damaging if the apparatus is limited to reflex actions that were adequate as a method of handling external stimuli. To serve this new need certain neurones—the ego complex—become specialized. They are different in that they maintain a reservoir of energy. They have learned "to store a quantity of energy sufficient to meet the demands for specific action." Their function is to bind or store drive energy and unpleasure. The apparatus, having learned to tolerate a store of *ego energy*, now has the capacity for a new function, the storage of *drive energy*.

Consistent with this is Freud's definition of the ego as "a group of neurones which is constantly cathected and thus corresponds to the *vehicle of the store* required by the secondary function" (Project 323), and later the ego is "a complex of neurones which hold fast to their cathexis, a complex, therefore, which is for short periods at a constant level" (*S.E. 1* 369). The constant level is maintained by an expansion of the number of neurones comprising the ego. "If the level of cathexis in the ego-nucleus rises, the extent of the ego will be able to expand its range; if it [the level] sinks, the ego will narrow concentrically" (Project 370).

The term "constant" in the Project, according to this interpretation, refers to a *constantly present* quantity of ego energy that can keep drive tension for a time at a constant level, that is, below the discharge threshold, and at the same time is available to meet the demands for specific action. Both the absolute quantity of ego energy and stored drive energy can vary. As ego energy increases in amount, greater numbers of neurones become involved in the network. This increases the capacity for the storage of drive energy, which then can increase in absolute amount but, being bound in the ego, does not increase the pressure for discharge.

The reserve energy that the apparatus learns to tolerate and that is called here ego energy must differ in some way from drive energy whose binding and discharge it governs. It must be either a different form of energy (indifferent or neutral) or at least a different mode of drive energy (neutralized). In fact Freud does postulate an ego energy that is different from drive energy when he suggests that its source may be the initial release of unpleasurable quantity (Project 324). Freud also suggests that ego energy may originate as drive energy which was absorbed by the contact barriers during its passage from one neurone to another (Project 301, 322).

Since the ego energy is neutral or neutralized, the problem of pressure for discharge does not arise. However, the maintaining of a constant cathexis in the ego neurones might be a burden to the mental apparatus. The supposition would even be consistent with the periodic need for sleep, during which time the ego energy is reduced and the ego network of neurones "narrows concentrically." It seems more likely, however, that it is the functions which the ego performs (delay of discharge and reality testing) that are exhausting and require a periodic rest, rather than simply the necessity of maintaining a constant energy investment in the apparatus.

To the extent that there is a mechanism by which the quantity of energy may increase without an equivalent rise in the tension level, it is still possible to speak of a homeostatic equilibrium. An appropriate image is perhaps a balloon that can expand as more air is blown into it, without a marked rise in air pressure. But the goal of constancy in terms of discharge of energy is no longer the immediate aim of the apparatus. Although the goal is still total discharge of drive energy, it is only to be discharged when the required need-satisfying object is really present in the outside world; until then the discharge is to be delayed.

Freud was somewhat indefinite about the relationship of the constancy principle to the pleasure principle. His views can be interpreted in the following manner. If the constancy principle is defined in terms of the conservation of energy and as the principle behind the discharge hypothesis, the pleasure principle "follows from the principle of constancy." Since energy cannot vanish and must not accumulate inside the apparatus, it must be discharged. At first it is discharged in a reflex manner (principle of inertia); next its discharge is regulated by affects (pleasure principle); finally its discharge is regulated by the reality principle in which delay, the avoidance of hallucinatory wish fulfillment (discrimination between memories and percepts), and exploration of the outside world (matching of memories and percepts) is possible.

With the advent of the ego the reality principle is said to dominate the pleasure principle, yet the relationship between the two is still complex. Freud wrote (*S.E. 14* 120) that "the activity of even the most highly developed mental apparatus is subject to the pleasure principle . . ." Following the development of the structural hypothesis, Freud stated that the instincts are to the id what percepts are to the ego. He wrote in *An Outline of Psycho-Analysis* (S.E. *23* 198):

> The id, cut off from the external world, has a world of perception of its own. It detects with extraordinary acuteness certain changes in its interior, especially oscillations in the tension of its instinctual needs, and these changes become conscious as feelings in the pleasure-unpleasure series. It is hard to say, to be sure, by what means and with the help of what sensory terminal organs these perceptions come about. But it is an established fact that self-perceptions–coenaesthetic feelings and feelings of pleasure-unpleasure–govern the passage of events in the id with despotic force. The id obeys the inexorable pleasure principle. But not the id alone. It seems that the activity of the other psychical agencies too is able only to modify the pleasure principle but not to nullify it; and it remains a question of the highest theoretical importance, and one that has not yet been answered, when and how it is ever possible for the pleasure principle to be overcome.

Hartmann has further elaborated the relationship of the reality and pleasure principles.[12] Under the reality principle there is not only a postponement of gratification and a temporary toleration of unpleasure, but as the apparatus develops, the "conditions themselves on which the pleasurable or unpleasurable character of a situation rest have been changed." This "reassessment of pleasure values" he describes "as a modification of the pleasure principle or perhaps as a partial domestication of the pleasure principle" in which the pleasure principle comes partly under the control of the ego and the superego.[14] Hartmann also makes the point that it is not the essential characteristics of the pleasure-unpleasure principle that change, but rather the conditions of pleasure and unpleasure. The "pleasure principle itself has a history (genetic and dynamic vicissitudes) too, besides the limitations imposed on it by the reality principle in the narrower sense of the term."[15]

The essential point is that the striving after pleasure is altered but not superseded, and remains the motivational force in all mental functioning.

Just as the pleasure principle is modified by the increasing complexity of the apparatus, so also the signals associated with it have a developmental history. Even the term pleasure-unpleasure series implies a continuum from the most primitive signals of tension and nontension to the later complex, highly organized, and more stable affect states.

This helps to explain a seeming paradox. Clinically it was observable that unpleasure as a feeling could be associated with a lack of interest, and that appetite and pleasurable feelings could occur with increasing appetitive interests. The most illustrative example of the latter is the pleasure experienced during sexual foreplay, which increases the sexual appetite and heightens the ultimate end pleasure. Elaborate explanations have been given which attempt to show that the primitive regulation by the pleasure principle still holds. These tortured explanations ignore the developmental aspect of the pleasure principle discussed by Hartmann. The apparent problem is resolved when the pleasure in increasing the pregratification tension is seen as a vicissitude of the drive rather than one involving the pleasure principle. The appetitive build-up does not create drive energy in a physiological sense, but increases psychic representation of the drive

[14] Hartmann, *Essays on Ego Psychology*, pp. 247, 248.

[15] Also see Hartmann's discussion of the role of the anticipatory function of the ego and its effect on the pleasure principle, *ibid.*, p. 39.

and thus is the opposite of repression. In the vocabulary of the early papers it can be said that foreplay increases the linkage between somatic libido and the psychosexual group of ideas. Even if, as in Freud's early schematic picture of sexuality, it also stimulates the release of new quantities of somatic libido, the ego's expectation of gratification (anticipatory function) keeps the situation from being threatening.

Should the situation end in frustration, it does not necessarily follow that because tension is increased and discharge does not take place, primitive unpleasure must occur. This would be the case only if the apparatus was still entirely regulated by the pleasure principle and dealing with mobile energy, that is, if the ego network with its function of binding tension was not operating or was inadequate.

It is the whole point of the improvement of the apparatus that tension can be bound. This decreases the impact of unpleasure, reduces the necessity for discharge, and allows delay. What would have been overwhelming unpleasure is now a tolerable sense of frustration. As a result of this change the apparatus no longer serves the primary function of immediate discharge, is no longer regulated only by affects, and can avoid the hallucinatory vividness of memories. Instead, it is regulated by the reality principle and operates under the domination of the secondary process. The explanation for these changes is the cathectic modification, the binding of mobile energy.

In addition the expanding range of consciousness and the role of verbal representations increases the range of memories that can be recalled. This results in greater and firmer control of drives and affects. The basis for this increase in the range of what can be thought about, so that it includes the unpleasurable as well as the pleasurable, has been described by Freud in his paper on "Negation." Under the reality principle, notice can be taken of all the memories, unpleasurable as well as pleasurable, since the impact of the quantity of unpleasure produced is reduced. This is the essential fact that makes possible the function of the reality principle and secondary process. Until there was a way for the apparatus to inhibit the development of unpleasure (*S.E.* 5 601), the reality principle and the function of reality testing could not occur.

The perfection that the apparatus achieves remains vulnerable to regression. Freud points out that the "gap in the functional efficiency of our mental apparatus . . . makes it possible for thoughts which represent themselves as products of secondary thought activity, to become subject to the primary psychical process." This gap is the source of dreams and of the psychoneuroses. They result from the historical fact that "Primary processes are present in the mental apparatus from the first while it is only during the course of life that the secondary processes unfold and come to inhibit and overlay the primary ones" (*S.E.* 5 603).

What remains of the all-important constancy principle? It simply seemed to justify the discharge hypothesis; or at best can be said to be the theoretical basis by which the ego as a network of constantly cathected neurones comes into existence. Again one is reminded of the etiological equation. Just as its value was that it helped Freud focus on the sexual life of his patients, so the constancy principle justified him in his emphasis on stimuli that originate from inside the apparatus.

When a clear distinction is made between ego and drive energy, total discharge of drive energy (to the extent that this is possible) remains the biological goal, and it is the ego network with its reserve of energy that regulates the timing of this discharge.

The discharge hypothesis, which was the mainstay of the early economic views, seems to have steadily decreased in value as an analytic concept. The early papers stressed the importance of the concept, partly because the goal was to understand psychical functioning in terms of the natural sciences (i.e., quantitatively) and also because genetic and dynamic factors had not yet been formulated. The early papers, therefore, focused on focal brain potentials and their need to be discharged. Freud's emphasis soon turned to formulations involving drive energy, first described as endogenous stimuli, and in the Project called simply quantity.

Throughout the early papers Freud still hoped to keep clear the difference between the physiological and nonpsychological level and the psychological. This partly accounts for what the editors of the *Standard Edition* (*3* 62–68) have described as the confusing terminology of the early papers. They comment that no clear definition or distinction occurs in the usage of such terms as "sums of excitation," "quota of affect," or "affect" used alone. Since it is generally true of Freud that he did not expect of himself nor desire careful semantic distinctions, it seems most likely that the ambiguity of the terms reflected the need for flexibility. The term "sums of excitation," at first primarily neurological and later a somatic drive frame of reference, was intended to describe the most somatic level. The term "quota of affect" retained the implication of a quantitative approach and bridged the gap between the somatic and the psychic. "Affect" alone was at the psychic and clinical level. The concept of excitation and discharge takes as its prototypical example the epileptic attack or the sexual act in men. Both are rooted in the soma, achieve expression at the psychological level, and end in discharge. Economic formulations involving the discharge concept historically represent a striving toward this type of neurophysiological or "biological" framework.

Alternate to this is the more subjective and psychological orientation involving a wish leading to the experience of satisfaction or gratification. Current analytic formulations employ both frames of reference that can only describe the same phenomena in different terminology: nothing new is added. The origin of this double reference clearly comes from Freud. Particularly in his early papers (and most specifically in the Project), however, his goal was to bridge the gap.

When Freud realized that the exploration of the physical basis for the psychoneuroses was premature, he dropped the distinction between somatic and psychical libido and referred to the energy that the apparatus had to cope with simply as instincts or drive energy, defined as the demand the body makes on the mental apparatus.

Along with this change the emphasis shifted to the tracing of the economic vicissitudes inside the apparatus. This cathectic hypothesis is best exemplified by the libido theory, an economic and developmental view that involves the developmental shift from oral, anal, and phallic stages of development, and that also involves the concept of condensation and displacement as well as the more theoretical concepts of mobility of cathexis and primary process. These concepts have been extraordinarily productive, and they rank among Freud's most valuable contributions.

In contrast, the discharge hypothesis has not been as useful at an explanatory level. An example is the explanation of wit, which describes the discharge of an excess of psychic energy in laughter. The excess energy is conceived of as being released from its function of inhibition. The economic explanation is perhaps less meaningful than a dynamic approach that would emphasize symbolism and unconscious fantasy.

It would perhaps be possible to trace through Freud's writings the disadvantageous consequences of this overemphasis on the discharge concept. The error of Freud's first (toxicological) theory of anxiety can be understood as a miscarriage of the economic point of view that stressed the dis-discharge concept. He explained neurotic anxiety not as a response to danger but as an energy vicissitude (that is, transformation and discharge of dammed-up libido). He wrote that the affect of anxiety (real anxiety) occurs when the psyche "feels unable to deal by appropriate reaction with a task (a danger) *approaching from outside;* it finds itself in the *neurosis* of anxiety if it notices that it is unable to even out the (sexual) excitation originating from within. . . . *In the neurosis, the nervous system is reacting against a source of excitation which is internal whereas in the corresponding affect it is reacting against an analogous source of excitation which is external*" (*S.E. 3* 112 1895*b*).

In this interesting paragraph Freud relates anxiety to danger, but as a result of his preoccupation with the quantity of excitation, he shifts to an energic view, and emphasizes the *analogy* between external danger and internal excitation, rather than seeing them as identical. He corrected this in 1926 in "Inhibitions, Symptoms, and Anxiety," saying that the statement was not incorrect but did not go below the surface of things. Anxiety in the neurosis is then described as differing "in no respect from the realistic anxiety which the ego normally feels in situations of danger, except that its content remains unconscious and only becomes conscious in the form of a distortion" (*S.E. 20* 126).

Another disadvantage of the discharge hypothesis was its application to the problem of affects. The concept that unpleasure occurred when there was a rise in tension and that pleasure coincided with a fall in tension led to the belief that affects were a form of drive discharge, rather than a report of the economic state of the organism. Thus affect theory became chained to a simple economic formula based on the discharge hypothesis.

When Freud's hope of understanding the psychological and the physiological jointly was of necessity laid aside for some future date, the discharge concept should perhaps also have been temporarily relinquished. This does not imply that the concept of psychic energy and the economic point of view should have been discarded, only that its more concretistic form (excitation-discharge) was no longer as meaningful. With all its faults, the discharge concept had the value of preserving the physiological substrate in psychoanalytic theory and was an effort toward understanding the complex problem of the compulsion to repeat.

Freud's efforts to understand this problem are presented in his monograph, *Beyond the Pleasure Principle* (*S.E. 18* 7–64), and his paper, "Analysis Terminable and Interminable" (*S.E. 23* 216–253). The latter involves the concept of id anxiety and id resistance.[16] These terms and the problem they represent are not fully understandable in psychological terms alone. They clearly involve a psychobiological frame of reference, which is not only the original psychoanalytic frame of reference, but the current one as well.[17] These problems are best understood in terms of preverbal functioning and are closely allied to the problems of psychosomatic disease and of imprinting.

The current value to psychoanalytic theory of the economic approach has been commented on by Hartmann, Kris, and Loewenstein (*Drives, Affects, Behavior* 34, 35), who write, "Propositions concerned with energy transformation constitute generally an essential part of psychoanalytic theory." The authors point to their essential relevance to dream psychology and argue that concepts of fusion, defusion, and neutralization are central to the understanding of adaptation, sublimation, and the concept of secondary autonomy. They add that concepts of energy transformation "establish a link between . . . theory dealing with instinctual drives and ego psychology."

[16] The problem of id resistance and the repetition compulsion led Freud to the formulation of the death instinct. See Schur, "Phylogenesis and Ontogenesis of Affect- and Structure Formation . . . ," p. 275, and Lipin, "The Repetition Compulsion and 'Maturational' Drive-Representatives," *International Journal of Psycho-Analysis,* 44 4 (October 1963), 389.

[17] Hartmann, *Ego Psychology and the Problem of Adaptation,* p. 34.

6. *Affects*

FREUD EXPRESSED what are now the accepted formulations concerning the affect of anxiety in his 1926 monograph, "Inhibitions, Symptoms, and Anxiety" (*S.E. 20* 87–174), a complex paper in which he revised his earlier ideas. The paper is less well written and organized than most of Freud's work. Ernst Kris, in a personal communication, attributed this to Freud's illness and his feeling that he had little time left. In order to understand the current psychoanalytic theory of affects in general and anxiety in particular, a historical view is essential, and the letters and the Project serve a function here comparable to that of the Rosetta Stone.

In Freud's early publications he distinguished two components of a wish: the idea (the instinctual representative which, if it were in the ego, would be an idea) and the affect or "quota of affect" (*S.E. 14* 153).[1] The term quota of affect referred partly to what was later termed drive or instinct and partly to an energy that registered in consciousness as feelings. Psychical representation of the instinct came about when an idea was invested with affect energy.

The model behind this concept was the schematic picture of sexuality described in Draft G (*S.E. 1* 202). A sexual idea, when invested with slowly accumulating sexual energy,

[1] For editors' comments, see *S.E. 3* 66.

became a conscious sexual wish. Repression of an "incompatible" idea (that is, one that could not be integrated with other wishes by the ego) consisted of separating the quota of affect from the idea. Being robbed of its energy, the idea was turned into a weak one and was no longer able to achieve consciousness (*S.E. 14* 153). The affect charge could then be displaced to another idea or transformed and discharged as neurotic anxiety. This was the toxicological theory of anxiety, in which repression, the separation of the quota of affect from the idea, led to a toxic accumulation of energy that burdened the apparatus and required discharge. Affects were the consequence of conflict and represented discharge into somatic channels of transformed somatic libido. Repression in this formulation was the *cause* of anxiety.

One consequence of these early formulations was that affect and drive became intimately associated. For example, in *Studies on Hysteria* Freud refers to emotions as the overflow of excitation (*S.E. 2* 91). Breuer speaks of emotions as reducing excitement and says "their only purpose is to level out the increase of excitation and to establish psychical equilibrium" (*S.E. 2* 202).

A much more elaborate affect theory was described in the Project and involved the concept of unpleasure. Unpleasure could originate in three different situations.

The first and simplest situation was one in which unpleasure occurred as a result of the slow accumulation of drive tension in the apparatus. Unpleasure was associated with this rise in tension that was psychically experienced as a wish. In *The Interpretation of Dreams* a wish was defined (*S.E. 5* 598) as a current "in the apparatus starting from unpleasure and aiming at pleasure . . ."

A second condition in which unpleasure occurred was when discharge of tension failed to lead to gratification (Project 370). This unhappy event resulted in "a complete generation of unpleasure" (Project 326). The term unpleasure here is the economic equivalent of the affect of frustration or disappointment. Freud speaks, however, of the "generation" of unpleasure, with the implication that the reaction is not only due to a failure to decrease tension, but may result in an *increase in tension*, that is, energy is generated or released.

A third source of unpleasure occurred as a consequence of the recall after puberty of a sexual experience from earliest childhood (see chapter 4). The stimulation of this memory is described as leading to a *fresh release of unpleasure* (Draft K, *S.E. 1* 221, and Project 322). The important point in this situation is Freud's description of a fresh release of unpleasure. What was only implicit in the second situation (generation of unpleasure) is quite explicit in the third situation.

The first situation described in energy terms the increasing urgency of an ungratified wish (Project 318); the second situation described the response to frustration and disappointment; and the third situation described a traumatic state of affairs in which the apparatus is overwhelmed by the influx of energy while in an unprepared state. This could result from an external painful stimulus or from the recall of an unmastered painful memory. The affect was one of helplessness. In all three situations, the affects (ungratified wish, disappointment, and helplessness) were explained as the consequence of an energy increase in the system.

In the first case, involving a slow increase in the pressure of a wish, the energy that accumulates is clearly somatic libido, which Freud thought of as a chemical secretion (Letter 75, *S.E. 1* 269). The rising level of tension is able to register directly on consciousness as unpleasure. The reduction of tension by discharge registers as pleasure. The mechanism of this pleasure-unpleasure registration is never clearly formulated in economic terms, but it can be described as signal unpleasure, since the unpleasure signals to the ego the state of tension in the interior of the apparatus. It could even be that the unpleasure experienced is derived from the transformation and discharge of some of the accumulating libido, but Freud makes no mention of this.

In the other two situations, the unpleasure results not from a slow accumulation of energy in the system, but from a sudden release of new energy (Project 320). The nature of this energy is left somewhat uncertain but it does not seem to be somatic libido. The unpleasure energy is similar to somatic libido in the sense that it is thought of as a secretion. In certain circumstances, however, it is released instead of libido. This similarity and difference between somatic libido and unpleasure is made clear in a number of references. When Freud writes (Project 321), "in both instances the endogenous stimuli consist of *chemical products* of which there may be a considerable number," he clearly distinguishes libido and unpleasure as different chemical products. He had also spoken of the stimulus for breathing as one of the endogenous stimuli (Draft E, *S.E. 1*, 194).

Unpleasure as an endogenous stimulus could be freshly released (secreted) in a variety of different situations of which we have named two—disappointment and the recall of painful memories. Most painful memories registered fully in consciousness at the time of their occurrence and aroused defense. By repeated recall they could be "tamed." This came about by the ego's binding of the freshly released unpleasure (Project 381). Sexual memories from childhood that involved abandoned erotogenic zones (mouth and anus) were exceptions to this process of binding. In the normal person the recall of memories involving abandoned erotogenic zones no longer had an exciting effect and therefore created no economic problem. In persons who had never, during development, abandoned the mouth or anus as sources of erotic stimulation, these zones when stimulated by memories remained actively able to produce libido and a perversion resulted. If during maturation the zones had been abandoned so that they no longer produced libido, they might still, because of early childhood stimulation and the memory of this, remain active but release not libido but unpleasure (shame and disgust). Because the ego had not registered these experiences as traumatic at the time of their occurrence, their recall led to repression. The unpleasure resulted in a turning away from this early memory or from any experiences associated with it (Letters 52 and 75), rather than to its mastery.

It seemed necessary to postulate these two sources of unpleasure. The first described how a wish representing a rise in drive tension (libido) registered as (signaled) unpleasure. The concept of a fresh release of unpleasure was needed to account for repression (Letter 75, *S.E. 1* 269), and for the fact that a memory could later have more effect than had occurred at the actual time of the experience (deferred effect). There would be some advantages if the release of unpleasure could be separated from the bodily production of libido. If this could be done the concept of transformation would become unnecessary. In this connection Freud wrote (Draft K, *S.E. 1* 222):

> In my opinion there must be an independent source for the release of unpleasure in sexual life: once that source is present, it can activate sensations of disgust, lend force to morality, and so on. I hold to the model of anxiety neurosis in adults, where a quantity deriving from sexual life similarly causes a disturbance in the psychical sphere, though it would ordinarily have found another use in the sexual process. So long as there is no correct theory of the sexual process, the question of the origin of the unpleasure operating in repression remains unanswered.

He is even more explicit in Letter 75, of November 14, 1897, when he writes, "I have decided, then, henceforth to regard as separate factors what causes libido and what causes anxiety" (*S.E. 1* 271).

This resolution was abandoned and as a result the concept of unpleasure continued to have two sources. The first referred to a rise in tension (a wish), and pleasure to a fall in tension (discharge). The second meaning, even more decisive for affect theory, was Freud's belief that neurotic anxiety (as contrasted with realistic anxiety) was the result of the transformation of libido into anxiety. As long as he maintained that an intimate connection existed between libido and anxiety, affect of necessity had to be thought of as serving a discharge function.

In the metapsychological papers the economic aspect of affects entirely dominated Freud's mind. In the paper on "Repression," he repeats (*S.E. 14* 153) his earliest formulations. The instinctual representation is described as being composed of an idea (image or presentation) and a quota of psychical energy. In repression the two are separated and the quantitative factor (quota of affect) is transformed and discharged as an affect or as neurotic anxiety.

In his paper, "The Unconscious," Freud describes (*S.E. 14* 178) affects and emotions as "processes of discharge, the final manifestation of which are perceived as feelings." The aim of repression is not only the removal of the idea from consciousness, but also the inhibition of the instinctual impulse from being turned into a manifestation of affect. The discharge when it does occur is from the system unconscious (Ucs). It "passes into somatic innervation that leads to development of affect" (*S.E. 14* 187–188). Freud contrasts affects and ideas. They differ in that an idea is the cathexis of a memory trace,[2] while affects are secretory and vasomotor discharge processes. In this way they can be compared to motor actions: affects discharge to the interior; actions influence the outside world.

Affects that come from the system Ucs are always discharged as anxiety. Other affects are preconscious modifications of this basic affect, their new form depending on the substitute ideas in the preconscious to which they attach themselves.

[2] In contrast to this distinction, Freud also frequently described affects as the repetition of some earlier experience (*S.E. 16* 396, *20* 93, 133).

Freud described this sequence by dividing it into three phases (*S.E. 14* 182). The first phase, which he believed was frequently overlooked, consisted of "anxiety appearing without the subject knowing what he is afraid of." This is libido in the unconscious that is transformed into unpleasure and discharged as anxiety. In the second phase the unwelcome anxiety, which is uninhibitable, attaches itself to a remote substitutive idea. The anxiety can be discharged and its existence can be rationalized; the substitutive idea provides a passage across from the system unconscious to the system conscious and allows the discharge to occur. The substitutive idea, since it is remote from the original idea in the system unconscious, will stimulate less anxiety and can serve as a signal for further defense.

This formulation has come to be known as the conflict theory of affect, in which the affect served a safety-valve function for reducing drive tension when full discharge and gratification was blocked. Currently most analysts, for example, Rapaport,[3] subscribe to this view and see affect expression as serving to discharge a part of the drive energy. This part of drive energy is referred to as the "affect-charge."

Freud's next major paper on affects was his paper on grief and depression, titled "Mourning and Melancholia" (*S.E. 14* 243–258). His study of the Schreber case (*S.E. 12* 9–82) and his paper, "On Narcissism" (*S.E. 14* 73–102), had strongly influenced his theoretical formulations. Freud described the mourning process in terms of the withdrawal of cathexis from the object representation. The process involved the change of object libido into ego libido (*S.E. 14* 244, *20* 172). The formulation is reminiscent of the concept of "internal bleeding," which had originally been his explanation of melancholia (see chapter 3).

The goal of mourning or grief is, however, not the withdrawal of object cathexis, which would lead to indifference:

[3] "On the Psycho-Analytic Theory of Affects," *International Journal of Psycho-Analysis,* 34 3 (1953), 193.

rather the goal is the binding of the painful affects that occur when one recalls the person who has died and realizes the loss. Only after these painful feelings are bound or tamed can the thoughts of past pleasurable moments be recalled without the arousal of unpleasure. This view is consistent with the wish so many people have to dream of the lost object. When this dream can occur, part of the mourning must have been accomplished, since the dream can occur only if the pain that it would have aroused has been diminished.

The pleasure-pain principle applies to the regulation of the ego energy associated with affects. The goal of the mourning process is to bind the affect of grief so that thoughts along certain lines are not shut off. This is Freud's earliest description of the taming process (Project 381) and offers a more useful economic formulation of the grief reaction than the later one.

In the 1926 revision of his earlier concepts on anxiety, in "Inhibitions, Symptoms, and Anxiety" (*S.E. 20* 87–174), Freud's new structural hypothesis, with its emphasis on the ego's control of instinctual impulses, seemed to offer a solution to the cause for repression that had been so puzzling before. The major change was a shift from explanations based almost entirely on economic grounds to explanations that included dynamic and structural considerations.

Freud gave up the concept of the transformation of libido into anxiety; or, more precisely, he said it no longer interested him. This concept had first been enthusiastically described on February 7, 1894 (*Origins,* Letter 16, 80–87). Now he wrote (*S.E. 20* 162), "Our former hypothesis of a direct transformation of libido into anxiety possesses less interest for us now than it did."

In much the same vein he wrote (*S.E. 20* 140):

> At one time I attached some importance to the view that what was used as a discharge of anxiety was the cathexis which had been withdrawn in the process of repression. Today this seems to me of scarcely any interest. The reason for this is that whereas

I formerly believed that anxiety invariably arose automatically by an economic process, my present conception of anxiety as a signal given by the ego in order to affect the pleasure-unpleasure agency does away with the necessity of considering the economic factor.

Some reluctance to give up the idea entirely, however, appears in the next sentence when he continues: "Of course there is nothing to be said against the idea that it is precisely the energy that has been liberated by being withdrawn through repression which is used by the ego to arouse the affect; but it is no longer of any importance which portion of energy is employed for this purpose."

Freud also wrote (*S.E. 20* 161):

Formerly I regarded anxiety as a general reaction of the ego under conditions of unpleasure. I always sought to justify its appearance on economic grounds and I assumed, on the strength of my investigations into the "actual" neuroses, that libido (sexual excitation) which was rejected or not utilized by the ego found direct discharge in the form of anxiety. It cannot be denied that these various assertions did not go very well together, or at any rate did not necessarily follow from one another. Moreover, they gave the impression of there being a specially intimate connection between anxiety and libido and this did not accord with the general character of anxiety as a reaction to unpleasure.

The objection to this view arose from our coming to regard the ego as the sole seat of anxiety. It was one of the results of the attempt at a structural division of the mental apparatus which I made in *The Ego and the Id* [*S.E. 19* 12–66]. Whereas the old view made it natural to suppose that anxiety arose from the libido belonging to the repressed instinctual impulses, the new one, on the contrary, made the ego the source of anxiety. Thus it is a question of instinctual (id-) anxiety or ego-anxiety. Since the energy which the ego employs is desexualized, the new view also tended to weaken the close connection between anxiety and libido.

After Freud's discovery of unconscious processes, the non-psychological aspect of somatic libido was less emphasized and the actual neuroses came to mean the state in which drive tension was dammed up (*S.E.* *22* 93–95).[4] Unpleasure as a result of this dammed-up state remained part of Freud's theory of anxiety.

What the material was out of which anxiety originated was no longer an interest of Freud's, and yet almost without exception, after repudiating his concept of the transformation of libido into anxiety, he comments that it still remains a possibility. For instance, he wrote (*S.E.* *20* 141):

> We see, then, that it is not so much a question of taking back our earlier findings as of bringing them into line with more recent discoveries. It is still an undeniable fact that in sexual abstinence, in improper interference with the course of sexual excitation or if the latter is diverted from being worked over psychically, anxiety arises directly out of libido; in other words, that the ego is reduced to a state of helplessness in the face of an excessive tension due to need, as it was in the situation of birth, and that anxiety is then generated. Here once more, though the matter is of little importance, it is very possible that what finds discharge in the generating of anxiety is precisely the surplus of unutilized libido.

In his new formulations Freud recognized that one type of anxiety clearly originated from the ego (*S.E.* *19* 57; *20* 140, 161; *22* 85). It served a warning function alerting the ego to a danger and was therefore termed "signal anxiety." This reformulation established the identity of neurotic anxiety and realistic anxiety; both were a response to danger (*S.E.* *22* 93). Repression did not lead to anxiety but anxiety was the motive for repression. Signal anxiety occurred when a drive impulse in the id threatened to bring about a danger situation (loss of love, castration, guilt). The ego anticipates this consequence, gives a signal of anxiety, and the impulse is inhibited. This situation is typical of the psychoneuroses.

To Freud this explanation still left an important question unanswered. In his earlier theory the energy represented by

[4] Rangell, "On the Psychoanalytic Theory of Anxiety," *Journal of the American Psychoanalytic Association*, 3 3 (July 1955), 396.

the impulse could be accounted for; it was transformed and discharged as anxiety. The new explanation ought also to account for the energy involved in the id impulse.

In answer to this Freud wrote (*S.E. 20* 91–92):

> One question that arose was, what happened to the instinctual impulse which had been activated in the id and which sought satisfaction? The answer was an indirect one. It was that owing to the process of repression the pleasure that would have been expected from satisfaction had been transformed into unpleasure. But we were then faced with the problem of how the satisfaction of an instinct could produce unpleasure. The whole matter can be clarified, I think, if we commit ourselves to the definite statement that as a result of repression the intended course of the excitatory process in the id does not occur at all; the ego succeeds in inhibiting or deflecting it. If this is so the problem of "transformation of affect" under repression disappears. At the same time this view implies a concession to the ego that it can exert a very extensive influence over processes in the id, and we shall have to find out in what way it is able to develop such surprising powers.
>
> It seems to me that the ego obtains this influence in virtue of its intimate connections with the perceptual system—connections which, as we know, constitute its essence and provide the basis of its differentiation from the id. The function of this system, which we have called *Pcpt.-Cs.*, is bound up with the phenomenon of consciousness. It receives excitations not only from outside but from within, and endeavours, by means of the sensations of pleasure and unpleasure which reach it from these quarters, to direct the course of mental events in accordance with the pleasure principle.

Thus with almost a single stroke of the pen Freud disposed of the problem of "id anxiety," which until this revision had been the cornerstone of his anxiety theory. Until this moment all affect in the System Unconscious was neurotic anxiety (transformed libido). This was no longer true and the ego was described as the seat of all anxiety.

Yet Freud did not believe that this single view of anxiety

was an adequate explanation. He hoped to describe the earliest experience of unpleasure before it was tamed and could serve this signal function. This early anxiety he concluded had a different nature. He felt that the earliest and original danger was a helplessness in the face of overwhelming tension which could not be bound. This was described as the traumatic moment that occurred when regulation by the pleasure principle breaks down. In these moments the ego's capacity to cope with (bind or discharge) the quantity of energy impinging on it is inadequate and unpleasure results. The idea goes back to the concept of primary defense (Project 370)—noncathexis owing to the threat of unpleasure—and the breakdown of this defense, either from the lack of anticipatory preparation (Project 325) or from the influx of unmasterable quantity (Project 307), which acts like a "stroke of lightning" that can "do away with the resistance of the contact-barriers entirely . . ."

Freud described this when he wrote (*S.E. 20* 146), "In early infancy the individual is really not equipped to master psychically the large sums of excitation that reach him whether from without or from within."

An increase in tension "from without" was illustrated by the experience of birth, and later by the traumatic neurosis. The traumatic overwhelming of the apparatus could also arise from instinctual pressure (internal stimuli). In all three cases anxiety is not only being signaled as an affect, but is also being freshly created out of the economic conditions of the situation. Freud describes this, in much the same terms he used in the Project, as the "automatic and involuntary fresh appearance of anxiety" (*S.E. 20* 138). He recognized the fact that "the id can not have anxiety as the ego can" (*S.E. 20* 140), but on another occasion he wrote, "It [the id] can generate the sensory elements of anxiety" (*S.E. 23* 198). By this Freud apparently meant that the id was capable of the secretion of unpleasure, which was registered in in the ego as anxiety.

Freud then dealt with the problem of the transition from the automatic and involuntary fresh appearance of anxiety to the more controlled experience of anxiety (signal anxiety). Two factors played a role: one was the change in the *nature* of the danger situation and the other was the change in the *response* to danger. The response to danger changed because of the ego's increased capacity to tolerate tension (binding capacity).

The change in the nature of the danger situation could be attributed to the mother's role in caring for the infant (*S.E. 20* 137–138). The mother protects the child when the infant would otherwise experience a traumatic moment, an affect of helplessness. Because of her function as a need-satisfying object, the infant shifts from a fear of helplessness in the face of the economic situation to a fear of the loss of the object. In this all important change the fear of helplessness is transformed into the need of the object; the child's attention is also changed from a total preoccupation with inside bodily sensations and turned onto the outside world, beginning with the mother herself, who in normal development is the protector against helplessness and danger.

This transition was first mentioned, at least descriptively, in the Project (p. 318), where the child's screaming as a result of his helplessness brings help from the outside. In a footnote the *Origins* editor comments that it indicates the part played by object-relations in the transition from the pleasure principle to the reality principle or, in the way that we are considering it here, from the traumatic state of helplessness to the more controlled signal function of affect.

In schizophrenia, regression brings a revival of the earlier stage. The "world" again consists of torturing inner sensations and leads to the symptom of hypochondriasis and the delusion of the influencing machine.[5] In so-called borderline patients the mother has often failed in providing this comfort

[5] Tausk, "On the Origin of the 'Influencing Machine' in Schizophrenia," *Psychoanalytic Quarterly*, 2 (1933), 519.

and this turning outward toward objects is filled with danger.[6] In the phobic patient (for example, "The Case of Little Hans," *S.E. 10* 5), the parent comes to represent the danger that is resolved by displacement and leads to the phobic symptom.

Freud wondered if the two forms of anxiety, traumatic and signal, could be reduced to a single type. He was not hopeful about uniting them and he wrote (*S.E. 20* 110): "It will not be easy to reduce the two sources of anxiety to a single one. We might attempt to do so by supposing that, when coitus is disturbed or sexual excitation interrupted or abstinence enforced, the ego scents certain dangers to which it reacts with anxiety. But this takes us nowhere."

Although Freud felt no totally satisfying solution had been reached regarding anxiety, he continued to believe in its twofold origin. The two descriptions of anxiety differed in that the first (automatic) anxiety was based on an economic view (*S.E. 22* 94) and related anxiety to the *quantity* of libido in the apparatus. It has either no psychical content or at least very little. The second (signal anxiety) was based on a genetic and dynamic view and related to the *aim* of the libidinal impulse. Its occurrence depended on a memory of the earlier traumatic experience (*S.E. 20* 166) and also involved the anticipation of the possible loss of the object, loss of the object's love, punishment, castration, or guilt; that is, the content of the signal anxiety was specific to the particular developmental phase (*S.E. 20* 136–140). In the transition the ego has taken over and employed actively what was originally biological and experienced passively.

From this historical review of Freud's concepts concerning the genesis of affects an extraordinary parallel emerges between Freud's early views expressed in the Project and his later formulations as they are described in "Inhibitions, Symptoms, and Anxiety."

[6] Stewart, "The Development of the Therapeutic Alliance in Borderline Patients," *Psychoanalytic Quarterly*, 30 1 (January 1961), 165.

In the Project there are two basic forms of unpleasure: the first, in which tension increase (wish) registers in the ego, and the second, in which as a result of disappointment or trauma unpleasure is freshly released by the secretory neurones (Draft K, Project 320, 358). In "Inhibitions, Symptoms, and Anxiety," there are also two forms of anxiety: "signal anxiety" and automatic (freshly released) anxiety.

The narrower concept of the transformation theory and the discharge theory became of increasing importance and obscured the earlier dual nature of unpleasure. It is almost universally accepted that when Freud in 1926 published "Inhibitions, Symptoms, and Anxiety" he was advancing a new theoretical formulation concerning the problem of anxiety. It seems clear from a close reading of the Project that Freud *went back to an earlier theory* described in 1895. This earlier theory involved two forms of anxiety: signal anxiety and anxiety originating from the fresh release of unpleasure (economic anxiety).

When seen in this new light, the reasons given by Freud for the necessity to postulate the fresh release of unpleasure take on additional importance. In order to follow his reasoning it is necessary first to clarify Freud's use of the term "transformation of affect." Primarily it implied the transformation of libido into anxiety and was the central concept in the early description of the actual neuroses. It followed from repression, fulfilled the demands of the principle of constancy, and accounted for the affect or energy associated with an instinctual impulse. This aspect of the transformation of libido to anxiety which accounted for the origin and discharge of neurotic anxiety was "no longer of interest" to Freud in his new theory of anxiety.

The term transformation was also used to explain why an instinctual form of gratification was replaced by a later one. The concept of transformation from pleasure to unpleasure was an essential part of the developmental aspect of the libido theory and the emergence of genital primacy. The abandoned erotogenic zones in the psychoneurotic remained partially active, but instead of releasing libido, released unpleasure.[7]

The value of this second meaning of transformation was that it accounted for primary repression. This point is clearly stated by Freud in *The Interpretation of Dreams* (*S.E. 5* 604) when he wrote: "The fulfillment of these wishes would no longer generate an affect of pleasure but of unpleasure; and *it is precisely this transformation of affect which constitutes the essence of what we term 'repression'*."

Freud repeatedly stated his dissatisfaction with his formulations concerning the origin of unpleasure (*S.E.* 7 28, *18* 11), but he felt they were essential to any theory of repression.

This type of transformation of affect had first been described in Letter 75 (*S.E. 1* 269) and was at that time related to repression. Freud wrote: "A few weeks ago came my wish that repression might be replaced by the essential thing lying behind it;. . . . I have often suspected that something organic played a part in repression; I was able once before to tell you that it was a question of the abandonment of former sexual zones . . ." (*S.E. 1* 268). He then linked the change to the fact that humans by the fact of their upright carriage abandoned the pleasure in the sense of smell.

This idea persisted and was repeated in the case history of the Rat Man (*S.E. 10* 248) and the paper on *Civilization and Its Discontents* (*S.E. 21* 99).

In his published works Freud never fully developed any metapsychological explanation of the change in which the satisfaction of an instinctual impulse produces unpleasure in-

[7] The two uses of the term transformation can be related. The transformations are of libido into anxiety or the release of unpleasure instead of libido. If the order of events in the first concept is not the release of libido and then its transformation, but transformation and the release, the two become identical. The secretory neurones might, in both the actual neuroses and the psychoneuroses, secrete unpleasure instead of libido (vinegar instead of wine," see "Three Essays on the Theory of Sexuality," *S.E.* 7 224 footnote 1).

stead of pleasure. He referred to the problem (*S.E. 14* 146) when he asked:

> Why should an instinctual impulse undergo a vicissitude like this? A necessary condition of its happening must clearly be that the instinct's attainment of its aim should produce unpleasure instead of pleasure. There are no such instincts: satisfaction of an instinct is always pleasurable. We should have to assume certain peculiar circumstances, some sort of process by which the pleasure of satisfaction is changed into unpleasure.

The answer which he had already given in chemical terms in the Project was restated forty-seven years later, when he wrote in 1932 (*S.E. 22* 94–95):

> The *first and original repressions* arise directly from traumatic moments, when the ego meets with an excessively great libidinal demand; they construct their *anxiety afresh*, although, it is true, on the model of birth. The same may apply to the generation of anxiety in anxiety neurosis [actual neurosis] owing to somatic damage to the sexual function. We shall no longer maintain that it is the libido itself that is turned into anxiety in such cases. But I can see no objection to there being twofold origin of anxiety—one as a direct consequence of the traumatic moment and the other as a signal threatening a repetition of such a moment [italics added].

To account for "the first and original repressions," Freud postulated as he had in the Project that "the first anxiety would thus have been a toxic one" (*S.E. 22* 81). Freud is also reported to have stated this in the Minutes of the Vienna Psychoanalytical Society, November 17, 1909. The report states, "If we assume that there is no repression without an organic kernel then this organic repression must reside in the replacement of pleasurable sensations by unpleasurable ones."[8] Again he goes on to associate this with man's assumption of an upright posture and the reduction of importance of the sense of smell. Freud's frequent reference to the im-

[8] Jones, *Life and Work of Freud*, vol. 2, p. 444.

portance of man's upright posture has not been explored further. Perhaps the freedom that man achieved from olfactory sensory regulation allowed a change from limbic brain domination and permitted increasing cortical regulation. The latter permitted an awareness of the sense of awareness, the capacity for verbalization, and an expansion and greater control of the inner world. These were crucial to man's development and differentiation from other animals. These changes are part of development and maturation that we describe in a shorthand way when we say primary process is overlaid by secondary process. The change of function creates an almost impenetrable barrier between the earlier and later forms of mentation and results in what is called organic repression.

If organic repression can be accounted for in some such way as this, there is no need to invoke the concept of a new release of unpleasure (automatic anxiety) nor relate the early traumatic moments to the first and original repression. These early traumatic states are no different from signal anxiety except that the signal and response are crude and global. This is part of our development in which what is biological and passively experienced is then tamed and used actively.

We are left, as Freud was, with a less than satisfactory metapsychological explanation for the fact that earlier forms of instinctual expression (oral and anal) are in the process of development no longer main sources of gratification but become organized under the domination of the genitals when genital primacy is achieved. Nevertheless, with the abandonment of the transformation theory and the seduction hypothesis, the concept of the fresh release of unpleasure (traumatic anxiety) should also probably have been abandoned. A unitary theory of anxiety seems adequate for our understanding,[9] and the problem of organic and primal repression

[9] Brenner, "An Addendum to Freud's Theory of Anxiety," *International Journal of Psycho-Analysis*, 34 1 (1953), 18, and Rangell, "On the Psychoanalytic Theory of Anxiety," p. 389.

should be explained in developmental rather than economic terms.

The concept of signal anxiety as a derivative of traumatic anxiety also deserves some discussion. It is often used with two meanings, although they are not distinguished from each other. The term signal can refer to a signal *amount* of anxiety or unpleasure. The difference between unpleasure and anxiety is seen as a change in the quantity of energy involved. The change is in the nature of the signal. The term signal anxiety is also used to describe a *signaling function,* in which the function of anxiety is to signal to the ego the presence of a situation of danger (*S.E.* 20 126).

Both concepts are present in Freud's earliest theories concerning anxiety. ". . . the release of unpleasure was quantitatively restricted and its start was precisely a signal for the ego . . ." (Project 358).

Both the quantitative aspect and the signal function of anxiety require further discussion. It seems incorrect to explain the change from overwhelming unpleasure to controlled signal anxiety as a change in the quantity of unpleasure released, that is, a change in the nature of the signal. Rather the change should be viewed as a consequence of the ego's development. The same input exists but the existence of the ego with its increased binding power means the response will be different. The signal does not change but instead the response to the signal changes.

Pathological regression of the ego would then be seen as a loss in the ego's capacity to bind anxiety. Regression tends to reinstate the diffuse and global responses and also results in a change in what the ego reacts to as danger. In psychopathology the quality of the affect (signal anxiety–unpleasure), the nature of the response (signal–overwhelming), and the cause for anxiety (guilt–castration–separation) may all be altered by regression. A further elaboration occurs when the anxiety is defended against by symptom formation.

Whenever Freud spoke of the "traumatic moment," he spoke of the apparatus as being overwhelmed by the *quantity* of excitation (*S.E. 20* 137, 141, 146). This he felt required the concept of the fresh release of unpleasure. This totally quantitative explanation could have been avoided if Freud had utilized a field theory approach. Painful memories, instead of producing fresh energy release and a rise in endogenous stimuli, could be viewed as producing and resulting from a change in the nature of the energy toward a more mobile form. This would be a consequence of a reduction in the binding power of the ego. The increased mobility threatens the stability of the secondary process functioning and regulation by the reality principle. The threatened reappearance of primary process functioning and pleasure principle regulation characteristic of early drive organization is the source of the increasing sense of helplessness. The ego's original fear of drive needs was based on the mobility of the energies involved. When mobility threatens to return as a result of ego regression, it is preceded by signal anxiety, and if it does reoccur, the loss of ego function is evidenced by the overwhelming nature of the anxiety, which occurs in an unimpeded fashion. Unpleasure is "economically justified" in terms of a change in the mode of the energy rather than from a simple quantitative view. This formulation is hinted at (*Origins*, Letter 39, 144) in Freud's discussion of the reduction of the binding capacity of the lateral cathexes.

This view places the emphasis on the ego's fear of being overwhelmed by the mobility of the energy rather than its absolute quantity, and makes the concept of the fresh release of unpleasure, which was first advanced in the Project in terms of secretory neurones, no longer necessary. This explanation fits in with a point that Freud frequently emphasized: that an experience is made traumatic if it occurs unexpectedly, and if there has been no preparation for it. The anticipation of a traumatic experience increases the ego's capacity to bind. This suggests that regression of the ego and the reduction of its binding power is the danger, rather than the absolute quantity of excitation.

The *signaling function* of anxiety states that a small release of unpleasure alerts the ego to a situation of danger. Yet it is clear that anxiety cannot signal the existence of a danger situation; rather anxiety follows the perception of danger. The physiological aspects of anxiety clearly prepare the organism for flight or fight. But this leaves unexplained the psychical function of anxiety and raises a question about the function of affects in general.

The concept of a dual origin of anxiety strongly supported the idea that the earliest function of affects was drive discharge or tension reduction and that this was changed to a signal function. When the signal level of functioning failed, a traumatic experience occurred and affects again served a discharge need.

This formulation reflected the close tie between affects and drive discharge theory. As suggested earlier, when the seduction theory and the transformation concept were abandoned the hypothesis of a fresh release of unpleasure should also have been abandoned, along with the affect-discharge hypothesis. The most parsimonious view of anxiety would then be that at first it manifests itself in the diffuse state of unpleasure and is the early ego's passive response to danger. External danger is responded to because key stimuli produce automatic patterned responses, including internal secretory changes that function as protective devices. Internal danger is at first almost indistinguishable from physical pain (Project 320).[10] Pain or appetitive need has a total impact and the response is global. Later this total response is tamed via maturation and object ties and when combined with the anticipatory function of the ego, the signal function can occur.

This sequence parallels Freud's views of the development of thought. Thinking and anxiety have much in common, and the parallel becomes even more apparent when the similarity between thought as trial action and anxiety as a signal is

[10] See also Ramzy and Wallerstein, "Pain, Fear, and Anxiety," *Psychoanalytic Study of the Child*, 13 147.

recognized. Thinking which is described as trial action can also be described as serving a signal function, whereas anxiety as a signal is a response to a (fantasied) trial action.

With this parallel in mind, it is desirable to review the development of thought. In *The Interpretation of Dreams*, Freud spoke of the hallucinatory wish fulfillment as the precursor to thought (*S.E.* 5 567). In the absence of the object that could provide gratification, a perceptual identity is hallucinated. This hallucination occurs while the psychic apparatus functions with mobile energy and under the regulation of the pleasure-unpleasure series. The wished-for object can achieve consciousness only when the memory trace representing it can be hypercathected with drive energy. This occurs by displacement and condensation of drive energies characteristic of primary process. The development of structure (thresholds for discharge) and the binding of energy allow delay and inhibit the drive hypercathexis that would result in recall via hallucination. Thought as trial action can occur only when energy is bound, creating a high potential. This high potential allows small energy transmission through a variety of alternative pathways. This can be described as a trial run (*S.E.* 5 599). The difficulty is that there is no means by which the thought could reach consciousness. The perceptual quality of an hallucination had the disadvantage of creating the expectation of gratification, but it also guaranteed the registration of the memory trace in consciousness. The binding of the mobile energies did away with the hallucinatory vividness and therefore the traumatic disappointment, but it also shut off the usual pathway by which the memory trace might reach consciousness. Only with the employment of attention cathexis, a neutral (i.e., nondrive) energy, could the memory trace achieve consciousness but not hallucinatory vividness. The additional fact of verbal representation increased the ease by which memories could be brought to consciousness.

In effect, the whole developmental process from hallucinatory wish fulfillment to thought as trial action involves a means of avoiding a traumatic experience.

Freud's view of this developmental sequence is often overlooked because hallucinatory wish fulfillment is regularly described as serving a discharge function, that is, providing gratification. Hallucination produces the expectation of gratification, but this goal is seldom achieved. Freud clearly states that the major function of the dream is not discharge of drive energy, but a binding of the energy. He writes (*S.E.* 5 578):

> Thus there are two possible outcomes for any particular unconscious excitatory process. Either it may be left to itself, in which case it eventually forces its way through at some point and on this single occasion finds discharge for its excitation in movement; or it may come under the influence of the preconscious, and its excitation, instead of being *discharged*, may be *bound* by the preconscious. *This second alternative is the one which occurs in the process of dreaming*. The cathexis from the *Pcs.* which goes halfway to meet the dream after it has become perceptual, having been directed on to it by the excitation in consciousness, binds the dream's unconscious excitation and makes it powerless to act as a disturbance.

He then goes on to say: "Dreaming has taken on the task of bringing back under control of the preconscious the excitation in the *Ucs.* which has been left free; in so doing, it discharges the *Ucs.* excitation, serves it as a safety valve and at the same time preserves the sleep of the preconscious in return for a small expenditure of waking activity" (*S.E.* 5 579).

It seems that the phrase involving the discharge of the system unconscious has been interpreted to mean gratification rather than the binding of tension. Dreaming interrupts "deep sleep" long enough to bind the impulse in much the same way that impulses would be bound in the waking state, although the route to consciousness is different. Thus it both interrupts sleep and is at the same time the guardian of sleep. Viewed in another way, the hallucinatory wish fulfillment aspect of dreams is a precursor to two important ego functions; it is the precursor to the anticipatory function of the ego and is a primitive form of what will become the ego's capacity for delay.

The ability to visualize an object (revive a memory) or imagine a line of action and its consequences has its origins in hallucinatory wish fulfillment. The capacity to delay also depends on first the visualization associated with a wish and then the binding by the preconscious. Forceful wishes that cannot be gratified are associated with strong affects. These wishes and their associated affects repeatedly achieve consciousness and require repeated efforts at binding.

The line of reasoning that allows us to understand the transition from hallucinatory wish fulfillment to thought as trial action can also be applied to the understanding of the transition from unpleasure to signal anxiety. At the beginning automatic responses to perceptions and regulation by gross affects (unpleasure) occur. Perceptions are soon associated with memories. The *means by which the memory is brought to consciousness is its affective meaning.*

As we know, verbal representation provides quality to thoughts that allows their representation in consciousness, and permits "more delicately adjusted performances" (*S.E.* 5 574). Just as perceptions having quality can attract the freely mobile attention cathexis and achieve consciousness, so thoughts that are verbally represented also have quality and can achieve consciousness. As a result they interrupt the automatic (unconscious) domination of the pleasure principle in the regulation of the psychic apparatus; thoughts add a new dimension to the sensory regulation of the apparatus.

In this connection Freud writes (*S.E.* 5 616): "Excitatory material flows in to the *Cs.* sense-organ from two directions: from the *Pcpt.* system, whose excitation, determined by qualities, is probably submitted to a fresh revision before it becomes a conscious sensation, and from the interior of the apparatus itself, whose quantitative processes are felt qualitatively in the pleasure-unpleasure series when, subject to certain modifications, they make their way to consciousness."

The finer regulation of the functioning of the apparatus by conscious affects (derivatives of the pleasure-unpleasure series) is described in the following paragraph (*S.E. 5* 616):

> We know that perception by our sense-organs has the result of directing a cathexis of attention to the paths along which the incoming sensory excitation is spreading: the qualitative excitation of the *Pcpt.* system acts as a regulator of the discharge of the mobile quantity in the psychical apparatus. We can attribute the same function to the overlying sense-organ of the *Cs.* system. By perceiving new qualities, it makes a new contribution to directing the mobile quantities of cathexis and distributing them in an expedient fashion. By the help of its perception of pleasure and unpleasure it influences the discharge of the cathexes within what is otherwise an unconscious apparatus operating by means of the displacement of quantities. It seems probable that in the first instance the unpleasure principle regulates the displacement of cathexes automatically. But it is quite possible that consciousness of these qualities may introduce in addition a second and more discriminating regulation, which is even able to oppose the former one, and which perfects the efficiency of the apparatus by enabling it, in contradiction to its original plan, to cathect and work over even what is associated with the release of unpleasure. We learn from the psychology of the neuroses that these processes of regulation carried out by the qualitative excitation of the sense organs play a great part in the functional activity of the apparatus. The automatic domination of the primary unpleasure principle and the consequent restriction imposed upon efficiency are interrupted by the processes of sensory regulation, which are themselves in turn automatic in action.

Freud then goes on to relate this "new process of regulation" to the regulation by thought processes. He omits from his discussion (however, see *S.E. 22* 89) the regulation by *affect* that precedes but is later further modified by thought regulation.

What is suggested here is that quality and the achievement

of consciousness of the inner world first occurs by the perception of affect.[11]

The two sensory surfaces of consciousness (perception of the external world and of the internal world) do not come about only when thought processes achieve the capacity to register on consciousness through the acquisition of verbal representation (*S.E.* *5* 574). The two surfaces exist from the beginning, and the function of affects is to provide the quality needed to allow registration.

Brierley first described this when she wrote of affects as a mode of consciousness.[12] However, she limited affects to drive tension increase and placed them "topographically and in time-order in the middle of the instinct-reaction arc." She implies that as drive tension increases beyond a certain threshold, the ego responds with anxiety and initiates a defense. As a result of recent studies on perception,[13] this can be described in a somewhat different way. Drive tension and discharge or defense probably occur automatically and at an unconscious level. The role of affects is to allow the process to achieve consciousness, as a result of which finer, more discriminatory regulation becomes possible. The function of anger can be used as an illustration of this thesis. A stimulus leads to a response of fight. At the same time there is a physiological preparation of the body for the action and a psychical affect (quality) of anger that allows or demands the focus of attention (hypercathexis) onto the situation. The affect anger also insures that consciousness of the situation will be maintained; that is the hypercathexis of attention and consciousness will not be distracted by other irrelevant stimuli.

In the same manner a distinction should be made between

[11] Hartmann, *Ego Psychology and the Problem of Adaptation,* p. 57.

[12] Brierle, "Affects in Theory and Practice," *International Journal of Psycho-Analysis,* 18 (1937), 256.

[13] C. Fisher, "A Study of the Preliminary Stages of the Construction of Dreams and Images," *International Journal of Psycho-Analysis,* 5 1 (January 1957), 5.

sexual drive and sexual affect. The affect provides a persistent quality and permits the registration in consciousness of impulse that otherwise could have led to actions carried on as an automatic response.

Affects then belong in the stimulus-response arc in the same place as perceptions and thought. They aid the apparatus by providing quality to what otherwise would be only quantitative cathectic shifts occurring in "some deepest stratum of the mind." By providing quality they attract the hypercathexis of attention and result in conscious registration. Consciousness, which monitors the inside as well as the outside world, is able to register the inside world, since affects allow and even demand attention. Affects, like their precursor pain, are hard to ignore. In the sequence pain-affects-thought, pain is the most demanding and thought the least demanding of attention. Pain also allows the least freedom of response and thought the most. Affects are one of the representatives of the inner world, as perceptions represent the outer world; both are part of the fabric of consciousness. They function as built-in rewards and punishments, ensuring that the individual's behavior will fulfill the necessary biological cycles (drives, sleep, and the like), and also allow these motivations to appear in consciousness by lending quality to the impulses. The pleasure-pain principle in this sense is not limited to drive regulation alone; it is a general regulatory principle of cathectic economy. Pain, affects, and thoughts are at various stages the mechanisms by which the automatic cathectic regulation can be raised to consciousness and to less automatic regulation.

This view also has implications for our understanding of the functions of the superego. These functions are derived from the pleasure-unpleasure series, and represent the internalization of painful danger situations derived from object relations (loss of the object, loss of object's love).

The sequence of pain-unpleasure-anxiety and guilt is related to the conscience aspects of the superego, whereas the sequence of relief-pleasure-reward and self-love is related to the ego-ideal aspects of the superego.

In the light of this formulation, what then becomes of the discharge hypothesis (safety valve function) of affects? Most often the evidence for drive tension reduction is seen in the secretory activity and the random or organized motor responses. These motor responses are identical in situations of danger, whether the danger is from the outside or the inside (drives). We do not speak of anxiety in response to external danger as having a tension-reduction function. It does not therefore seem correct to assume that affects reduce tension, or that they initiate secretory activity or even motor activity. Their sole function from the beginning is to make possible the conscious representation of economic shifts within the organism. That is to say, they always serve a communicative function whether gross or signal, and permit what otherwise would go on at an unconscious level to achieve consciousness. By keeping the danger situation in the center of consciousness, the ego is in a better position to deal with immediate reality, whether it is to defend against danger or to ensure gratification.

7. *Early Metapsychology*

FREUD'S SCIENTIFIC goal was not simply to understand psychopathology, but to develop a general psychology that would describe the laws governing all of psychic functioning. This meant that he had to describe a structural model, the energy shifts by which it ran, and the functions it served. These three questions are essential to the study of any machine: How it is built? What makes it run? What function does it serve? In psychoanalysis this complete formulation—the structural, economic, and dynamic views—is defined as the metapsychological presentation (*S.E. 14* 181).

Freud's first efforts toward a metapsychological explanation were presented in Draft G, when he described the "Schematic Picture of Sexuality." A somewhat different approach was given in Letter 52, when he described the various registrations of perception and memories. This description is an early version of the "picket fence" model that was elaborated in chapter 7 of *The Interpretation of Dreams* and that was part of the topographical point of view. In 1923, in *The Ego and the Id*, Freud developed the structural model in which the psychical apparatus is divided into the id, ego, and superego. It is the most frequently used model in current psychoanalytic theory.

However, Freud's most ambitious efforts to describe a

working model of the mind are contained in the Project. Of this effort he once wrote (*Origins*, Letter 32, 129):

> . . . the barriers suddenly lifted, the veils dropped, and it was possible to see from the details of neurosis all the way to the very conditioning of consciousness. Everything fell into place, the cogs meshed, the thing really seemed to be a machine which in a moment would run of itself. The three systems of neurones, the "free" and "bound" states of quantity, the primary and secondary processes, the main trend and the compromise trend of the nervous system, the two biological rules of attention and defence, the indications of quality, reality, and thought, the state of the psycho-sexual group, the sexual determination of repression, and finally the factors determining consciousness as a perceptual function—the whole thing held together, and still does.

On reading the Project, one is struck with not only the many highly condensed ideas that are presented, some of which were developed by Freud as much as thirty years later, but also with the large number of ideas to which he never returned. Most of these latter ideas lie in the area of what has become the special interest of the psychologist. These include the roles of perception, memory, thought, affect, and so forth. Because of Freud's increasing exposure to problems of psychopathology, his interest focused more and more on the problems of instinctual conflict and its vicissitudes. In this sense, the Project can be viewed as a notebook outlining many problems, some of which, because of the lack of time, had to be neglected.

In some of Freud's later papers, it is as if he assumed a knowledge of the neuronic model presented in the Project and therefore could present his ideas in a brief and condensed fashion. Certainly a familiarity with the Project enriches our understanding and clarifies some ambiguities. An example of this can be seen in Freud's discussion of censorship in dreams, imposed by the resistance (*The Interpretation of Dreams, S.E. 4* 308, *5* 530). The discussion becomes more easily understandable if we visualize a network of neurones as described in the Project, with contact barriers and changing resistances based on facilitation and fluctuations of neurone cathexis. Chapter 7 in *The Interpretation of Dreams* is a revised and reformulated version of the Project, and although chapter 7 is less painful in its effort toward mechanical consistency, it is also less explicit and less detailed. The two versions are both valuable for the clearest presentation of Freud's ideas. The concepts of primary process, the pleasure-unpleasure principle, bound cathexis, attention cathexis, the principle of constancy, and the association by simultaneity are not only first described in the Project, but in many ways are more fully and clearly described there than in Freud's later writings.

It may be that the Project served Freud in much the same way that it is useful to us. The use of concrete images in formulating and organizing complex ideas is a universal experience. Freud first developed a quite mechanical model with concrete images of its functioning. This then remained useful to him in thinking about the problem and in presenting it later in a more abstract (less mechanical) form.

A. *The Structures Involved*

The theoretical neurones of the system were, as in the reflex arc, divided into sensory and motor neurones. The sensory neurones had to serve two mutually exclusive functions. They had to be able to receive perceptions from the outside world but remain fresh and unmodified, ready to record new impressions. They also had to store perceptions for later recall, that is, to be altered by experience so that they could serve the function of memory.

This dual and mutually exclusive function required that the sensory neurones be divided into two subgroups. The first of these was made up of permeable neurones, offering no resistance and retaining nothing. These were called the Phi (ϕ) neurones and served as receptors to external stimulation. The second group of sensory neurones was impermeable, offering resistance, and was modified by the passage of quantity. These neurones were termed the Psi (ψ) neurones and served the function of psychical processes in general. Freud suggested that the Phi and Psi neurones were actually the same but, being exposed to different amounts of energy because of their different milieus, they functioned differently.

The Psi (ψ) neurones were further subdivided into nuclear and pallial neurones. The nuclear neurones were intimately associated with the soma and were gradually filled by energy from that source. The pallial neurones became the switchboard, memory warehouse, and energy reservoir needed to meet the "exigencies of life."

Finally, to complete the structure, Freud was forced to postulate a third set of neurones, which he designated the Omega (ω) neurones. Their assumption was necessary in order to account for the content of consciousness: the awareness of sensations and qualitative differences in perceptions. A purely quantitative approach was adequate to treat psychical processes as long as they occurred independently of consciousness, but was inadequate to portray qualitative differences. Freud finally located the Omega neurones (ω) between the Phi (φ) and the Psi (ψ) neurones. He described them as actually a further subdivision of the Psi (ψ) system, characterized by the fact that they were capable of containing only a very small quantitative cathexis.

The Omega (ω) neurones, representing awareness of the quality of a perception, must be permeable and behave like organs of perception. Freud suggested that the Phi (φ) neurones conveyed not quantity to the Omega (ω) neurones, but periodicity–a temporal aspect or frequency of the neuronic motion. Freud describes this as occurring by a process of induction. When this periodicity registers on the Omega (ω) neurones, it gives evidence that the perception is real. Periodicity transferred from the terminal organs via the

Phi (ϕ) neurones, registers on the perceptual neurones (ω) as quality and produces consciousness and the indication of reality. Transmission of quality is "not durable; it leaves no traces behind and cannot be reproduced" (Project 310). This definition of consciousness, that it is the sense organ for the perception of psychical qualities (*S.E. 5* 615; *14* 192; *19* 13), remains one of Freud's most fundamental contributions.

Recollection of an experience, which is a function of Psi (ψ) neurones, occurred without stimulation of the Omega (ω) neurones (i.e., without quality). In this fashion perceptions and recollections were normally distinguished. Recollections remained unconscious except for their capacity to register as pleasure or unpleasure.

The nerve cells in the apparatus were thought of as having many branchings, each in contact with other neurones. As a result of their interconnections they formed a complex network. Certain pathways, because of high resistance, ended as nearly blind alleys. These were termed lateral cathexes, and energy could accumulate and be temporarily stored in them.

B. *Energies of the Systems and Their Relationship to Structure*

1. Energies of the Phi (ϕ) System.

The sensory stimuli from the outside world start from the terminal organ and are transmitted by the Phi (ϕ) neurones to the motor system as in the reflex arc model (Project 314). In addition, as the structure is elaborated the Phi (ϕ) neurones transmit *only* a characteristic period to the perceptual neurones (ω), where they register as quality (sensations) and result in consciousness. The effect of the registration is to signal an indication of reality to the perception. Since only periodicity is transmitted, no energy is normally added to the system. The exception to this is stimuli that register as pain. These stimuli were described as the eruption of large amounts of energy into the system, overwhelming the screen barriers and demanding immediate motor reaction, usually flight from the stimulus. Pain is dramatically compared to a stroke of lightning (Project 307).

2. Energies of the Psi (ψ) System.

The usual source of energy with which the apparatus must cope originates in somatic (endogenous) sources. It accumulates by summation and is transmitted from the interior of the body via the free nerve endings into the nuclear portion of the Psi (ψ) neurones. The actual *transmission* of quality into the Psi (ψ) neurones does not evoke sensation, that is, does not effect the perceptual neurones (ω) and therefore, unlike other energy transmissions, does not register in consciousness. This is because the Psi (ψ) neurones have only a monotonous period that does not register as quality in the perceptual (ω) neurones. However, there is an important pathway of communication between Psi (ψ) neurones and the perceptual neurones (ω). The Psi (ψ) neurones are capable of contributing to the perceptual neurones (ω) an awareness of the amount of energy stored in the Psi (ψ) neurones. This is done through the affects of pleasure and unpleasure, which appear as a conscious sensation. Pleasure and unpleasure are defined as the perceptual neurones' (ω) registration of the height of tension in the Psi (ψ) neurones; or more accurately, since the perceptual neurones (ω) are related to the Psi (ψ) neurones as far as quantity is concerned, like intercommunicating pipes, a rise of tension in Psi (ψ) results in an increased tension in perceptual neurones (ω). These quantitative variations in the perceptual (ω) neurones register in the only way they can, as quality, that is, the sensation of unpleasure, which automatically achieves consciousness. Affects in this formulation function as indicators and offer a means by which quantity can register as quality and achieve consciousness.

Thus only periodically does the energy in the Psi (ψ) neurones become capable of acting as a psychical stimulus.

This occurs when there is no discharge, and the nuclear neurones become filled. "Once the path of conduction has been re-adjusted, no limit is set to this accumulation. Here ψ is at the mercy of Q [quantity] . . ." At this level the endogenous act as a stimulus continuously" (Project 317, 316). When the influx of energies from endogenous sources is no longer intermittent but is constant—"a continuous influx of quantity"—the perceptual (ω) neurones become hypercathected, producing a sensation of unpleasure and forcing the body's dilemma (need) on consciousness. This is described as the free Psi (ψ) energy becoming riveted (*Origins*, Letter 39, 144). In this circumstance quantity in Psi (ψ) can attract consciousness independently of the cooperation of the perceptual neurones (ω) or stimuli from the Phi (φ) neurones.

There is another form of energy in the Psi (ψ) system that is termed the "free psychical energy of attention." It is part of the energy reservoir stored in the apparatus under the constancy principle and aids the apparatus in its efforts to deal with the "exigencies of life." Freud is somewhat unclear whether this is a modified form of drive energy or has a different origin. It is stored in the pallial portion of the Psi (ψ) neurones and is part of the complex of neurones that is termed the ego. The energy accumulates as a result of the inhibition of discharge and the continued production of endogenous quantity. This energy is described as free, meaning mobile and freely available to the ego to serve its functions. It is to be distinguished from unbound (free) *drive* energy, which presses for discharge. The function of this freely moving attention cathexis is to hypercathect perceptions (periodic scanning) and fix them in the center of conscious awareness.

3. Energies of the Omega (ω) System.

The perceptual neurones (ω), stimulated by transmission of periodicity from the Phi (φ) system, organize and excite the energies in the Psi (ψ) system, ". . . that is, indicate the direction to be taken by the free psychical energy (of attention)" (*Origins*, Letter 39, 142). This "exciting" effect describes the organizing effect of a perception on an appetitive state. For example, the sight of food can create or add to a state of hunger. Freud describes this as a "process of induction" (Project 310).

The above descriptions make it clear that there are five different ways in which neurones can affect one another in terms of their energy content.

(*a*) By transmission of quantity–transmission and discharge in the Psi (ψ) neurones.

(*b*) By transmission of periodicity, ϕ to ω, (as though it were a process of induction).

(*c*) When the level of quantity stored in Psi (ψ) registers in the perceptual neurones (ω) as quality, that is, sensations of pleasure (decrease) or unpleasure (increase).

(*d*) By excitation, in which the perceptual neurones (ω) have an organizing effect on Psi (ψ) energies. This is restated as the processes that are excited in Psi (ψ) by conscious sensations.[1]

(*e*) When memory traces in the Psi (ψ) neurones achieve such a degree of intensity that they can force themselves on the Omega (ω) as if they were perceptions (hallucinations). This hallucinatory vividness can lead to the expectation of gratification and total discharge (i.e., primary process).

C. *Working Assumptions*

Freud began his monograph by limiting himself to the laws of natural science, hoping to explain mental functioning

[1] In looking back to Draft G, we can see in what way it is an early version of the formulation presented in the Project. There is a similarity between the perceptual neurones (ϕ) and the psychosexual group of ideas (PsG). The group of ideas, like the perceptual neurones, are stimulated from the external world (ϕ neurones) and from the terminal organ, where endogenous stimuli accumulates (Psi [ψ] system). Both in turn are early versions of the structural hypothesis.

without recourse to any vitalistic assumptions. Therefore he postulated an energy (quantity) and a unit of structure—the neurone. The basic theoretical model was a reflex arc in which energy input was immediately discharged. This was described as the primary function of the neuronic system (later the psychic apparatus): to bring the tension state back to zero, then termed neuronic inertia, and later known as a biological principle—the Nirvana principle. As long as the stimulus (for example, pain) arose in the outside world and could be discharged by action and without dependence on the outside world, this primary functioning remained adequate. Those methods of discharge that not only provided discharge but also cessation of stimulus (flight) were preferred. But this simple state of affairs soon required modification, since the energy input also arose from the soma and was associated with appetitive needs (endogenous stimuli) that could be gratified only by specific reactions, that is, involved dependence on objects in the external world. The dependence on the objective world was termed the "exigencies of life," a phrase that described an appetitive need which could be gratified only in the presence of the drive object. Since objects in the outside world were essential for gratification, immediate discharge of a tension state without regard for the outside world was impractical and damaging. Immediate random discharge and flight were useless in dealing with endogenous sources of stimuli. In order to make possible the required delay in discharge and to bring about the possibility of the required specific reaction, the neuronic system must store a reserve supply of energy. With this reserve the system is prepared to meet the "exigencies of life" (delay in the absence of the drive object). The primary function of the apparatus, total discharge and zero tension, is for this reason changed to a secondary function, the maintaining of an optimum tension (principle of constancy).

While the system operated under the primary function, energy passed through the neurones unimpeded, toward immediate discharge. To serve the secondary function the neurones had to be capable of storing energy. This required the concept of a "cathected neurone" in which the neurone was "filled" with quantity without transmission of this excitation, that is, the concept of a bound energy. The energy in the neurone could increase or decrease, altering the ease of transmission of drive energy (i.e., reducing resistance), but not contributing to the quantity transmitted. This ability of the neurone to bind energy made it possible for the neuronic system to operate under the principle of constancy, that is, serve its secondary function.

These modifications and elaborations of the system led Freud to write, ". . . the structure of the nervous system would serve the purpose of *keeping off* Qή from the neurones and its function would serve the purpose of *discharging* it" (Project 306). This is a puzzling sentence, since it is clear that structure and function are inseparable. It can be understood as a condensed statement that the first structure had as its function the reception of stimuli and their immediate discharge. This proved unsatisfactory and the structure required elaboration so that discharge could be delayed. The fact of immediate discharge characteristic of the functioning of the early system is an unavoidable consequence of its primitive structure. Primary process—hallucinatory wish fulfillment and its inevitable traumatic failure—is a damaging, painful experience from which, while it operates, the organism must be protected.

The concept of primary process was one of Freud's most significant contributions. He described it as a normal aspect of mental life, occurring as a result of the high mobility of drive cathexis, which becomes manifest through the mechanisms of displacement and condensation (*S.E. 5* 588, *14* 186). Even after it is replaced by secondary process functioning, it remains latent and capable of again becoming operative.

The *necessity* for discharge or the need for retention of quantity under the principle of constancy operates only in the extremes of high and low tension, at which point the functional efficiency of the system has already broken down, and the system is in danger of returning to the inefficient level of operation characteristic of its primary function. This occurs in certain circumstances that promote *regressive* functioning. One of these is the threat of pain. The memory of pain is capable of producing excessively strong release of unpleasure and requires "repeated 'binding' from the ego before this facilitation towards unpleasure can be counterbalanced." While untamed the memories have a sensory quality, promote discharge and a tendency toward primary functioning (Project 335, 381).

A second circumstance that leads to regressive functioning is sleep. During sleep there is a "*lowering of the endogenous charge in the ψ nucleus* [both nuclear and perceptual neurones] which makes the secondary function superfluous . . . And here, as is immediately clear, we have the *precondition of psychical primary process*" (Project 336); "this is owing to the lack of ego-cathexis" (Project 338).

Freud described the potential return of the apparatus to the level of primary process functioning, as the gap in the functional efficiency of our mental apparatus (*S.E. 5* 603), "which makes it possible for thoughts, which represent themselves as products of the secondary thought-activity, to become subject to the primary psychical process." As a fact of central importance in his general psychology he adds, "In consequence of the belated appearance of the secondary processes, the core of our being, consisting of unconscious wishful impulses, remains inaccessible to the understanding and inhibition of the preconscious." In the language of the Project, this core of the unconscious would be stated as processes in the Psi (ψ) neurones involving mnemic material (unconscious memories) which are never capable of becoming conscious (primary repressed).

In situations other than pain, which overwhelms the ego's binding capacity, and sleep, when the ego's cathexis is normally reduced, the functioning of the ego should provide more control over the discharge of drive energy. However, the existence of a core of unconscious wishful impulses inaccessible to preconscious inhibition means that mankind always lives under the threat of a regression to this more primitive kind of psychic functioning that we term psychoneurotic or psychotic illness.

D. *The Development and Function of the Model*

The goal of the Project was to present a model that could account for psychic functioning. It was to account for memory, how memories were distinguished from perceptions, the nature of hallucination, the function and origin of affect, what the basis and function of thought was, and its relation to experience. In addition the model was to account for abnormalities in psychic functioning. Freud felt as a result of his clinical experience that the basic problem with which the apparatus had to cope was the bodily needs as represented in the drives, and that the regulation of the flow of drive energy was the main function of the psychical apparatus. Freud used the term motive to describe this capacity to regulate and direct the flow of energy through the apparatus. Used in this sense, motive does not initiate behavior, but directs ongoing processes, that is, provides the system with selectivity and choice as to the pathway to be taken and the timing of action (discharge). The simplest structure that allows motive (selection) is formed by the contact barriers. They are a built-in resistance to the flow of energy. The first and simplest source of motivation (selection) is the fact that quantity can overcome resistance. Energy under this type of regulation takes the path of least resistance.

Freud quickly adds a complication to this primitive form of functioning. The pathway that will be followed by one level of quantity may be quite different from the pathway followed by a greater quantity. In the first instance, the smaller quantity may meet an insurmountable resistance in one neurone, *a*, and therefore be distributed via *b* and *c* neurones. A larger quantity might follow *b* and *c* neurones, but *also* can overcome the resistance in *a*. In fact, once the resistance to passage in the *a* neurone is available, by far the greatest amount of energy may follow this otherwise unavailable pathway. Freud describes the receptivity of a neurone (once the resistance is overcome) as the "breadth of path" of the neurone (Project 375). The "breadth of path" is constant in a neurone and independent of the resistance at the contact barrier.

This type of regulation is closely akin to the reflex arc and does not provide any protection from a passage of energy that leads to unpleasure nor provide any guarantee of a pleasurable outcome.

A second source of motive (selection) is the lowered resistance in the contact barrier that is the result of earlier repeated passage of quantity. The level of resistance may be suspended as the flow of energy goes through the barrier, and then be restored after discharge, but at a somewhat lower level than before the passage. The lowering of the resistance at the contact barrier as a result of the passage of quantity is termed facilitation. The next time energy goes through the system it will tend to follow a previously used pathway. Memory is represented by these facilitations, or more accurately in the difference between facilitations. Thus previous experiences will influence the next passage of quantity leading to the same outcome. Hence the endogenous stimuli (drives or appetitive needs) only periodically become psychical stimuli. Neither of these primitive forms of regulation distinguishes between a pleasurable and unpleasurable discharge.

The pleasure-unpleasure regulation of energy flow is made possible by the intercommunication between the perceptual neurones (ω) and the Psi (ψ) neurones, where quantity in Psi (ψ) registers as quality in the perceptual neurones (ω). Selection is based on *association by simultaneity*. When unpleasure (increased tension in Psi [ψ]), which registered as unpleasure in perceptual neurones (ω), is, by discharge, turned into pleasure, the registration of the object by which the reduction in tension occurred is associated with the specific action associated with it. These two associations remain linked. When the need is again presented to the perceptual neurones, the memory of the object is also cathected. The increased cathexis of the second neurone (memory of the object) makes possible an easy flow of energy from the need to the memory of the satisfying agent. The cathexis of the second neurone operates to reduce the resistance in the contact barrier between the two neurones and this regulates the flow of energy along this channel. In this sense, cathexis of the second neurone is seen to be the equivalent of facilitation. This provides a "motive force" in that it effects the selection of the pathways for discharge. A wishful state produces an energic flow toward the memory-image of the object of the wish (wishful alteration).

When an association of simultaneity results in the experience of unpleasure, a memory trace occurs representing the relief brought about by the disappearance of the pain-giving object. This biological (reflex) experience is utilized by the psychic apparatus, which attempts to reproduce the state of this "disappearance." In terms of the Project, this means cathecting some neurone other than the neurone associated with the pain. The raising of the contact barrier that prohibits the association becomes, in later analytic theory, the concept of anticathexis.

The determinant of selectivity at this stage of development is based on past experience, that is, *memory*. Recall of the past is the significant directing force in relation to the pathways taken by excitation: an experience of satisfaction leaves a memory trace and creates a primary wishful state as the motive force; an experience of pain leaves a memory of unpleasure and creates primary defense.

Memory of these experiences provides this motive or aim as long as the wishful idea is kept cathected (Project 329). Although the system is regulated by memories, this should not be taken to mean conscious memory, but rather unconscious memory traces. Consciousness at first is supposedly achieved only by perceptions, the affect of pleasure or unpleasure, and by memories that have intense (sensory) investment, that is, pain and hallucinatory wish fulfillment.

In spite of this elaboration, the system still operates under the primary function, immediate discharge, since there is no capacity for delay. This form of function is termed primary process and the system is still regulated by the pleasure principle.

Primary process functioning under the pleasure principle, however, is more complex than the simple reflex discharge. Many alternative pathways are present and discharge through the system is regulated by past experience (unconscious memory of pleasurable or painful energy shifts). The more desirable pathway is automatically chosen.

Besides the lack of ability to delay discharge, there is also no mechanism by which the cathexis of a wish can be inhibited. Therefore the wishful cathexis in the Psi (ψ) neurones quickly reaches such a quantitative level that by flow back it registers on the perceptual neurones (ω) as quality. This results in hallucinatory vividness and leads to discharge independently of outside reality.

The next determinant in the regulation of discharge and the selection of correct pathways depends on the existence of an ego, with its capacity to bind cathexis, allowing for a delay in drive discharge. Freud describes (Project 369) the ego as being composed of nuclear neurones of Psi (ψ), which receive endogenous energy from somatic pathways. These Psi (ψ) neurones are distinguished from other Psi (ψ) neurones in that they retain a constant cathexis and have available a reservoir for the storage of energy. To serve this function of storage Freud suggested that the neurones which were part of the ego were laterally connected with other ego neurones and formed a complex network. Energy, instead of going in an unimpeded fashion through these neurones toward motor discharge, was switched via these lateral connections off the main route of travel. These neuronic branches were termed the lateral cathexes and served the function of storing and binding energy. The origin of the ego complex was not clear, but was related to the basic experience of unpleasure that follows inappropriate and premature motor discharge. It was described as a "biological acquisition" based on primary defense.

The system learns not to cathect the wished-for image too fully, since it will lead to wishful hallucination and primary process discharge. It also learns not to initiate discharge until certain conditions are fulfilled on the perceptual side. When these restrictions are not followed, unpleasure energy is released. It may be that this energy itself is then used as the original energy of the ego neurones. Once these restrictions are followed, further energy accumulates in the system. The outflow of energy is impeded but the inflow continues. As a result an ever widening group of nuclear neurones becomes invested, that is, the ego network is increased in size.

The energy stored or bound in the neurones raises their potential. This energy is not transmitted, but is in a "state of quiescence" (*S.E.* 5 599). The effect of this high level of energy in the neurone is *to reduce the resistance to the passage of energy*. As a result, when the major quantity of drive energy is bound in the lateral cathexes, the remaining smaller amount of energy can travel along a cathected neurone, whereas before only a much larger quantity could overcome the resistance (Project 334). This is described as a strong cathexis and a weak displacement.

The existence of an ego complex of neurones with their capacity to bind cathexis enables the system to delay discharge. The delay is made possible by the binding of cathexis, which leads to a dampening down of internal stimuli

(*S.E.* *5* 617, *14* 220). The system employs the time thus made available to ensure that the outside circumstances are appropriate for gratification of the drive. The delay gives time for indications of reality to arrive. Freud's later concepts of reality testing are based on this earlier concept. Percepts that disappear as a result of action are judged as real in contrast to wishes (*S.E.* *14* 119, 232). Hartmann has elaborated the formulation which points out that reality testing must not only distinguish ideas from perceptions but also involves subjective versus objective judgments.[2] Errors here lead not so much to distortions of perception as to distortions of concept formation. The system is, as a result of the strong cathexis and weak displacement, able to make "trial runs" through a variety of paths using small amounts of energy, and is thus able to test out which pathway will be most gratifying. This is the definition of thought (Project 334, 368). Thought is made possible in part by the fact that small quantities of energy are able to pass along neurones that contain bound energy, and for the first time an unpleasurable idea (pathway) can be cathected and explored. The employment of small amounts of cathexis guarantees a release of only signal unpleasure (*S.E.* *5* 602). The system can "cathect and work over even what is associated with the release of unpleasure" (*S.E.* *5* 616). Freud describes this as the "key to the whole theory of repression" (*S.E.* *5* 601). He later (*S.E.* *5* 617, *14* 146) elaborates on this statement, stating that repression at the beginning is aimed at the closing out of interfering intensities of stimuli. But because of the dynamic aspect of the unconscious, the intent of repression miscarries and becomes as a consequence the source of conflict, substitute formations and symptoms.

Dr. René Spitz describes the onset of thinking as trial action as beginning in the second month after birth![3]

When this function of a trial run of cathexis is working,

[2] *Essays on Ego Psychology*, p. 241.

[3] Spitz, *A Genetic Field Theory of Ego Formation*, p. 24.

the need or wish requiring specific action is matched against the reality of the outside world (guaranteeing the success of the specific action). If the two are found to coincide, pleasurable discharge of larger quantities is permitted. If the wished-for situation does not match the outside situation, a search to modify and find the required external object can occur. This defines the function of cognition, which can occur as a result of inhibition of discharge, trial action, and a waiting until the wishful cathexis of a memory and a perceptual cathexis coincide. During this trial run, the trial cathexis of a potentially unpleasurable path produces a moderate signal of unpleasure (signal anxiety) and redirects the search to more profitable paths. This search involves *remembering*, analyzing the perceptual image (cognition), and *judgment* as to its capacity to result in gratification (suitability for specific action).

The binding capacity of the ego also means that the energy invested in an idea will remain committed to the idea and will not be subject to displacement and condensation, characteristic of primary process mobility. As a result, "When a process passes from one idea to another, the first idea retains a part of its cathexis and only a small portion undergoes displacement. Displacements and condensations such as happen in the primary process are excluded or very much restricted" (*S.E. 14* 188).

Binding by the ego offers a mechanism that results in a reduction in the drive investment of a wish. Before this inhibition the wish could easily achieve hallucinatory intensity. That is, the wish via flow-back from the Psi (ψ) neurones could register as quality on the perceptual neurones (ω). Whereas actual perceptions always give an indication of quality and achieve consciousness, memories at this stage of development of the apparatus do so only when highly invested. By binding the energy invested in the wish, the level of energy is reduced below that which would register on the perceptual neurones (ω) and result in hallucinatory vividness (Project 439). "It is accordingly *inhibition by the ego which makes possible a criterion for distinguishing between perception and memory*" (Project 326).

The final important consequence of the ego's storage of energy through its binding capacity is that it can be used to manipulate facilitations. The principle was already described in the "association by simultaneity" theory, in which it was stated that energy passes more easily from one neurone to an adjacent cathected neurone than to an uncathected one. The cathexis of a further neurone is equivalent to a facilitation in that it lowers the resistance at the contact barrier. The energy stored in the lateral cathexis of the ego network can be employed to cathect neurones and thus divert facilitation. "Since cathexis can be changed, it lies within the choice of the ego to modify the passage (of association) from ω [perception] in the direction of any purposive cathexis" (Project 377).

It is clear from this description that there are two ways in which these methods by which the ego regulates the flow of energy may break down. The wishful cathexis may be so strong that it overthrows the binding capacity of the ego, ignores the signal of inappropriateness from the perceptual neurone and seeks gratification in spite of the absence of the object in reality. It is a faulty functioning of the apparatus along earlier, more primitive lines and leads to the painful experience of disappointment and frustration. The other situation in which the system may fail to function adequately in pursuing a wishful cathexis is when the signal of unpleasure is ignored. The trial cathexis of a neurone which led to signal unpleasure should lead to primary defense. This is a raised resistance to energy flow along these lines, and a search for the correct channel of cathexis that would lead to pleasure. The quantity involved in the wish may be so great that it overcomes the resistance and leads to discharge, when this pathway can only repeat a painful experience.

The common factor in both failures is the amount of energy involved. The investigative process must, for purposes of accuracy and defense, involve only small quantities. If the trial run involves too great a quantity of energy, the barriers against discharge (lateral cathexes) are overwhelmed. Under these circumstances, either the reality of the external world or the earlier experience of failure is ignored. The first involves hallucinatory wish fulfillment with its inevitable disappointment (primary process); the second involves the failure of primary defense (ignores past experience of unpleasure).

It is important to recall that up to this point in the development of the apparatus, it functions almost independently of consciousness. Although the regulation at an early stage employs memories for the direction of the impulses into certain channels, these memory traces are not necessarily accompanied by consciousness, and when they do reach conscious representation, it is with the hallucinatory vividness of a perception. Even the formation of the ego, with its capacity to bind energy, permitting delay, thought, and the inhibition of the wish so it is not confused with perception, does not, except for perceptions, usually involve consciousness. The next great advance in the more stable functioning of the apparatus involves the wider employment of the function of consciousness.

Freud's view of consciousness was an unusual one. He made no attempt to explain how quantity is changed into quality by the excitation of the perceptual neurones (ω). His goal was "establishing a coincidence between the characteristics of consciousness that are known to us and processes in the ω neurones which vary in parallel with them" (Project 311). He did not view consciousness as an epiphenomenon added to the essential and all-important physiologico-psychical processes, nor did he feel that all mental processes were represented in consciousness, that is, that conscious and mental were identical. He felt that "consciousness is the subjective side of one part of the physical processes in the nervous system, namely of the ω processes; and the omission of consciousness does not leave psychical events unaltered but involves the omission of the contribution from ω" (Project 311).

First consciousness was related to perceptions and to the qualities of pleasure and unpleasure that were the consequence of changes in the level of tension in the nuclear portion of the Psi (ψ) neurones. The function of consciousness was greatly enlarged when the system developed a deployable, mobile but nondrive energy under the ego's control. This energy was termed the attention cathexis. Its function was to add cathexis to the perceptual neurones (ω) that were excited by perceptions of objects in the outside world.

The importance of objects in the outside world developed from experiences of satisfaction. The first time an object was perceived, the energy involved was of a small quantity. Only after the experience proved pleasurable or unpleasurable would it take on meaning and the investment of the object involve a greater quantity of energy. When an appetitive state reappeared, the apparatus developed a state of expectation in which the Psi (ψ) neurones were precathected by the energy of the wish. If the needed object was then actually perceived, the perceptual neurones (ω) were already alerted. This was later described by Freud as meeting the sense impressions halfway (*S.E. 12* 220). This occurred when the state of expectation was generalized so that all indications of quality received by the perceptual neurones (ω) were periodically scanned (hypercathected) by the attention cathexis of the Psi (ψ) neurones. The ego arranged that the attention cathexis would follow the indications of quality and would lead to the perceptual neurones (ω) being stimulated. By this mechanism the attention cathexis is drawn to that portion of the perceptual neurones (ω) being stimulated and makes the perception more distinct "but not more vivid" by its hypercathexis (Project 340).

The fact that the ego invests the attention cathexis first on the indication of quality and only secondarily on the perceptual neurones (ω) involves a considerable saving of energy. Only those perceptual neurones (ω) that have already been alerted and then stimulated by quality need be hypercathected. Since the indication of quality also is evidence that the stimulus is from the external world (i.e., reality), the system is assured that this important source of stimulus will be kept under surveillance. Attention cathexis is described as a biological acquisition (Project 370) and it leads Freud to a formulation of the biological role of attention: "*If an indication of reality appears, then the perceptual cathexis which is simultaneously present is to be hypercathected*" (Project 371).

Without the hypercathexis of the perceptual neurones (ω), an incoming stimulus would have traveled along associative lines (the paths of least resistance) until, after being split into ever smaller amounts, it would have met with insurmountable resistances and have been dissipated. The hypercathexis by the Psi (ψ) neurones, since it adds more energy to the impulse, insures that the associative pathways will spread over a larger part of the associative network and thus reach a wider number of memory traces before being dissipated.

Later, in *The Interpretation of Dreams*, Freud points out that the chain of associative thoughts may not end in dissipation, but can and will continue if the thoughts are invested with energy from unconscious wishes. The present description is not so much a contradiction of the later example as it is a description of one possible vicissitude. (See *Origins* 420 and fn. 1, and Project 363).

The necessity for attention cathexis, in fact, is partly due to the inhibition of the wish which the binding of energy brings about. Before the capacity for binding developed, it was possible via condensations and displacements for a wish to reach a level of sensory intensity that forced it into consciousness (hallucination). The capacity to bind cathexis ruled out this form of the wish's registering on the perceptual neurones (ω) and limited the awareness of processes in the Psi (ψ) neurones.

Even the greater spread of cathectic transmission in the Psi (ψ) neurones, which attention cathexis offers, was insufficient for the most efficient functioning of the apparatus.

Therefore another modification is introduced into the system that will allow a periodic recharging of the chain of associations, so that if it is a valuable, purposive, or critical line of thought, the memory traces which have been aroused can give an indication of quality, be brought to consciousness, and again hypercathected by the attention cathexis. As a result the energy flow will not end by spreading into distant neurones, and weakened by the process of dispersal, be finally unable to overcome the resistance in the contact barriers and therefore brought to an end. What mechanism allows this recharging of the flow so that its pathway becomes almost interminable and capable of conscious attention by the ego?

This state of affairs is brought about by linking the energy flow to speech associations (Project 365, *S.E.* 5 574, 617). By the use of words, a motor act is introduced that registers as a perception and draws to itself the hypercathexis of "attention," making a train of thoughts capable of sustained investment. Even though in thought the motor action of speech is not fully performed, the motor image is a perception and as such possesses quality. The cathexis of a memory trace results in the stimulation of auditory and motor (verbal) associations. These associations arouse quality and, following the biological rule of attention, this report of quality will be hypercathected by attention cathexis. This allows the memory to enter into consciousness. These "*indications of speech-discharge* . . . put thought-process on a level with perceptual processes, lend them reality and *make memory of them possible*" (Project 366). The availability to the psychic apparatus of this type of consciousness greatly expands the "inner world" and greatly enhances the ego's control over both the inner and outer world.

This does not mean that all trains of thought become conscious. There are many trains of thought of which only parts sporadically enter into consciousness. This is likely to happen when a course of automatic (unconscious) association reaches an end or comes up against an obstacle or arouses an idea that is associated with an acceptable wish. Under these circumstances this part of the chain of thought may give rise to an indication of quality and, receiving hypercathexis of attention, appear in consciousness.

This is the nature of most ordinary thought-processes. The ego follows the course of association automatically and therefore most of the chain is unconscious, but there are "occasional *intrusions* into consciousness—what is known as conscious thinking with unconscious intermediate links, can through these be made conscious" (Project 373). The editor comments that this is Freud's earliest description of preconscious processes of thought.

The fact that thought can be associated with speech not only allows it to register on consciousness, but also gives it a stability and capacity to resist distortion and is thus the "*highest, securest form of cognitive thought-process*" (Project 374).

There is always a danger that this stability may be lost, as when under strong emotions attention cathexis is withdrawn from the thought process and the chain of thought becomes unconscious. The beauty of this self-regulating, self-reporting control of energy flow in the neuronic system can best be appreciated by a brief recapitulation of the mechanisms involved.

The original reflex arc model is first elaborated by the insertion of resistances at the contact barriers. This allows alternate pathways to be followed depending on: (*a*) quantity of energy involved; (*b*) facilitation of pathways; (*c*) the associations built up through experience (association by simultaneity), that is, cathexis or decathexis of adjacent neurones.

The displacement of quantities under the system thus far described is regulated by the pleasure-unpleasure principle, and primarily involves perceptual consciousness.

Further security, delay, and finer discriminations are made possible by: (*d*) the ego with its lateral cathexes, which inhibit flow, raise the cathectic level of the neurones (binding), and permit trial runs with small quantities (thought). At this stage of development the inhibitory function of the ego dampens the vividness of the memory image, so that it will not be treated as a percept (hallucination) and lead to primary process discharge.

The ego has available to it the perceptions and the storehouse of memories in terms of pleasure and unpleasure. The trial run serves to match the percept with the remembered and wished-for object. Since this "thought activity" is carried on at a high bound cathexis with small quantities in flow, it does not threaten a traumatic release of unpleasure. When the system is functioning adequately, that is, when there is a high ego cathexis, only signal unpleasure (signal anxiety) is released.

Greater efficiency in the control of energy flow requires a freely displaceable energy not requiring discharge (i.e., neutral rather than drive energy). This is described as attention cathexis.

Consciousness, which is defined as the "sense organ for the perception of psychical qualities" (*S.E. 5* 615), is greatly enlarged by the employment of attention cathexis. At first consciousness is dependent on perceptual stimuli and changes in Psi (ψ) tension that qualitatively are registered in the pleasure-unpleasure series. Speech (a motor discharge) becomes a new and important form of perceptual stimulus that is linked to memories. Through the use of speech and auditory associations, memories achieve quality, which permits them to receive hypercathexis from the attention cathexis and thereby achieve consciousness.

Thought processes when they achieve consciousness can be not only purposeful, but also theoretical. Thoughts are able to explore not only the pathways to gratification, but *all* possible paths independently of the outcome. This is possible only when all memories, both pleasurable and unpleasurable, are available (Project 440, *S.E.* 5 600). This situation can occur only when there is a capacity to inhibit the release of unpleasure.

Although the Project was written in 1895, it is clearly the major work of Freud's first ten years devoted to psychoanalysis. Most of Freud's basic ideas were first developed there and then were illustrated by their application to the understanding of mental functioning in dreams. The choice of dreams to illustrate these discoveries shows Freud's extraordinary ability to make felicitous choices, for of all normal mental phenomena, dreams can best illustrate both the most primitive functioning (primary process) and the overlay by more elaborate functioning (secondary process). The study of dreams also allowed a discussion of the mental mechanisms involved in primary process (condensation, displacement, formation of compromises, and the like), as well as repression, reversal, and other methods of censorship. Finally, even the technique and goal of therapy could be illustrated by the interpretation of dreams.

The existence of infantile sexuality and its role in psychopathology was the other major discovery in this first decade. Freud again showed his genius in the imaginative application he made of this discovery. A knowledge of infantile sexuality made it possible to understand the perversions, the psychoneuroses, and normal sexuality. All of this was foreshadowed in the letters to Fliess, particularly Letter 75.

The Interpretation of Dreams (1900) and the *Three Essays on Sexuality* (1905) have been described as Freud's "most momentous and original contributions to human knowledge" (*S.E.* 7 126). From our review it is clear that the main outlines of these discoveries were made in the first ten years. It therefore comes as something of a surprise to realize how long it took to complete the discoveries as expressed in the libido theory. As the editors of the *Standard Edition* point out (*12* 316), the various stages of libidinal development were described only after many years of clinical observation. The autoerotic stage was described in 1905, the narcissistic stage in 1911, the anal-sadistic stage in 1913, the oral stage in 1915, and the phallic stage not until 1923.

The case study of the Wolfman provides clinical illustration of many of the concepts developed in this early period. For example the deferred effect of a traumatic scene is discussed (*S.E. 17* 112), as well as the transformation of libido into anxiety (*S.E. 17* 113). The problem of trauma and its relation to primal repression, first discussed in the Project (p. 368), is also illustrated in the Wolfman case (*S.E. 17* 111). The concept is more fully developed in the 1926 monograph, "Inhibitions, Symptoms, and Anxiety" (*S.E. 20* 94).

A detailed presentation of Freud's efforts to formulate the problem of repression is as yet unwritten. We have seen its beginnings in the tables presented in various drafts and letters (*S.E. 1* 211, 230, 234, 237); yet fifty years later Freud had reached no fully satisfying formulation.

Another unfinished piece of work deals with the problem of perception and consciousness. The major outlines of Freud's approach are developed in the Project and described in *The Interpretation of Dreams.* He returned to the subject briefly in 1925 ("A Note upon the 'Mystic Writing Pad,'" *S.E. 19* 227, and "Negation," *S.E. 19* 235), where he emphasized the active and intermittent aspect of consciousness.

Only recently have these problems begun to be restudied, as for example in such work as that of E. Kris, "On Preconscious Mental Processes,"[4] C. Fisher, "A Study of the Preliminary Stages of the Construction of Dreams and Images,"[5] and G. Klein's "Consciousness in Psychoanalytic Theory."[6]

Fortunately for the student of psychoanalysis, Freud's concept of the ego has been fully reviewed by Hartmann.[7] The pathology of ego functions, however, has not been as fully described. The development of this concept extends from Draft K and the first paper on the neuropsychoses of defense (*S.E. 3* 185) to Freud's last paper, "Splitting of the Ego in the Process of Defence" (*S.E. 23* 275).

Much remains to be done. Although the immediate goal of this book was to review the first ten years of psychoanalysis, its other purpose will have been utilized if it stimulates the reader to a further study and appreciation of Freud's ideas.

As Hartman has written, "Among great scientists there are those who confront the world with strikingly new facts; but there are also those who not only demonstrate new facts but also teach the world to look at them in an entirely new way, thereby also changing the forms or modes of our thinking. There are only a few in our time whom we would put into this second category. But there is no doubt that Freud is among them."[8]

[4] *Psychoanalytic Quarterly*, 19 4 (October 1950), 540–560.
[5] *Journal of the American Psychoanalytic Association*, 13 2 (January 1957), 5–60.
[6] *Ibid.*, 7 1 (January 1959), 5–34.
[7] *Essays on Ego Psychology*, p. 268.
[8] *Ibid.*, p. 296.

Bibliography

ANDREWS, DONALD HATCH. *The Symphony of Life*. Lee's Summit, Mo.: Unity Books, 1966.

APFELBAUM, BERNARD. "Ego Psychology, Psychic Energy, and the Hazards of Quantitative Explanation in Psycho-Analytic Theory," *International Journal of Psycho-Analysis*, **46** 2 (April 1965), 168–182.

BEARD, G. M. *Sexual Neurasthenia, Its Hygiene, Causes, Symptoms, and Treatment*. New York, 1884.

BERGMAN, PAUL, and SYBILLE K. ESCALONA. "Unusual Sensitivities in Very Young Children," *Psychoanalytic Study of the Child, 3–4* 333–352. New York: International Universities Press, Inc., 1949.

BERNFELD, SIEGFRIED. "Freud's Earliest Theories and the School of Heimholtz," *Psychoanalytic Quarterly*, **13** 3 (1944), 341–362.

BRENNER, CHARLES. "An Addendum to Freud's Theory of Anxiety," *International Journal of Psycho-Analysis*, **34** 1 (1953), 18–24.

BRIERLEY, MARJORIE. "Affects in Theory and Practice," *International Journal of Psycho-Analysis* **18** (1937), 256–267.

CANNON, W. B. *The Wisdom of the Body*. New York: W. W. Norton & Company, Inc., 1932.

COLBY, KENNETH. *Energy and Structure in Psychoanalysis*. New York: Ronald Press Company, 1955.

ERICSON, ERIK HOMBURGER. "Freud's 'The Origins of Psycho-Analysis,'" *International Journal of Psycho-Analysis* **36** 1 (January–February 1955), 1–15.

FISHER, ALAN E. "Chemical Stimulation of the Brain," *Scientific American*, **210** 6 (June 1964), 60–69.

FISHER, CHARLES. "Psychoanalytic Implications of Recent Research on Sleep and Dreaming," 2 parts, *Journal of the American Psychoanalytic Association*, **13** 2 (April 1965), 197–303.

———. "A Study of the Preliminary Stages of the Construction of Dreams and Images," *ibid.* **5** 1 (January 1957), 5–60.

FREUD, SIGMUND. "Abstracts of the Scientific Writings of Dr. Sigm. Freud" (1877–97 [1897]), *Standard Edition of the Complete Psychological Works of Sigmund Freud*, **3**, 227–256. London: Hogarth Press, 1962.

———. "The Aetiology of Hysteria (1896), *Standard Edition*, **3**, 191–221, 1962.

———. "Analysis of a Phobia in a Five-Year-Old Boy" (1909), *Standard Edition*, **10**, 5–149, 1955.

———. "Analysis Terminable and Interminable" (1937), *Standard Edition*, **23**, 216–253, 1964.

———. "An Autobiographical Study" (1925 [1924]), *Standard Edition*, **20**, 7–74, 1959.

———. *Beyond the Pleasure Principle* (1920), *Standard Edition*, **18**, 7–64, 1955.

———. "A Case of Successful Treatment by Hypnotism" (1892–93), *Standard Edition*, **1**, 117–128, 1966.

———. "Civilization and Its Discontents" (1930 [1929]), *Standard Edition*, **21**, 64–145, 1961.

———. "'Civilized' Sexual Morality and Modern Nervous Illness" (1908), *Standard Edition*, **9**, 181–204, 1959.

———. *Collected Papers*. Edited by James Strachey. Vol. 5. London: Hogarth Press, 1950.

———. "Constructions in Analysis" (1937), *Standard Edition*, **23**, 257–269, 1964.

———. "Contributions to a Discussion on Masturbation" (1912), *Standard Edition*, **12**, 243–254, 1958.

———. "The Disposition to Obsessional Neurosis" (1913), *Standard Edition*, **12**, 317–326, 1958.

———. "Dostoevsky and Parricide" (1928 [1927]), *Standard Edi*tion, **21**, 175–194, 1961.

———. "The Dynamics of Transference" (1912), *Standard Edition*, **12**, 99–108, 1958.

———. *The Ego and the Id* (1923), *Standard Edition*, **19**, 12–66, 1961.

———. "Formulations on the Two Principles of Mental Functioning" (1911), *Standard Edition*, **12**, 218–226, 1958.

———. "Fragment of an Analysis of a Case of Hysteria" (1905 [1901]), *Standard Edition* **7**, 7–122, 1953.

———. "From the History of an Infantile Neurosis" (1918 [1914]), *Standard Edition*, **17**, 7–122, 1955.

———. "Further Remarks on the Neuro-Psychoses of Defence" (1896), *Standard Edition*, **3**, 162–185, 1962.

———. "Heredity and the Aetiology of the Neuroses" (1896), *Standard Edition*, **3**, 143–156, 1962.

———. "Hypnosis" (1891), *Standard Edition* **1**, 105–114, 1966.

———. "Inhibitions, Symptoms and Anxiety" (1926), *Standard Edition*, **20**, 87–174, 1959.

———. "Instincts and Their Vicissitudes" (1915), *Standard Edition*, **14**, 117–140, 1957.

———. *The Interpretation of Dreams* (1900), *Standard Edition*, **4–5**, 1953.

———. "Introductory Lectures on Psycho-Analysis" (1916–1917 [1915–1917]), *Standard Edition*, **16**, 1963.

———. *Jokes and Their Relation to the Unconscious* (1905), *Standard Edition*, **8**, 1960.

———. "A Metaphysical Supplement to the Theory of Dreams" (1917 [1915]), *Standard Edition*, **14**, 222–235, 1957.

———. "Mourning and Melancholia" (1917 [1915]), *Standard Edition*, **14**, 243–258, 1957.

———. "Negation" (1925), *Standard Edition*, **19**, 235–239, 1961.

———. "The Neuro-Psychoses of Defence" (1894), *Standard Edition*, **3**, 45–61, 1962.

———. "New Introductory Lectures on Psycho-Analysis" (1933 [1932]), *Standard Edition*, **22**, 5–182, 1964.

———. "A Note Upon the 'Mystic Writing-Pad'" (1925 [1924]), *Standard Edition*, **19**, 227–232, 1961.

———. "Notes Upon a Case of Obsessional Neurosis" (1909), *Standard Edition*, **10**, 155–318, 1955.

———. "Observation of a Severe Case of Hemi-Anaesthesia in a Hysterical Male" (1886), *Standard Edition*, **1**, *25–31*, 1966.

———. *On Aphasia* (1891), New York: International Universities Press, Inc., 1953.

———. "On the Grounds for Detaching a Particular Syndrome from Neurasthenia Under the Description 'Anxiety Neurosis'" (1895 [1894]), *Standard Edition*, **3**, 90–117, 1962.

———. "On the History of the Psycho-Analytic Movement" (1914), *Standard Edition*, **14**, 7–66, 1957.

———. "On Narcissism: An Introduction" (1914), *Standard Edition*, **14**, 73–102, 1957.

———. *An Outline of Psycho-Analysis* (1940 [1938]), *Standard Edition*, **23**, 144–207, 1964.

———. "On the Psychical Mechanism of Hysterical Phenomena: A Lecture" (1893), *Standard Edition*, **3**, 27–39, 1962.

———. *The Origins of Psycho-Analysis*, Letters to Wilhelm Fliess, Drafts and Notes: 1887–1902. Edited by Marie Bonaparte, Anna Freud, and Ernst Kris. Authorized translation by Eric Mosbacher and James Strachey. Introduction by Ernst Kris. New York: Basic Books, Inc., 1954.

———. "Preface and Footnotes to Translation of Charcot's *Lecons du Mardi de la Salpêtrière (Poliklinishe Vorträge)*" (1892–94), *Standard Edition*, **1**, 133–143.

———. "Preface to the Translation of H. Bernheim's *De la Suggestion et de ses applications à la therapeutique* (Paris: 1886; 2d ed. 1887). German translation 1888–89. *Die Suggestion und ihre Heilwirkung (Suggestion and Its Therapeutic Effects), Standard Edition*, **1**, 75–85, 1966.

——— and Joseph Breuer. "Preliminary Communication" (1893), *Standard Edition*, **2**, 3–17, 1955.

———. "The Psychical Mechanism of Forgetfulness" (1898), *Standard Edition*, **3**, 289–297, 1962.

———. "Psycho-Analysis and Telepathy" (1941 [1921]), *Standard Edition*, **18**, 177–193, 1955.

———. "Psycho-Analytic Notes on an Autobiographical Account of a Case of Paranoia" (1911), *Standard Edition*, **12**, 9–82, 1958.

———. *The Psychopathology of Everyday Life* (1901), *Standard Edition*, **6**, 1960.

———. "A Reply to Criticisms of My Paper on Anxiety Neurosis" (1895), *Standard Edition*, **3**, 123–139, 1962.

———. "Report on My Studies in Paris and Berlin" (1956 [1886]), *Standard Edition*, **1**, 5–15, 1966.

———. "Repression" (1915), *Standard Edition*, **14**, 146–158, 1957.

———. "Review of August Forel's *Hypnotism*" (1889), *Standard Edition*, **1**, 91–102, 1966.

———. "Screen Memories" (1899), *Standard Edition*, **3**, 303–322, 1962.

———. "Sexuality in the Aetiology of the Neuroses" (1898), *Standard Edition*, **3**, 261–285, 1962.

———. "Sketches for the 'Preliminary Communication' of 1893" (1940–41 [1892]), *Standard Edition*, **1**, 147–154, 1966.

———. "Splitting of the Ego in the Process of Defence" (1940 [1938]), *Standard Edition*, **23**, 275–278, 1964.

——— and Joseph Breuer. *Studies on Hysteria* (1895), *Standard Edition*, **2**, 1955.

———. "Three Essays on the Theory of Sexuality" (1905), *Standard Edition*, **7**, 126–243, 1953.

———. "Types of Onset of Neurosis" (1912), *Standard Edition*, **12**, 229–238, 1958.

———. "Uber den Ursprung der hinteren Nervenwurzeln in Rückenmarke von Ammocoetes," S. B. *Akad Wiss. Wien* (Math. –Naturwiss. K 1., III Abt., **75**, 15, Jan., 1877.

———. "The Unconscious" (1915), *Standard Edition*, **14**, 159–209, 1957.

———. " 'Wild' Psycho-Analysis" (1910), *Standard Edition*, **9**, 221–227, 1957.

GREENACRE, PHYLLIS. "Re-Evaluation of the Process of Working

Through," *International Journal of Psycho-Analysis*, **37** 6 (November-December 1956), 439–444.

———. *Trauma, Growth, and Personality*. New York: W. W. Norton & Company, Inc., 1952.

Hartmann, Heinz. "The Development of the Ego Concept in Freud's Work," *International Journal of Psycho-Analysis*, **37** 6 (November-December 1956), 425–438.

———. *Ego Psychology and the Problem of Adaptation*. New York: International Universities Press, 1958.

———. *Essays on Ego Psychology: Selected Problems in Psychoanalytic Theory*. New York: International Universities Press, Inc., 1964.

———, Ernst Kris, and Rudolph M. Loewenstein, "The Function of Theory in Psychoanalysis" in *Drives, Affects, Behavior*. Edited by Rudolph M. Loewenstein. New York: International Universities Press, Inc., 1953, 13–37.

Hoffer, Willi. "Mouth, Hand and Ego-Integration," *Psychoanalytic Study of the Child*. **3–4**, 49–56. New York: International Universities Press, Inc., 1949.

Holt, R. "Beyond Vitalism and Mechanism: Freud's Concept of Psychic Energy," in *Science and Psychoanalysis*, edited by J. H. Masserman. New York: Grune and Stratton, Inc., 1967. Vol. 11, pp. 1–41.

Holzman, Philip S. "A Note on Breuer's Hypnoidal Theory of Neurosis," *Bulletin of the Menninger Clinic*, **23** 4 (July 1959), 144–147.

Jones, Ernest. *The Life and Work of Sigmund Freud*. 3 Vols. New York: Basic Books, Inc., 1953–57.

Jouvet, M. "Telencephalic and Rhombencephalic Sleep in the Cat," *The Nature of Sleep*. Edited by G. E. W. Wolstenholme and M. O'Connor. Boston: Little, Brown and Company, 1960.

Klein, George S. "Consciousness in Psychoanalytic Theory," *Journal of the American Psychoanalytic Association*, **7** 1 (January 1959), 5–34.

Kris, Alexander. "On Preconscious Mental Processes," *Psychoanalytic Quarterly*, **19** 4 (October 1950), 540–560.

Lipin, Theodore. "The Repetition Compulsion and 'Maturational' Drive-Representatives," *International Journal of Psycho-Analysis*, **44** 4 (October 1963), 389–406.

Lorenz, K. "The Nature of Instincts," *Instinctive Behavior*. Edited by C. Schiller. New York: International Universities Press, 1957.

Magoun, H. W. "An Ascending Reticular Activating System in the

Brain Stem," *The Harvey Lectures* 1951–52. Series 47. New York: Academic Press, Inc., 1953. Pp. 53–71.

MARUZZI, G. "Active Processes in the Brain Stem During Sleep," *The Harvey Lectures.* New York: Academic Press, Inc., 1963. Pp. 233–297.

MODELL, ARNOLD H. "The Concept of Psychic Energy," *Journal of the American Psychoanalytic Association*, **11** 3 (July 1963), 605–618.

PROVENCE, SALLY, AND ROSE C. LIPTON. *Infants in Institutions.* New York: International Universities Press, Inc., 1962.

PUMPIAN-MINDLIN, EUGENE. "Propositions Concerning Energetic-Economic Aspects of Libido Theory; Conceptual Models of Psychic Energy and Structure in Psychoanalysis," *Annals of the New York Academy of Science*, **74**, 4 (January 23, 1959), 1038–1065.

RAMZY, ISHAK, AND ROBERT S. WALLERSTEIN. "Pain, Fear, and Anxiety," *Psychoanalytic Study of the Child*, **13**, 147–189. New York: International Universities Press, Inc., 1958.

RANGELL, LEO. "On the Psychoanalytic Theory of Anxiety," *Journal of the American Psychoanalytic Association*, **3** 3 (July 1955), 389–414.

RAPAPORT, DAVID. "On the Psycho-Analytic Theory of Affects," *International Journal of Psycho-Analysis*, **34** 3 (1953), 177–198.

SCHUR, MAX, (ed.). *Drives, Affects, Behavior.* Vol. 2. New York: International Universities Press, Inc., 1965.

———. "Phylogenesis and Ontogenesis of Affect- and Structure-Formation and the Phenomenon of Repetition Compulsion," *International Journal of Psycho-Analysis*, **41** 4–5 (July-October 1960), 275–287.

SNYDER, FREDERICK. "Progress in the New Biology of Dreaming," *American Journal of Psychiatry*, **122** 4 (October 1965), 377–391.

———. "Toward an Evolutionary Theory of Dreaming," *American Journal of Psychiatry*, **123** 2 (August 1966), 121–136.

SPITZ, RENÈ. *A Genetic Field Theory of Ego Formation.* New York: International Universities Press, Inc., 1959.

———. "Hospitalism: An Inquiry into the Genesis of Psychiatric Conditions in Early Childhood," *Psychoanalytic Study of the Child*, **1** 53–74. New York: International Universities Press, Inc., 1945.

STEIN, MARTIN H. "States of Consciousness in the Analytic Situation: Including a Note on the Traumatic Dream," in *Drives, Affects, Behavior*, Vol. 2. New York: International Universities Press, Inc., 1965.

STEWART, WALTER A. "The Development of the Therapeutic Alliance in Borderline Patients," *Psychoanalytic Quarterly*, **30** 1 (January 1961), 165–166.

TAUSK, VICTOR. "On the Origin of the 'Influencing Machine' in Schizophrenia," *Psychoanalytic Quarterly*, **2** (1933), 519–556.

TINBERGEN, N. *The Study of Instinct*. New York: Oxford University Press, 1951.

ZILBOORG, GREGORY. "Freud's Fundamental Psychiatric Orientation," *International Journal of Psycho-Analysis*, **35** 2 (April 1954), 90–94.

Index

ABOUT THE AUTHOR

Walter A. Stewart, M.D., is Clinical Associate Professor of Psychiatry at Einstein College of Medicine, and was previously on the faculty of Columbia University College of Physicians and Surgeons. He is a graduate of Dartmouth College, took his M.D. at Johns Hopkins University, is a graduate and a faculty member of Columbia's Psychoanalytic Clinic for Training and Research, and is a faculty member of the New York Psychoanalytic Institute. He has published frequently in the *Psychoanalytic Quarterly*, the *Journal of the American Psychoanalytic Association*, and other professional journals, and is on the editorial board of the Annual Survey of Psychoanalysis. He is a member of the American Psychoanalytic Association, the American Psychiatric Association, and the American Academy of Science.

GEORGE ALLEN & UNWIN LTD

Head office:
London: 40 Museum Street, W.C.1

Trade orders and enquiries:
Park Lane, Hemel Hempstead, Herts.

Auckland: P.O. Box 36013, Northcote Central, N.4
Barbados: P.O. Box 222, Bridgetown
Beirut: Deeb Building, Jeanne d'Arc Street
Bombay: 15 Graham Road, Ballard Estate, Bombay 1
Buenos Aires: Escritorio 454-459, Florida 165
Calcutta: 17 Chittaranjan Avenue, Calcutta 13
Cape Town: 68 Shortmarket Street
Hong Kong: 105 Wing On Mansion, 26 Hancow Road, Kowloon
Ibadan: P.O. Box 62
Karachi: Karachi Chambers, McLeod Road
Madras: Mohan Mansions, 38c Mount Road, Madras 6
Mexico: Villalongin 32, Piso, Mexico 5, D.F.
Nairobi: P.O. Box 30583
New Delhi: 13-14 Asaf Ali Road, New Delhi 1
Ontario: 81 Curlew Drive, Don Mills
Philippines: P.O. Box 4322, Manila
Rio de Janeiro: Caixa Postal 2537-Zc-00
Singapore: 36c Prinsep Street, Singapore 7
Sydney, N.S.W.: Bradbury House, 55 York Street
Tokyo: P.O. Box 26, Kamata

Sigmund Freud

INTRODUCTORY LECTURES ON PSYCHO-ANALYSIS

'No serious critic of psycho-analysis should omit to read it; no serious student can afford to neglect it.' *Lancet*

'Certainly the clearest and most comprehensive and complete account of the subject which has yet appeared.' *Saturday Review*

'We are in the presence not only of the scientific mind, but a mind gifted with a genius for exposition and polemical reasoning, a mind that combines the experimental genius of a Pasteur with the expository power of a Huxley or a Tyndall.' *New Age*

'The best book with which to commence the study of psycho-analysis.' *British Medical Journal*

'An ideal introduction to the study of psycho-analysis. The book cannot be too highly recommended.' *Journal of Neurology*

Edited and Selected by B. Nelson

FREUD AND THE TWENTIETH CENTURY

Freud's exploration of dreams, myths, symbols and the imaginative profundity of man's inner life will probably prove to be the most important twentieth century advance. Virtually everybody has some knowledge of Freud's ideas but what is really needed is a good account of his work and its effects on modern life which is accurate and really readable. This admirable symposium answers all the requirements. It covers the tremendous effect of psycho-analysis on philosophy, religion, literature, art and society. Each chapter is by an acknowledged expert who can write for the layman and not only for the expert.

The chapters are of a very high standard and in placing together widely differing views they are of exceptional interest.

Sigmund Freud

THE INTERPRETATION OF DREAMS

This entirely new translation of Freud's most important work contains a number of features not to be found in any previous edition, whether in English or German. Freud made a great many changes and additions to the book over a period of some thirty years, and the present edition indicates for the first time the exact nature of these changes and additions and the dates at which they were made, thus enabling the reader to trace the gradual development and modification of Freud's views. This edition also includes numerous explanatory notes and an historical introduction, as well as enlarged and revised bibliographies and very full indexes. In preparing the translation Mr. Strachey has enjoyed the advantage of regular consultation with the author's daughter, Miss Anna Freud.

'This book, with the new contribution to psychology which surprised the world when it was published (1900), remains essentially unaltered. It contains, even according to my present-day judgment, the most valuable of all the discoveries it has been my good fortune to make. Insight such as this falls to one's lot but once in a lifetime.' FREUD in the Foreword of this edition.

LONDON: GEORGE ALLEN & UNWIN LTD